What the critics
release, *Bodies*.

"Inspector Buck
drinking, womanizing, racist cop who does whatever and
whoever he needs to in order to get what he wants . . . This novel
is basically a 'slice of life' story of about one year of Buck's life
and crimes (both committed and solved) . . . an extremely dark
novel, not for everyone . . ."

—Ted Hertel, *Deadly Pleasures*

"Saffiotte is a real sonofabitch, but he's also our guide through
this 200 pages of depravity . . . The unnamed city is a character
unto itself, and it reminded me of the Frank Miller graphic novel
(and movie) *Sin City*. It's a rat-filled, fetid sore of a slum where
Italian immigrants sell rotting vegetables on busted pushcarts.
Wolfson's descriptions are vivid and stay with you as the pages
fly by . . . a hardboiled classic from an era when the genre was
still finding its feet."

—*Paperback Warrior*

"Plenty of hard-edged banter, muscular prose and clever riffing
on jazz melancholy in this cruel and poignant tale. The
denouement is blistering and devastating. P.J. (Pinkus Jacob)
Wolfson matches James M. Cain for raw emotional power. This is
noir that puts an end to the scientific debate about whether
absolute black exists—this is it, despair that rings so true it
hurts."

—Paul Burke, *Crime Time*

I was a Bandit

by
Eddie Guerin

Introduction
by
Jeff Vorzimmer

An Imprint of Stark House Press

I WAS A BANDIT
Copyright ©1929
by Double, Doran & Company, Inc.

Published by Staccato Crime
An imprint of Stark House Press
1315 H Street
Eureka, CA 95501, USA
griffinskye3@sbcglobal.net
www.starkhousepress.com

Preface ©2021 by Jeff Vorzimmer

All rights reserved under International and Pan-American Copyright
Conventions.

ISBN: 978-1-951473-69-3
Staccato Crime: SC-002

All Staccato Crime titles are edited and produced
by David Rachels and Jeff Vorzimmer.
Book series design by ¡caliente!design, Austin, Texas.

Without limiting the rights under copyright reserved above, no part of this
publication may be reproduced, stored, or introduced into a retrieval system or
transmitted in any form or by any means (electronic, mechanical, photocopying,
recording or otherwise) without the prior written permission of both the
copyright owner and the above publisher of the book.

First Staccato Crime Edition: November 2021

Foreword to
Staccato Crime

A dozen years ago, my friend Allan Guthrie recommended to me an obscure crime novel from 1931, *Bodies Are Dust* by P. J. Wolfson. I immediately set out to find a copy, but there were none to be found anywhere in the vast universe of the internet. I turned to my local librarian for help, and she suggested I try the interlibrary loan network, which libraries use to borrow books from other libraries around the world.

As my librarian searched the interlibrary database for *Bodies Are Dust*, she arched her eyebrows and said, "It seems there only ten copies of the book in libraries worldwide."

I was similarly surprised and said, "That's fewer copies than the Gutenberg Bible," of which there were 49 in libraries and museums at that time.

"Of the ten copies," she added, "two of them are here in Austin."

When *Bodies Are Dust* arrived at my local library, I was thrilled to actually have a copy in my hands. As I opened the book I noticed someone had scrawled on the title page, "Very vicious—should not be in library." I laughed out loud. Flipping to the back of the book where due dates were stamped, I saw that it had been checked out many times in the 1930s and 40s, but the date stamped just above mine was March 27, 1948. No one had borrowed this book in over sixty years!

About the same time that Allan Guthrie was recommending *Bodies Are Dust* to me, my friend David Rachels (not coincidentally, the co-editor of this series) was also searching for a copy. Luckily, David found a 1952 paperback reprint that Gary Lovisi was willing to part with for less than fifty dollars. He and I have found that this is the case with too many outstanding crime books from the early twentieth century—if you're lucky enough to find a copy, you also have to be lucky enough to afford it.

As I write, there is one copy of *Bodies Are Dust* for sale on Amazon, eBay, or AbeBooks, and that copy is in French. When an English-language copy appears, it might be an affordable paperback (affordable, that is, if it is in tattered condition), or it might be an expensive hardcover ($800-$1000, depending on condition and whether it's a first or second edition).

Staccato Crime will solve this problem by publishing affordable paperback editions of difficult-to-find noir fiction and true crime from the Jazz Age, 1899-1939. Our hope is that when a friend recommends to you an obscure work of early twentieth-century American crime, you will be able to find a copy here—and also, that Staccato Crime will lead you to recommend these books to your friends.

Jeff Vorzimmer
Austin, Texas

New and Forthcoming Titles
From Staccato Crime

Eddie Guerin was one of the first criminals to achieve worldwide infamy in almost real time. New technology made this possible. First, the telegraph made mass-communication national, and then the laying of the transatlantic cable made it international. So, when Eddie Guerin and his cohorts robbed the Crédit Lyonnais in France on July 2, 1888, the story appeared in the next morning's newspapers in the United States.

When Guerin and his associate, Billy Connors, were picked up 22 days later in London, the story made the afternoon editions of American papers that same day. These stories marked the beginning of Eddie Guerin's international notoriety.

Guerin had achieved local notoriety in Chicago as early as the age of 17, when he was already being referred to regularly in the *Chicago Tribune* as the "infamous" or "notorious" Eddie Guerin:

> Last evening Eddie Guerin, the notorious, was arrested by Sergt. Ryan . . .
> —*Chicago Tribune*, Jan. 12, 1878

> The notorious Eddie Guerin was got "dead to rights" early last evening . . .
> —*Chicago Tribune*, Feb. 3, 1878

> The sneak-thief who was caught going through the tobacco store at the LaSalle Street tunnel . . . was yesterday taken to the Armory where he was there identified at once as the notorious Eddie Guerin . . .
> —*Chicago Tribune*, Mar. 17, 1878

On Tuesday, January 4, 1887, at the age of 26, Guerin made the front page of the *Tribune* for the first time, and his name was soon known nationwide after he shot a police officer, Detective Thomas Treharn, in what Guerin characterized as a personal dispute.

Guerin claimed that he and a buddy had been seeing the police officer's wife and that the officer had drawn on him first with the intent to kill him. Guerin fled to Canada, where he lived openly in Windsor with a fellow safe-cracker, Jack Rogers, as late as the summer of 1887.

By June 1887, Guerin was working as a safe-cracker in England, where he was arrested in Manchester for bank robbery on August 23. That particular story was covered by only one newspaper in the States, appearing on the front page of the *Standard-Union* of Brooklyn the following day. It was noted in the article that he and Billy Connors had been previously arrested in Brooklyn on December 10, 1884.

A year later, on July 2, 1888, when the Crédit Lyonnais was robbed of 250,000 francs (the equivalent of $1.4 million today), it was given scant coverage on either side of the Atlantic, but when Guerin and two associates were arrested for the crime on July 24 in London, it was suddenly front page news in both Europe and the States. Only when the robbery was attributed to Guerin did it seem newsworthy.

Early in 1889, Guerin was extradited to France from England, where he had fled, for trial. On May 20, he was sentenced to ten years in prison in Rion. Nothing of significance about Guerin appeared in the newspapers as he served out his full term. After his release, he was deported and forbidden ever to enter France again.

But Guerin was persuaded to return to Paris in early 1901 by an old acquaintance, safe-cracker Gustav Muller, a.k.a. George Miller. Miller was putting together a team to rob the American Express Office on the Rue Scribe in Paris. He recruited Guerin because Eddie was a veteran safe-cracker himself and also spoke fluent French.

They pulled the job on April 26, 1901, and got away with around $250,000 (the equivalent of $8 million today). Five days later, Guerin was caught while leaving Paris by train with the notorious female criminal Chicago May. Somehow May eluded the police, but she was apprehended five weeks later, after returning to Paris.

Twelve and a half months elapsed before Guerin was put on trial (though he remembers it as nine months). The trial, which lasted only two days, was covered by every major American newspaper. On June 14, 1902, Guerin and Miller were sentenced to life at Devil's Island, the penal colony in French Guiana.

Three years later, Guerin again appeared on the front pages of American newspapers after a daring escape from the penal colony. Guerin escaped not from Devil's Island itself but from Cayenne on the French Guiana mainland. Guerin claimed that no man had ever escaped from Devil's Island, but the newspapers weren't about to let the facts get in the way of a good story, and they reported in breathless prose how Guerin had killed and devoured two fellow escapees while at sea to become the only prisoner to have ever escaped the island.

For months afterwards, newspapers around the world ran purported personal accounts with headlines such as HOW I ESCAPED FROM DEVIL'S ISLAND and THE ONLY MAN TO ESCAPE FROM DEVIL'S ISLAND. In reality, Guerin's friend Pat Sheedy was selling these tall tales, and Guerin learned about them only after he reached Chicago and saw the headlines. For nearly two decades, Guerin's name had been selling newspapers, and he hadn't made money from any of it.

The last straw may have come belatedly in December 1927, when a failed Guerin assassin, recently released from prison, published "Why I Shot Eddie Guerin" in *True Detective Mysteries*. Remarkably, there was still interest in the Guerin name, and in 1928 he was able to sell the rights to his life story. Guerin was approaching 68, a broken and remorseful man.

The first review of *I Was a Bandit* appeared in the *New York World* in early 1929, and it was favorable. Through March, this review was syndicated nationally. In an era when there were no laws prohibiting criminals from profiting from the publicity of their crimes, the book sold well.

In 1936, upon the death of his sister, Guerin inherited one-fifth of her estate, valued at $67,000 (the equivalent of $1.3 million today). But Guerin's final score, legal though it was, did not stick any better than those that landed him in prison. In 1940, at the age of 80, he died penniless in the town of Bury, just north of Manchester, England. He was buried in a pauper's grave.

Fortunately, for lovers of true crime, Eddie Guerin left a rich legacy with his autobiography, *I Was a Bandit*. Not only does it detail his exploits in lucid prose, it touches on the lives of every major criminal of the late-nineteenth century and early twentieth century, the likes of which include Chicago May Churchill, Sophie & Ned Lyons, Billy Burke. Max Shinburn, Marm Mandelbaum, Shang Draper, and "The Napoleon of Crime" Adam Worth.

Eddie Guerin
newspaper engraving, 1936

Notes on Previous Editions Consulted

Two editions of Eddie Guerin's autobiography were published simultaneously in Britain and the United States in late 1928. Although this London edition, titled *Crime: Autobiography of a Crook*, has a 1928 copyright date and claims to be a "first edition," textual evidence suggests that it was typeset later than the New York edition, which has a 1929 copyright date. Many of the typographical errors of the New York edition appear to have been corrected in the London edition.

Both editions were consulted in the preparation of this edition, and differences between them were reconciled on the side of cultural consistency. For example, the chief administrative official of a prison appears as "Warden" in American prisons and "Governor" for similar British institutions. The same is true of prison guards, designated as such in American prisons and as "warders" in British prisons. Similarly, "jail" appears as "gaol" in reference to those in Britain.

It also must be noted that Guerin was an Englishman by birth and although he implies that he was very young when he emigrated it is likely Guerin retained some Briticisms in his speech. For example, his use of the uniquely British word *fortnight*, designating a period of two weeks, appears in both New York and London editions. Such British or American words that appear in both editions have been maintained, regardless of context, although American spelling has been maintained throughout.

Endnotes have been added to clarify or correct factual errors and to give the full names and years of birth and death of historical figures.

Eddie Guerin, head-and-shoulders portrait., ca. 1900.
Retrieved from the Library of Congress,
https://www.loc.gov/item/2006680253/

This is not what one could call in any shape or form a pretty story. It is the plain unvarnished tale of a man who has been a notorious criminal from his boyhood days, and it is printed only because it will prove, in a way that all the prison statistics in the world cannot prove, that you can't win at the crooked game.

"As a man sows, so shall he reap," and without a doubt Eddie Guerin has paid not once, but many, many times a heavy price for the crimes he has committed. It will be for the reader to judge how far he is to blame for the life he has led. His case is typical of hundreds of other professional criminals who have been thrown into prison at an adolescent age, at a time of life when the youthful mind is naturally in its most impressionable state.

It should be borne in mind by the readers of this story that when Guerin first made his acquaintance with a prison cell— over fifty years ago—there was absolutely no provision in existence for the special treatment of juvenile offenders. As a matter of fact, Guerin served his apprenticeship in lawlessness in what was possibly the worst school in the world—Chicago.

The people of a well-ordered country like England can have little or no conception of the wild criminal life which existed in the United States of America for a good many years after the war between the North and the South. Cold-blooded murder was looked upon as an almost everyday occurrence, while such comparatively trifling offenses as robbery under arms, sticking-up banks, dynamiting safes and other forms of getting money easily were regarded with a tolerant eye unknown in any other country making any pretense of civilization. Naturally, also, the justice meted out to the offenders—when they happened to be caught—was of a somewhat rough-and-ready nature.

What would our reformers of these enlightened days say to a boy of fifteen being thrown into a penitentiary crowded with murderers, bank robbers, burglars, sneak-thieves and hobos, or, as we know them in this country, tramps? Yet this is what happened to Guerin, and as he had the misfortune to be a boy who had lost his father and whose naturally adventurous disposition led him into all sorts of scrapes, it is not to be wondered that the environment of prison life in the bad old days of America quickly made him an out-and-out crook.

Guerin rose to great heights in his profession, in fact, he became what the penny novelist likes to call a "King of the Underworld." His sensational escape from the penal settlement of French Guiana in the early part of the present century, after having been condemned to life-long imprisonment for blowing up the safe in the offices of the American Express Company in Paris, made him for a time the most notorious person in the world. The dare-devil character of the man who could free himself from the horrors of that terrible convict depot—the last of its kind in the world—so strongly appealed to the sympathy of his fellow-beings that when he was ultimately recaptured in London there arose a widespread cry to refuse the extradition that the French Government demanded.

It had been only a little time previously that civilization had been even more deeply stirred by the case of Captain Dreyfus, the French army officer who had been convicted on perjured evidence of the worst possible type and transported to Devil's Island as a traitor to his country. The events that happened afterward, when the plot against Dreyfus was brought to light, and the world had an opportunity of learning how the French Government treated its prisoners, brought about a revulsion of feeling which had much to do with Eddie Guerin being saved from the horrors of ending his life in a French convict settlement.

But, of course, Guerin largely had nobody but himself to blame for being condemned to penal servitude for life. He had already served in France ten years' imprisonment for a bank robbery and he ought to have realized that the French penal code is not exactly merciful. But when a man has more or less definitely embarked upon a life of crime and has served his apprenticeship in it for a good many years it is extremely difficult to make him see the error of his ways. Prison life has few terrors for the old hands. They know the ropes and they are up to all the tricks of the trade. Chaplains may preach at them, governors may give them excellent advice as they take their discharge, but to all practical intents and purposes it resolves itself into a case of needs must when the devil drives.

Guerin says—and one cannot doubt him—that nobody will employ an ex-convict. Furthermore, very few such men possess the strength of mind to make a clean break-away from their old and vicious associates. Another thing is that having once made big money easily they find it almost impossible to work for wages, that is, of course, unless they be men endowed with very great determination. Guerin makes no pretense of having been ill-treated by the world. His only complaint is that for a trivial little offense which in these more thinking days would be met by a period of probation he was unceremoniously pitched into a common jail to learn the nefarious trade of a criminal.

In many ways, no doubt, the story he has to tell will cause our reformers to ponder a little, as it may also achieve the purpose for which it is written, namely, to prove to the youth of the present generation that criminality in any shape or kind, be it burglary, bank robbery, the picking up of unconsidered trifles, or, in fact, any infringement of the biblical commandment that "Thou shalt not steal," cannot, and does not, pay.

It would also be as well to point out that Guerin himself furnishes a classic example of the indubitable fact that you can't win at the Great Game. Here is a man who in the heyday of his criminal career was right at the top of the tree. His name was known from one end of the world to the other. He possessed the perhaps doubtful satisfaction of knowing that his photograph, his finger-prints, his dossier, and everything about him, were to be found in the archives of the police of America, France and England as that of a man reckoned to be one of the most daring bank robbers in the world. In his own sphere of life he has enjoyed a notoriety comparable only to that of a champion boxer or a celebrated beauty of the stage. But for all the profit it has brought him he might just as well have remained in the obscurity in which he was born. As he looks back on the last fifty years and there comes to his mind the long vista of the prison cells he has known, and as he thinks of all the best years of his life wasted behind bars and bolts, it must be bitterly brought home to him that there is no reward either in this life or the hereafter for the man who deliberately makes war on society.

Fifty years is a very long time and it is somewhat sad to reflect that any man could not have realized long before that period had elapsed that the game isn't worth the candle. Guerin is an old man now—he is sixty-seven years of age—but the mental awakening which might have made him realize the error of his ways did not come soon enough to enable him to make the fresh start in life which might have been possible had some one taken him in hand at an early age. Unfortunately, his first taste of jail came at a time when the idea of curing crime by kindness was not seriously thought of. The system in those days—all over the civilized world, America, France and England—was terrorism, brutality, starvation, flogging, transportation, everything, in fact, that would tend to brutalize the victim of it. We all know that things are rapidly changing for the better, but nevertheless the results of the old regime are still in evidence. In Eddie Guerin one sees an illuminating instance of a man who has been made a criminal by the stupidity of a blind officialdom.

This book is quite truthful and it possesses the inestimable virtue of dealing with nothing but bare facts. Possibly it may shock a good many people, but after all that does not greatly matter. If it succeeds in doing the good it is hoped and intended to do it will more than have achieved its purpose.

S.T.F.[1]

Chapter One
THE ROAD TO RUIN

I am going to take stock of my life. I don't know that it will be a particularly profitable task, but nevertheless I think it may prove interesting. After all, it is quite a useful thing occasionally to stop and make a mental survey of all that has happened in the past and to ask yourself what are you going to do with your future.

I have reached the comparatively ripe age of sixty-seven, and if I am ever going to have any wisdom in this life I should have it now. I realize full well that I have been guilty of the most incredible foolishness. Only a man out of his senses, or inherently wicked, could waste his life as I have wasted mine.

Let me draw a mental picture of myself! I see a rather quizzical face with a pair of shrewd blue eyes, a nose which has taught the wary ones to fight shy of me, and a thatch of white hair which I am sure makes me look more like a respectable clergyman than anything else. A keen observer might decide, on closer examination, that I could not possibly claim the Church as my occupation, but I would certainly defy anyone who did not know me to make an accurate guess.

One way and another, I suppose, I am not a bad advertisement for prison life. I look well and I feel well. My appetite is pretty good and I have not ruined my digestion swilling the magnums of champagne which the get-rich-quick company promoters higher up in the Great Game have done and for which they pay a price many years afterward.

When I have made money I have spent it. I have nothing at all to show for the fifty odd years I have been at "work," nothing but a certain amount of experience and the firm conviction that crime does not pay. I am quite certain it is not a profession I would adopt if I had my time over again, and while I do not intend to whine about it, it might be as well if I explained the beginning of my life and how I first fell from the path of rectitude.

I was born, so my parents informed me, in London, in the year 1860[2], being taken to the United States when quite a little child. Naturally, I do not recollect very much about my early days in London, but the matter is of more than passing importance because forty odd years afterward, when the French Government made application to have me extradited from England in order that I should return to Devil's Island to serve a sentence of transportation for life, I found myself faced with the terrifying proposition of proving that I was indeed of British nationality.

All the records of my birth had disappeared, the Great Fire of Chicago, which took place in 1871[3], destroying practically everything connected with my family. But fortunately for me, my father, an Irishman who had emigrated to the States with the idea of making a fortune and then coming back to his native land, uncompromisingly refused to relinquish his British citizenship. It was this fact that brought about my salvation in 1907, after lying in H.M. Prison, Brixton, for fourteen long, weary months awaiting the verdict that meant either freedom or death.

The British Attorney-General could not prove that I had been born in America, which would have meant that my extradition was merely a matter of form, but the proceedings would probably have dragged on indefinitely had it not been that my lawyer, the famous Richard Muir, ferreted out the all-important fact that my father had always remained a British subject.

At the end of a case which proved to be historic I left the court a free man and, I might also add, a marked man. The sensation of my unexpected release was followed twenty-four hours later by a greater drama when a Yankee gunman hired by the notorious Chicago May[4] attempted to assassinate me in the streets of London. However, I shall come to that episode of my eventful life in due course.

The Chicago of my early days, when I was about eleven years of age, was wooden-built. There were rickety board walks along the street and practically all the houses were made of wood, flimsy, ramshackle dwelling-houses and shops thrown together by the people who came pouring in aflame with the stories of the wealth that could be had for the asking. The Great Fire started through a woman named O'Leary who used to supply us with milk. She had gone to milk her cows one night, taking a lamp with her. One of the animals kicked the lamp over and thus began one of the greatest fires in the history of the world.

The reader of this story will require no particularly vivid imagination to depict my early life. My father died long before I was out of my teens, leaving my poor old mother to struggle along as best she could. She had some relatives in the town, but I don't suppose they took much interest in her and I am quite prepared to believe that she found it hard enough to provide the bare necessities of life without bothering very much about my schooling.

In after-years it was often bitterly brought home to me how much I had lost, and what I had paid, for the want of proper parental control. The influence of a father and a mother to whom you can look for everything and whose guidance can firmly set your feet on the ladder of life is an asset that you can never properly appreciate until it is too late. I was too young when my father died[5] to realize what it meant.

School had no attraction for me whatever. There was no compulsory education then as there is now. Tired of the humdrum life at home and the everlasting poverty which obtruded itself at every turn, I ran away from school and got a job on a boat where I was employed as a bell-boy. It was one of the first steamers that ran on Lake Michigan and went up to Milwaukee. I stayed on this boat for a season and following that became a call-boy for a month at the Adelphi Theatre in Chicago.

It is slightly amusing to recollect, in the light of after-events, that they were then playing at the theater *Ali Baba and the Forty Thieves*. I don't know that it made any particular impression on me, or that it imbued me with the idea of becoming a thief myself. At any rate I did not last long in the theatrical profession.

I then became what used to be known in America as a candy butcher, that is, I sold peanuts, candy, newspapers, cigars, and other odds and ends on the trains. I was a pretty smart-looking youngster in those days and never found the slightest difficulty in getting a job, although I never stuck to it long. I wanted to be out and about earning money. The idea of making a few dollars a week never appealed to my restless nature, which I suppose is one of the reasons why I never stayed on the straight and narrow path.

The Chicago of the 'seventies was a wild and woolly affair. Public-houses and pool rooms, gambling establishments of all kinds, red-light houses kept by foreign women, were open all night long, and with no one to exercise any control over my habits I drifted into the pool rooms at a time when I should have been home in bed. I was only fourteen years of age when I obtained a job as a cash boy in the Marshall Field store in Chicago, the same place where Mr. Gordon Selfridge made his beginning. Well, if I had stuck to my work there is no saying that I, too, might not have become a millionaire like Mr. Selfridge. The opportunity was there, but I could not see it.

Running about with money appealed to me well enough, though I could not earn sufficient to satisfy myself. Seven or eight months I lasted in the Stores, and then I became a Western Union telegraph boy delivering telegrams about the city. But here again the pay did not come up to my requirements. Night after night I would be playing pool and gambling in dollars, until I began to look round for ways and means of raising more money. The only opportunity I could see of getting any was to steal. Delivering telegrams as I was to all sorts of private houses and business establishments, I found there were plenty of chances of pilfering small articles. These I used to sell and for a time played pool to my heart's content.

However, this sort of thing could not continue indefinitely. I was only just fifteen years of age when the police took me into custody for stealing a box of cutlery from a place to which I had been sent. They threw me into a cell with a collection of tramps and old-timers who seemed to be much amused at my boyish tears at being locked up.

"Cheer up, kiddo," they all said to me, "it won't be long before you're used to it. Keep smiling and you'll be all right."

I shall never forget my first taste of prison life. They put me in what was known as the House of Correction and I went numb with horror at the sights I saw. There were blacks and whites of all ages and sizes, and the place stunk like a sewer. Men were lying about the floors smoking, spitting, cursing, idling away the time until they were dealt with. They laughed when they saw me, asked me what I had done, and amusedly poked each other in the ribs when I said I was in for nicking a box of cutlery.

Night time came and with it no hope of my release. The big Irish policeman who had arrested me good-naturedly said he would let my mother know and see if she could not do something for me. But I am afraid I had long ago estranged any sympathy at home. A guard came along and hustled me into a cell, rudely requested me to stop blubbing, and left me locked up feeling as miserable as it was possible for any boy to feel. I got nothing to eat all night. In the morning a trusty came along, shoved some bread and coffee inside the cell, winked at me, and left me to my wretched thoughts until ten o'clock, when I was taken to the police court and charged.

There was quite a bunch of us to be dealt with. Chicago was full of criminals then, as it is now. I was taken to the court, heard as in a dream the evidence that was given against me and just dimly remembered being informed by the jailer that I would go to the Sessions for trial.

What a tragical farce! Fifteen years of age, barely old enough to know better, flung like a dog into a filthy prison crowded with all the thugs and thieves in Chicago. Regularly night after night while awaiting trial I cried myself to sleep, bitterly promising myself that I would never do anything wrong again. Most of my fellow-prisoners were kind enough. They gave me food to supplement the mush, a sort of porridge we had for breakfast, slung me pieces of meat to eke out the scanty diet, and asked me if I would like a chew. Boy-like, I tried to masticate some tobacco, but it only made me feel worse than ever. I went about hardly knowing what I was doing until the time came, a fortnight later, to appear at Sessions.

I had nobody to defend me. My poor mother would have nothing to do with me, so, taking the advice of the men in the prison, I pleaded guilty and was sentenced by the Judge to nine months' imprisonment. I hardly heard what he said. I had been in a trance from the moment the police arrested me and I was still bereft of my senses when they took me back to the prison and shoved me into a cell about four feet wide and seven feet long. My mother, broken-hearted, would not come to see me, and the only people to whom I could turn for any sympathy were the other men in the jail.

For over a week I lay there without any exercise whatever. I asked the trusty who came round with the food what I could do about it.

"Say you want to see the Captain," he advised me. "But mind you be mighty civil to him, kid, or else he will jump on your toes. He's a pretty slick customer if you start sassin' him."

I did not feel in the mood to "sass" anyone and I must say it was in a very humble tone that I asked one of the guards for permission to see the boss.

"What do you want him for?" demanded the fellow suspiciously. "Ain't you satisfied with what you've got?"

"It isn't that, sir," I replied meekly. "I want to know if I can't have something to do."

"You stop where you are and don't make a nuisance of yourself," snarled the guard, banging the door, "or else I'll give you something to remember. Who do you think you are, saying you want to see the Captain? You wait until the Captain wants to see you."

I did not know what was going to happen to me then. I expected to be put on bread and water or suffer some other dire fate. At night the prison was a place of horror. I could hear the negroes wailing in their cells, occasionally a foul-mouthed burst from some irate prisoner demanding something he couldn't get. But about eleven o'clock the following morning the bolts on my cell door clanged and I saw the Warden, a big, full-blooded Irishman, in company with a couple of guards.

"Stand to attention!" rapped one of them.

"Well, what's the matter with you?" inquired the Warden, scowling at me. "What do you mean by sending for me?"

My heart dropped right into my boots and for a time I could only stutter.

"Please, s-s-s-sir, couldn't you give me something to do?"

"Do!"

"Yes, s-s-sir," still more meekly.

"Huh! So you're starting to make trouble already? What is it you want to do?"

I explained as best I could that I must do something or I would go mad.

"Oh, give him something," grunted the Warden, moving away.

I discovered then the foolishness of making yourself known in a prison. It is far better to say nothing and do nothing—just let them do what they like with you. In that way you don't get singled out.

A few days after seeing the Warden—I found out that his name was Captain Mack—I was put to work in a sort of factory where they knitted stockings. I couldn't knit and the guard who had charge of the place couldn't teach me, so he made me a sort of dispatch clerk. I had to pack the stockings in a box to be sent away to be sold, and it was not long before the idea came to my mind of trying to make my escape. Even in those early days I had no inclination to remain in prison any longer than was absolutely necessary. I used to lie awake at night thinking how I could get out, and it occurred to me that the long boxes in which I packed the stockings might provide the means.

A pretty daring scheme for a boy of fifteen, if you like! By keeping close observation every day I soon discovered that the boxes were taken out of the prison as soon as we came back from our midday meal. The plan I had in mind was nothing less than to be carried out myself in place of the usual consignment of stockings.

But I had to get some one to help me. Little Eddie, as everybody termed me, was quite well liked, and I fastened upon a man named George O'Donnell, who seemed quite friendly towards me, as my accomplice. His eyes glistened as I told him of my scheme.

"My God, kid!" he exclaimed admiringly, "you've sure got some gumption. But tell me how are you thinking of getting out of the box? It'll have to be nailed down."

"I've thought of all that," I said. "If we get a set of false nails and just get the box lightly nailed down I can burst the top off as soon as I get down to the depot."

I wanted O'Donnell's help to hammer the false nails down, and of course I had to trust him. I got the nails all right and everything was fixed for me to get into the box and be carried out of the prison, put on the express wagon and taken outside the gates. The time came to put my plan into execution, but just at the very last moment when I was ready to climb into the box O'Donnell came over to me and whispered:

"I can't do it, Eddie, I'll sure be copped. You'll have to find some one else."

"You dirty skunk!" I hissed back at him. "Are you going to 'snitch'?"

"Not me," said George. "But it's no good, Ed. They'll be sure to get you."

There was no help for it. I had no stockings to put in the box and it had to go out empty. The following day it reached its destination and then, by Jove, wasn't there a hullabaloo! The next thing I heard was that Captain Mack wanted me and I knew that I was in for trouble. He had me down to the office, closely guarded by a couple of men three times my size.

"Ah!" he cried the moment he saw me, "so now I know why you wanted some work. What have you got to say for yourself?"

"I don't know what you're talking about," I replied, looking him full in the face.

"You don't, hey?"

"No, sir."

"I'll tell you," he bawled at me angrily. "You sent an empty box out of the prison yesterday. You thought you were going in it, didn't you?"

"But I'm sure I don't know anything about it, sir," I said as boldly as I could, though I could feel the blood draining from my face. I had a premonition then that some one had given me away and I made a mental vow that whoever the snitch was he would pay for his treachery.

The Captain did not waste much time questioning me.

"Call up O'Donnell," he ordered brusquely.

One look at my confederate was quite enough. The dirty dog would not meet my eye.

"What do you know about this affair, O'Donnell?" asked the Captain. "You're in this and if you don't spill the whole story I'll give you something you'll remember to your dying day."

O'Donnell didn't need much urging. Then and there he snitched, put everything on me, and was then hustled out of the room, leaving me to be dealt with.

"Now then, you," said the Captain, fixing me with a liverish eye, "what do you think is going to happen to you?"

"I can't say, sir," I replied, quite truthfully for once.

"But I can," the Captain shouted. "What you'll get is a first-class beating up. I'll teach you to break out of prison. By the time I'm finished with you you'll wish you were dead."

He was almost as good as his word. The guards took me away and put me into a solitary cell where they could keep a close watch on me. I got nothing but bread and water to eat, no books to read, nobody to whom I could talk. I could see them on the *qui vive* for something they could find to punish me. The week I remained in that silent cell brought home to me as nothing else could have done the awful precariousness of crime.

The beating-up I expected didn't come and I fondly hoped the Captain had forgotten all about it. But, alas! one morning a couple of guards came along, unceremoniously yanked me out of the cell, and pulled me along to a place where there was an iron register over the stairs going up to the first terrace of cells. Hanging over it was a pulley with a long rope. Miserably wondering what was going to take place next, I saw the Warden come along.

"Get hold of him," he ordered the two guards. They put a pair of handcuffs on my wrists, put a hook between them, and then pulled me up the stairs and dropped me down again until I almost fainted. For something like ten minutes they kept on with the torture. Up and down I went, screaming blue murder and calling Mack and the guards all the names I could think of. I was on the verge of unconsciousness when they finally hauled me up, took the handcuffs off my wrists, and flung me into a dungeon, with a basin of water and a lump of bread to keep me alive. Nobody came near me. My wrists were lacerated, my head almost bursting with pain. But I stuck my tongue between my cheeks, resolved to show no fear. Twenty-four hours elapsed, when the guards came again, told me to get up, and escorted me to one of the punishment cells on the first range, where they kept me without exercise of any kind for three whole months.

This is the plain, undeniable truth. Just imagine, a boy fifteen years of age being subjected to torture for the perfectly natural desire of wanting to escape! No one came near me except the man who put the food in my cell and occasionally a hypocritical, sniveling old chaplain who besought me to give up my evil ways and lead an honest life. I rudely told him to go to the devil, for which he promised to report me to the Warden.

The days and nights went by. The prison stunk as usual, while incessantly I could hear the bickering and fighting that went on in the hall below. The jail received its usual quantity of prisoners and just as religiously spewed them out. The bad men were brought in, paid their graft to the fixers who abounded in Chicago at that time, while all the time I lay in my tiny, noisome cell but dimly realizing the truth that I was already well on the way to being an out-and-out bad man myself.

It never occurred to me then that you couldn't win. As far as I can remember my only thoughts were those of revenge. Bitterly did I clench my teeth, cursing the swine who had betrayed me, and just as vengefully did I swear that if this was the way the world treated you when you had committed some trivial crime, then you might just as well do something big and deserve the punishment you got.

Fifteen years old! God, when I look back and think over it all it appears almost unbelievable. I am quite certain I had nothing inherently wrong with me. I could truthfully plead the lack of a proper upbringing, but it never occurred to my boyish brain that I was merely the victim of an iron-bound law which refused to distinguish, or at any rate did not take the trouble, between mere youthful waywardness and incorrigible criminality. But I don't mind saying that by the time I came out of that Chicago House of Correction I felt in no mood to listen to any good advice.

I felt vindictive towards the whole world when they finally turned me out of the prison gates with nothing but what I stood up in. The morning I took my departure I promised one of the guards who had taken part in the manhauling that I would pay him for what he had done.

"Get out before you come to any more harm," he growled at me. "You're too young to know what you're talking about."

I don't suppose he was to blame for what he had done, but that aspect of the matter did not appeal to me. A year or two afterward, when I had gone a little further down the slippery path of wrong-doing, I waylaid him and had a stand-up fight.

Chapter Two
APPRENTICED TO CRIME

Discharged from prison! I wonder how many of my readers appreciate what it means to be turned loose on the world barely sixteen years of age, in a city where everybody scornfully flings it at you that you have been in jail?

If I had known then what I know now I would have cleared out of Chicago forthwith, done anything, in fact, to stop myself drifting still further into crime. But of course I was too young to realize the actual position. My mother and my relatives naturally gave me a cool reception when I went home. One way and another they drummed it into me that I had disgraced the family for evermore, and, boylike, I resented it.

But a very short time elapsed before I again got into trouble. I had a faithful friend, Irish as I was, named Paddy Fitzgerald. Paddy was a regular broth of a boy, up to anything and, like myself, thoroughly devil-may-care. His mother kept a few cows and supplied her neighbors with milk. Paddy himself had some pigeons in the barn over the cowshed. We made that our headquarters and from it sallied forth foraging for what we could find. A grocer's shop yielded up a case of pies, a box of ginger, and some honey. We took it up into the barn, hid it among the hay, and for a day or two lived like fighting cocks.

Unfortunately, Paddy's disappearance and mine caused a little excitement. His mother heard us talking when she came to milk the cows. She brought Paddy's grandfather out with a pitchfork.

"By gum, I'll catch the young rascals," wheezed the old chap, prodding the hay. That soon made us scurry. We got away all right, but we did not go home again. The pies, etc., had put the police on our track and my mother told me the best thing I could do was to clear out for good. She wanted no more trouble with me, while I don't mind confessing that I was equally anxious to have none. No doubt it was a stupid thing for my mother to have done, but she, poor soul, had quite enough on her shoulders without a reprobate like me to worry the life out of her. Still, I have never ceased to regret that in my youthful foolishness I cleared out of Chicago caring not a nickel as to what happened. But the call of the road was in my blood and off I went, fully confident of being able to get a living somewhere.

For some little time Paddy and I wandered about the country doing odd jobs. We fell in with the yeggmen[6], the hobos, the bums and all that vast traveling fraternity of crooks who used to get their living by various forms of robbery. The hobos and the bums soon disgusted me. I was never one for jumping trains and being unceremoniously flung off by a burly conductor, any more than I could lower myself to panhandling grub the way the hobos did. If I wanted anything I took it. I did not believe in asking.

By the time I had reached the mature age of seventeen I had become a regular follower of Barnum's Circus all over the States. Not that I wanted to see the show. Oh dear, no! I was serving my apprenticeship in all sorts of little things, such as the three-card trick, the thimble and pea, and all those humorous little variants of "finding the lady" which go to provide a living for all the nimble-fingered.

There were always plenty of "mugs"[7] to be found in the big towns visited by the circus. Barnum himself I never saw. He must have had fully a dozen shows on the road touring all over the States. At any rate, they attracted a tremendous amount of attention. There would be a spectacular parade through a town at which you would see all the hayseeds gaping with open mouths at the elephants and the clowns and all the weird human freaks of which Barnum was so fond. Hard on their trail would come all the "magsmen,"[8] the "spielers,"[9] the "dips,"[10] the "broadsmen"[11] and the "pickers-up."[12] That was my job. Being but a novice at the business all I had to do was to keep my weather eye skinned for the coppers.

Old Phineas knew all about the gang of human wasps that used to sting his customers, so he always had his own coppers attached to his shows. These traveling 'tecs[13] on arrival at a town would go to the local men and tell them what to look out for, but in nine cases out of ten they were wasting their time. The local men did not want to be told anything—as is the habit of the village "rozzer."[14] So it wasn't much trouble to get the three cards and the thimble and pea going while the ballyhoo men crowded round and started betting like blazes. The rustics would join in and be skinned of their dollars in less time than it takes me to write about it, while I, feeling very important, looked this way and that for a policeman's uniform.

What a game! I might have gone on with it indefinitely if I had not grown rather tired of having a dollar or two slung at me for my day's work.

It was only chance, after all, that made me an out-and-out thief. Paddy Fitzgerald and I, still following the circus, were walking down a street in Columbus, Ohio, one day, when we passed a big grain merchant's store. Paddy, like myself, wanted to get some money, and by that time we knew quite enough of the tricks of the trade to make a start. We saw the shopkeeper standing at the door.

"You keep him talking while I get in the back way and see what I can find," I said to Paddy. "Mind you, don't you let him go till I'm out again."

Paddy, nothing loth, immediately went up and started spieling, but apparently he made a mess of the job. Busily engaged in rifling a safe in the office at the back I failed to hear the shopkeeper come in.

"Hello, you, what's your little game?" he shouted, making a rush at me.

No time to stand on ceremony; I just skedaddled as fast as my legs could carry me, down into the main street with the man behind me screaming for the police. Paddy had tumbled something wrong. He had disappeared already. Off I flew, dodging half a dozen people who tried to stop me. I flung away the money I had obtained, thinking the owner would, pick it up and so let me get away. Suddenly a burly copper pounced upon me, threw me to the ground, and sat on my panting body till the grain merchant came up and charged me with stealing his money. He, too, was blowing hard.

"Officer! Officer! This young scoundrel has robbed me. Ask him what he means by it?"

With a two-hundred pound policeman sitting on my chest I couldn't say anything, and when I was hauled to my feet I had no fight left. With a crowd of about two hundred people following me I was taken up the street to the local jail right opposite the very place I had robbed! I came to know that grain merchant's shop very well during the next three months. The window of my cell overlooked it.

Once more did I have the opportunity of appreciating the fact that a criminal life wasn't quite so profitable as it appeared. I had only got a miserable one hundred and twenty-five "shin plasters" (dollar bills) out of the safe opposite and I had lost them all in my vain attempt to distract the enemy! I believe I also threw away a wad of fifty-cent bills; I certainly do know that I had nothing to show for the little adventure.

There was nothing radically wrong with the prison. They treated you much better than they did at Chicago. All the prisoners were allowed a certain amount of exercise every day, the niggers in one part and the whites in another. For the remainder of the time everybody played cards and did no work worth speaking of. At night time, of course, we were locked up. The only fly in the ointment was that they kept me there for three months before they brought me for trial.

I will give Paddy Fitzgerald his due. He sent me fifty dollars with which I could brief a lawyer to defend me. I got a man named Converse, who afterward became a Senator. However, for all the good he did me I might just as well have kept my money in my pocket.

I must have been quite a smart-looking youth in those days. The Warden had a pretty little Swedish maid named Kattie, who took quite a fancy to me.

"Ah, you poor boy!" she said to me in her fascinating broken English. "What haf you done that you should be in prison?"

"Well," I replied, "it's like this. A man over the way lost some money from his safe. He seems to think I took it."

Poor girl, I think she fully believed in my innocence, so I tried to get her to help me to escape. But her big blue eyes opened wide with fright when I suggested her smuggling me into the Warden's house and thence out into the street.

"Oh, no, Eddie, I could not do that. It will surely cause the most terrible trouble."

"Come on, Kattie," I said to her. "You'll come to no harm. As soon as I am away I'll send you some money and we'll get married."

But Kattie, if she did look young and unsophisticated, had enough sense in her little head not to be beguiled into anything like that.

"No, Eddie, I must not do that," she said. "You have been foolish, and it will be more foolish still to run away now."

One way and another Kattie and I did quite an amount of harmless flirting and possibly our relationship might have become a little closer had not Justice intervened. I was absolutely thunderstruck when, despite all the efforts of my attorney, I received the sentence of two years hard labor in the Ohio Penitentiary. Two years for nothing! This is no game, I thought. If you get two years without really robbing anyone, how much will you get if you relieve them of a few thousand dollars? Once more, if I had had any intelligence then, I might have paused in my career of crime and asked myself was it really worth while.

Kattie stuck to me like a brick for some time after I had been sentenced. She used to call at the prison and leave me fruit, but she wasn't allowed to see me, which was just as well. After a time she ceased to come and I lost trace of her altogether. When I had been discharged and had left Ohio I wrote to her at the Warden's house but I never got a reply. So that ended that little romance.

There was no monkey business about the life in the Ohio Penitentiary. You were not allowed to talk and all the prisoners had to march the lock-step from the cells to the dining-room and from the latter place to the workshops.

The lock-step! You fell into a long wriggling queue with your hands on each other's shoulders doing a sort of elephantine dance that would send you into convulsions of laughter if you saw it on the stage. But it was certainly no joke in the Penitentiary. If you talked you were at once reported for punishment. Still, we used to do it all the same. The names we used to call the guards—unheard by them—would have made their blood curdle if they had only known.

Seventeen years of age and a full-blown convict! Heaven only knows what my mother must have thought of it all. So far as I was aware she knew nothing about my being in prison now and I don't mind saying that I had not the slightest intention of enlightening her. The life did not cow me in the least. I was a regular spitfire in those days, ready and willing to fight on the slightest provocation. My fellow-convicts rather admired me, making me even more mettlesome.

One fine morning, when I must have been feeling a little too fresh, I made a sad mess of things. One of the guards, a big German-American whom I hated like poison, ordered me to take my place in the lockstep gang between two buck niggers.

"Not me," I said. "I don't march between any niggers. I'm a white man."

"So! A white man, are you? Get in the line or I will haf you before the Warden."

"Get in yourself, you big Dutch stiff," I replied rudely. "Who do you think you're talking to?"

It looked like developing into quite a nice little row, and everybody was squinting at me out of the corner of their eyes, wondering what I would do next. The two niggers looked murder, but the guard sensed the danger and shoved me back into the cell, where I spent the remainder of the day wondering what was going to happen to me. I know I cursed the folly which had made me lose my temper.

They didn't mean to let me go unpunished. The following morning they hauled me in front of the Chief Guard, Irish like myself. The Dutchman told his tale, I told mine, after which the Chief had a few rude things to say about drawing the color line inside a prison.

"You impudent little dog," he said to me. "Who the hell do you think you are, to say what you'll have and what you won't have here? Take him away," he ordered his men. "We'll give him something that will make him behave himself."

They took me over to the solitary cell, stripped me stark naked, put me into a bath with two inches of water in it, handcuffed me behind my back, and tied a bandage over my eyes. I hadn't the faintest idea what was going to happen to me. I half expected a flogging. I knew, of course, that preparations to some end were going on around me, but I certainly had no inkling of what they were until I suddenly felt a terrible sting which made me jump up in the bath about three feet. Once, twice, thrice the dreadful pain shot through me. My yells must have been heard in the street outside. They took the bandage off my eyes, when I saw what they had been doing to me—giving me electric shocks. I came to know it afterward as the "sting," and no doubt it was the forerunner of the electrocution which is now the method of execution in different parts of America.

Sting it certainly did; I never wanted another dose of it. It wouldn't be so bad if you knew it was coming. The unexpectedness of it was absolutely agonizing. A little discreet questioning among my fellow-prisoners elicited a bit more information about it. The punishment was usually administered by a convict who got a remission of his sentence for doing it and you were stung in much the same way that a prisoner in an English jail receives a certain number of strokes with the cat. One day they stung a man to death and that put an end to it.

Life in the Ohio Penitentiary could do nothing but send me still further headlong to ruin. The stinging I received made me more vicious than ever, while the company I kept—more or less compulsorily—didn't tend to improve my morals. They put old-timers in my cell, depraved men of the worst possible type who took a savage delight in teaching me all they knew. I must have been a pretty apt pupil. By the time I was eighteen I think I knew as much about crime as anybody in the prison.

Occasionally I met men I knew. In the days when I had been traveling Barnum's Circus I came across dozens of yeggmen, bank-busters and all the vast brotherhood of the underworld who live by their wits. They just laughed when they saw me in the Pen and told me I would surely make good before I had finished.

This Ohio Penitentiary was, I think, the stiffest prison I have ever known, and in its way the organization was marvelous. Apparently the State authorities tried to make it self-supporting, and from what I could see of it they must have succeeded. There were cigar factories, roller mills, tin shops, boot factories, blacksmith shops, all inside the prison walls and all of them run by contractors to whom the State hired the convicts at a wage of fifty cents a day. They were all sweaters, these contractors. Their idea was, naturally, to get all the labor they could out of the men. The guards stood in, so one way and another the life inside the jail was as bad as it could be.

Worst of all were the rolling mills; the men who worked there were nothing better than slaves, and I have seen prisoners deliberately drop molten lead on their feet in order that they might get out of the place and be sent to the prison hospital. The poor devils would have committed suicide had it been humanly possible.

The prison discipline was terrific: I have never known anything like it. You were not allowed to walk and you got no exercise worth speaking of. When you got up in the morning you cleaned your cell, marched to the dining-room in lock-step for your breakfast, which usually consisted of bread and coffee and sometimes hash. From there we went to work, where we remained until noon. Once more did we lock-step our way to the dining-room, where a sanctimonious old gentleman said prayers—God knows what for—and then let us get on with our stew. It was about the only meal of the day worth eating, and I must say they always gave us plenty of it. At night time we came back for our supper, bread and tea and cheese, after which we were put back in our cells for the night to meditate upon our sins.

I remember one of the men of a poetical turn of mind composing the following little ditty which we used to hum under our breath:

With my one, two, three and four
  All in a line,
From shoe-shop to quarry each bloke
  Will keep time.
They work like a Turk, and it's back to your cell,
While a bloke's doing time in the Pen.

We also got a ration of tobacco each Saturday which helped to make life a little more bearable, but I don't mind saying the two years I spent there were easily the longest I have ever suffered. As I became more accustomed to prison life and came to know the game better the days passed much easier, but in any case I never wanted another dose of the Ohio Pen.

You could buy almost anything you wanted in the prison if you had the money, but I hadn't got any. Guards stationed on the walls with rifles made it almost impossible to get away. The only attempted escape I ever heard of was that of some men who set fire to the prison hoping to gain their freedom in the confusion. They did not succeed and the price they paid effectually deterred them from wanting to get outside again before their time was up.

I came out of the Pen in the depth of winter, thoroughly resolved to have nothing more to do with prison life. They discharged me with the usual suit of clothes and five dollars. I had no intention of going home. Instead, I took a long jump to New Orleans, where I stayed for a couple of years in a gambling house where they played faro night and day. In those days—the time would be 1880—New Orleans was easily the best town in the Southern States. They held a Mardi Gras every year which brought thousands of people into the place. I had a pretty good job in the faro joint keeping watch for the police and seeing that money wasn't pinched, and one way and another the life held a lot of attraction for a boy of twenty. New Orleans abounded with old French planters whose picturesque Panama hats and white clothes still linger in my memory. They were generous, free-hearted men who did not mind what they spent, and if I had only looked after myself I might have made a lot of money.

Everybody in the town spoke French. At night time the cafes and music-halls would be in full blast and you could go around the public-houses, where they had lovely Creole waitresses who looked almost white. Negroes from the plantations crowded into the town and were specially catered for in cheap places where they were waited upon by their own folk. The faro dens were almost invariably well conducted and I must say I saw very little fighting there. They still play the game in New Orleans, but to nothing like the same extent. The last time I saw the town it had lost a good deal of its old-time flavor. All the old French planters had gone. It had become Americanized in a way that destroyed the greater part of its charm. In the 'eighties it was a place where they worked by day and played by night. I have never come across a town quite like it.

I became pretty well known and if all had gone well with me—that is to say, if I had kept away from gambling myself—I might have ended up a rich man. I made a friend of Parson Davies, one of the well-known characters of the town who kept a big gambling joint. He was the man who took on John L. Sullivan, the world's heavy-weight champion, after Pat Sheedy had finished with him. The Parson also brought out Kid McCoy and many other celebrated boxers. I never heard how he came to be called Parson, though he certainly did look like one. But there was nothing particularly soft in his nature. A man more capable of looking after himself I never met. I came across him years afterward in Chicago, where he ran some of the biggest gambling joints in the town and made a huge fortune. Chicago of the 'eighties and 'nineties was a real gold-mine to the men who knew the ropes. But I am not begrudging the success they attained. If I had kept my head I could have had precisely the same opportunity.

New Orleans held me for a couple of years. The police knew nothing about me and I carefully kept out of their way. They did not bother the faro banks. Provided a man lost his money decently they let the joints go along just as they liked, leaving it to the boss to keep order. It was just as orderly as Monte Carlo. In most of the places there would be a couple of bouncers, big fellows who were ready to throw you out the moment you got a bit quarrelsome. But after all, they will do that at Monte. Life in New Orleans was pleasant enough for anyone, but I began to long for a bit more adventure. The horrors of the two years in the Ohio Pen had practically faded from my youthful mind, and so I set off again *en route* to the bustling town of Pittsburgh, Pennsylvania. What I meant to do I hadn't the faintest idea, but I know I wanted to make a touch. I had saved a few hundred dollars in New Orleans, but could not make enough to satisfy the longing I had for money.

It was about the end of 1881 that I went up the river from New Orleans to Pittsburgh on the old paddle steamer *Natches,* one of the Mississippi boats which is still remembered in the States. It used to tickle me to death to see the niggers shooting crap on the decks. The captains of these steamboats usually paid their crews before the vessel reached its destination, and some of the smart niggers almost invariably managed to win all the others' money shaking the bones, so that when they reached the journey's end they had nothing left and were forced to sign on again to get back. It was about the only way the captain could rely on a crew.

I found Pittsburgh a good town, plenty of life, gallons of booze, and a host of congenial company. It contained more crooks to the square yard than Chicago, and I had not been in the place more than a few days before I fell in with a yeggman named Joe Butts. Joe and I took counsel together to see what we could do. The Pennsylvania Railway Office looked good. Joe went out and did a bit of reconnoitering and came back with the information that the cashier seemed a bit of a mug. We could stall him without any trouble.

We hired a buggy and horse, drove up to the railway door, when I got down, went inside and told the cashier a gentleman wanted to speak to him outside. He fell like a lamb. I have no doubt I smiled at him reassuringly, and at any rate, while he and Joe were holding sweet converse, I remained inside the office and robbed the safe to the tune of something like seven or eight hundred dollars. Nor did I bother to say adieu. Like the Arab, I folded my tent and silently stole away—out of the back door. I did not want that cashier to see me anymore than I could help.

Experience had already taught me that it did not pay to give your victim any more opportunities of identifying you than were absolutely necessary.

I don't know what Joe was talking about outside. He might have been discussing freights to Oshkosh, Wis., for all I knew or cared. The moment I got the money from the safe—conveniently left open—I vamoosed. I stood not upon the order of my going, but went.

All might have gone well with us had Joe kept his mouth shut. We got out of Pittsburgh as soon as we could, a boat called *Katie Stockdale* taking us up to Cincinnati in Ohio, where, we discovered on our arrival, they were holding a big musical festival. Joe and I had a rousing good time for about three days, drinking and dancing and buying ourselves a new outfit. I did not know then what I ascertained afterward.

Before leaving Pittsburgh Joe had gone into a public-house, started boozing, and promptly blown the gaff to the proprietor. I suppose he had been boasting of the easy money he had got. Somebody must have heard him; it was a flashy sort of place frequented by the swell yeggmen, and likely as not the publican kept his eyes and ears open for what he could see and hear. No doubt when Joe began to talk he began to listen. Like most of his kidney, he stood in with the police, and although we succeeded in getting out of Pittsburgh the bulls must have been hot on our trail from the time we boarded the *Katie Stockdale.*

Of all this I remained in blissful ignorance. Joe and I had a thumping good time in Cincinnati. We had a go at the faro banks, played up our money like sports, while I treated myself to a diamond pin which cost me seventy-five dollars. That, and a brand-new rig-out, did not leave much of the money, but I felt so pleased with myself that I decided to go back to Chicago and give my old friends a look-up. What made me do it I can't say. Common sense ought to have told me that if I was going to be pinched for the Pittsburgh job Chicago, next to Pittsburgh itself, would be easily the worst town in the States for me to be seen in.

What did I care? Twenty-one years of age, vainglorious over the success of the job I had just pulled off, a flash suit of clothes and a diamond pin. 'Little Eddie has made good,' I could hear them all saying. In my own mind I meant to turn up at home with all the outward and visible signs of great prosperity.

I did not bother going home the night I arrived in Chicago. Foolishly, as it turned out, I made a tour of the various joints I knew, had a dozen or two drinks with different acquaintances, and doubtless thoroughly spread the news that I had come back. I was blissfully ignorant, of course, that the Pittsburgh police had circulated my description. But the following afternoon I heard all about it. Walking down the main street a couple of men from the central police office bailed me up.

"Hello, Eddie, back again?"

"Yes," I said, looking this way and that to see if I could make a bolt, "it's good to see the old town again."

"Well, you won't see it long," replied one of the 'tecs. "You're wanted in Pittsburgh, Ed. You'll have to come inside."

I showed fight, but it was no good. They grabbed me by the arm and banged me inside the police station before I could fully realize what had happened. Once again did it dawn upon me that I had made a sad miscalculation.

Chapter Three
REAL PENAL SERVITUDE

Life did not seem so sweet when I found myself back in the City prison. The bulls remembered me and only laughed sarcastically when I told them I did not know what I was in for. Quite evidently some one else did because I was not allowed to communicate with a lawyer and thus fight the extradition as I might have done.

It was the same old crowd I had known a few years before. Shyster lawyers walking in and out as though they owned the place, greedy bail-fixers touting the prisoners for their custom, burly policemen shoving everybody all over the place, caring not a damn whether they were innocent or guilty. They did not give me a chance to save myself. I appeared at the police court, found myself remanded in custody without saying a word in defense and spent a night in the cell awaiting the police from Pittsburgh.

The bulls of that town seemed to look upon me as, a tough nut. The Chief of Police, one Roger O'Mara by name, came for me himself. I came to know him very well afterward and he wasn't a bad sort of fellow. He put the bracelets on me and took me back with him to Pittsburgh, all the time being handcuffed to him. O'Mara told me one thing that might have proved useful. Joe Butts had got clean away and there was just a chance the cashier of the Pennsylvania Railway wouldn't recognize me. However, O'Mara settled that matter in his own fashion. He brought the cashier to the prison, let him have a good look at me, and said to him:

"That's the man, isn't it?"

The American police were always pretty free and easy in the way they did their work, and I remember years afterward when a detective-inspector from Scotland Yard arrested me for robbery at the Crédit Lyonnais in Lyons he did much the same thing. Pinkertons had sent a man over from America to get me identified as Eddie Guerin. The bank paid all expenses. They gave this policeman £2 a day and a traveling allowance which made the trip a nice little holiday. My captor brought him along and said, just the same as Roger O'Mara said: "That's Eddie Guerin, isn't it?" And only a fool would have answered "No."

Things looked pretty black in Pittsburgh. Most of the money had gone; a suit of clothes and a diamond pin was all I had left. But to give Joe Butts his due he sent me $200, which enabled me to get a lawyer and buy myself some decent food. Nevertheless, I could not get bail. The professional fixers fought shy of me. They must have known I would make a get-away if the opportunity came my way. Three long months I stuck in the Pittsburgh jail awaiting trial, and young as I was it made me feel sick to see the young boys and girls thrown into prison in the company of some of the worst criminals in America. Being a bit of an old hand myself I could feel the misery they felt and I went out of my way then to give them a bit of advice. I don't suppose they ever took it, but that is neither here nor there.

The lawyer who defended me got a hundred dollars, but all I received was three years. I gave another hundred dollars to a lawyer who was supposed to have influence with the Warden of the prison to get me a decent job, but I think he put the money in his pocket and bothered no more about me. They put me into a cell with a Dutchman, a German-American calling himself Hans Schmidt, burglar by trade, bad man in every possible way. I was not altogether unsophisticated myself, but the language this German used shocked even me.

The Allegheny State Prison where I had to serve my sentence possessed a terrible reputation. It was practically all solitary confinement and I should say that it contained the worst criminals in the whole of America. Pittsburgh, as I have previously mentioned, used to attract all the big bad men, and at the time I made my appearance there something like six hundred men were in the place, murderers, burglars, horse-thieves, boxmen, i.e. safe-breakers, most of them ready and willing to murder you at a moment's notice. And quite obviously the State authorities were under no delusions about the matter. The guards, dressed in civilian clothes, carried both pistols and clubs. They were ready to shoot you or give you a crack over the head the moment you opened your mouth.

I got away from the Dutchman as soon as I could. His filthy habits, the shockingly obscene language he used, appalled me. With a little bit of trouble I got into the cell of the librarian, a decent old fellow doing twenty years for burglary. They kept him locked up practically all the time. When I first saw him he was as white as a ghost and it made me realize if nothing else could do the almost unbelievable cruelty of the American prison system. This old fellow, who had committed a crime which would have got him, in England, no more than two years, had been locked up in one of the worst convict prisons in the world for nearly twenty years. I think they let him out in the fresh air about twice a year just to keep him alive. Anyhow, if I had had any brains, it might have dawned upon me when I saw him that it would pay me to keep out of prison in the future. But I doubt whether I even thought of the matter. The only thing that concerned me for the immediate present was to get out of Allegheny.

Being in the librarian's cell gave me the opportunity of getting round the prison and making the acquaintance of the officials. The Warden I rarely saw, but I came to know the Chaplain very well.

"Chaplain," I said to him one morning, "couldn't you get me some sort of job outside? I am not like one of the old-timers. I'll go mad if I don't get out in the fresh air."

"Well, Eddie," he replied, "you know what it is. They are not going to let young and active boys like you too near the walls. You might take it into your head to fly away."

"Not me, Chaplain. I know too much for that."

Anyhow, the Chaplain went off promising to see the Warden, with the result that I was shortly afterward transferred to the wash-house to take care of a little steam-engine. Then I began to get busy.

A little reconnoitering soon brought home the difficulties of the situation. The wash-house was in the open air all right, but I would have to climb over a sixty-foot wall to make my escape. However, I did not mean to be deterred, and I had a word with the carpenter, Tim O'Connor by name, serving fifteen years for house-breaking. He came to the wash-house one day to fix a hanger, and I took the occasion of having a little heart-to-heart talk.

"Tim," I said, "what's the chances of getting away from here?"

He looked at me in astonishment. Having been there over ten years the idea of leaving never seriously occurred to him.

"Well," he replied shaking his head, "the wall isn't so very high."

"Talk sense!" I retorted. "It is quite high enough to keep us in. You're a carpenter—couldn't you make a ladder?"

"Say, now, boy, who are you getting at? Do you think I want to go back in the solitary? Besides, if they caught you getting over the wall they'd drop you like lightning."

But Allegheny was getting on my nerves. I meant to get over that prison wall or die in the attempt. Night and day I worried Tim for a ladder until eventually he brought along some planks and a couple of clamps by which I might possibly get over the wall. The idea was to clamp the boards together, put them on the wash-house roof, crawl up and over the wall.

What happened was much what I expected. The clamps gave way, the boards fell and smashed one of the prison lamps, and in a very short space of time the guards were on my track. They couldn't definitely prove anything against me, but they took my job away from me and put me back into a solitary cell where for two months I remained until I was transferred to a newer and stronger prison up the river.

That didn't damp my spirits. The prison that could hold me when I meant to get out wasn't built in those days. The new place had not been completed, and the job they put me to—that of cleaning the cells—gave me the opportunity of examining the locks. If you've got the key of your cell you've pretty nearly got the key to freedom.

It took a long time to get that key, however. A man working in the cigar factory, Tommy Hall, helped me to make one that fitted both our cells, but it took a month, while all the time I kept my eyes skinned to see how we could get away. Among my duties I had to go down to the hall each morning and bring up the bread in company with a guard who watched me distribute it to the prisoners. When nightfall came I took the tray down after the guard had finished and by keeping a careful watch I got to know everything that took place. I noticed that after their nightly round the guards went to the middle of the prison and that the door leading to the yard was not locked because there were still armed men on the wall.

I told Tommy everything.

"Now, look here, Tommy," I said. "Before we can get far we shall have to have some money. What about you? Have you got anybody who will let you have any, because I haven't?"

"My sister will bring some," Tommy informed me, "but, of course, we will have to get a message to her."

"I can manage that," I said.

One of the men being discharged cheerfully agreed to call on Tommy's sister and tell her what was about to take place. It was risky, but we could do nothing else. As it turned out, we had nothing to fear. The sister wrote in for permission to see her brother, came along and kissed Tommy, and while she was doing it slipped a fifty-dollar bill out of her mouth into his. It was one of the cleverest tricks I have ever heard of.

Now for the grand get-away! In our wing of the prison there were five tiers of cells. When Tommy came in from the cigar shop the only guard we could see was the one in charge of the cell house. He made a double tour of his charges morning and evening, and he did not seem to suspect anything wrong. I had arranged with Tommy to make a dummy to put in his bed so that if by any fatal chance a guard did look into his cell he might not notice anything wrong.

In company with the guard I took the bread round as usual in the evening. Half-way, I had to go back to get some more. With the false key in my hand I let Tommy out of his cell, gave him the key, and then saw him slip away and hide himself in an empty cell in the bottom floor. The guard finished distributing bread and wished all his prisoners pleasant dreams. Then he locked me up for the night, said "Good night, Ed," to which I dutifully replied "Good night, sir," and for all he knew went to bed like a good, obedient boy. Off he went and everything became quiet.

Half an hour later I heard a key in the door of my cell. It was Tommy.

"Come on," he whispered, "it's all quiet downstairs."

Closing the cell door behind me I sneaked off behind Tommy, into the yard, and hid under a bridge which communicated with another part of the prison. We heard the "All right" bell ring and the guards march out to the Warden's office. There was nothing we could do until they were out of the way. As soon as the coast was clear we got into the engineering shop, put on a suit of overalls apiece and a blouse to hide the prison dress. Some one had carelessly left a ladder lying around. It was too short for our purpose, but Tommy climbed to the top while I came up behind him and let him stand on my shoulders. He scrambled to the top of the wall, hauled me up, leaving us with the problem of making a nasty jump on the other side.

Suddenly the watch-dogs started barking. It was then almost pitch dark. The guards on the wall began firing, but they could see nothing. Flat on our stomachs we crawled along to a sentry-box where food used to be hauled up the prison wall. Tommy went down the rope first and uttered a screech as he tore the skin off his hands. I came down sailor fashion and reached the ground without mishap.

By this time the prison bell was clanging madly. Bursts of flame from the guards' rifles were stabbing the darkness with light, but the men on the walls could not see us. In less than ten minutes we had jumped a freight train passing through Allegheny. We did not know where it went and we didn't care. Some hours later it pulled into Pittsburgh, where Tommy hunted up some good pals of his who hid us for a time while the hue and cry was hot.

I discovered later that they did not miss me at the prison until the following morning, when the guard waiting downstairs for my arrival with the bread box kept bawling in vain. Eventually he climbed upstairs to find me and on opening the cell door received the shock of his life. The bird had flown!

"Ed," said Tommy the day after our arrival in Pittsburgh, "this won't do. Every damn 'bull' in the city will be on the lookout for us. It's the quick get-away for you and I, boy."

I quite agreed. We were hiding in a boat house, a damp uncomfortable place, afraid to venture out. But Tommy had a pal who got us a horse and buggy, and like the good sport he was drove us to Oil City, Pennsylvania, a place then in the throes of a tremendous boom. Huge gushers of oil had been discovered in the neighborhood and if I hadn't been a fugitive from justice with a price on my head, liable to be shot at sight by any Sheriff, I might have stopped there and piled up a fortune for myself. Here again is an instance of the truth that you can't win at the crooked game. All around Oil City there were thousands of men staking out claims and selling them for huge sums. Tommy and I, both of us broke, dependent for our safety on the goodwill of a friend, could only think of making Canada as soon as possible.

Privately, also, I didn't fancy the crowd I saw round Oil City. There were half a dozen faro banks going and I knew some one would be sure to recognize me. So we jumped a train for Erie in the same State, hid ourselves away from prying eyes, and finished up by taking another train from the Niagara Falls into

Canada. Without any further incident we reached Toronto, where I knew some people who put us up and gave us the chance to get our bearings.

I felt just a little doubtful about being able to stop in Canada long. When I was at the old Allegheny State Prison a famous burglar named Miller got away in a shoe box in much the same fashion that I had attempted to escape from the jail in Chicago. He became known in consequence as Shoebox Miller, and he was a pretty tough customer. At the time I knew him he had a life sentence for burglary with violence, but he got away and safely landed in Toronto.

Then he did a very foolish thing. He had a sweetheart—and the bulls knew it. Shoebox wrote to her, but the police intercepted the letters, took out an extradition warrant, and sent it over to Toronto.

Shoebox strenuously denied his identity when the Toronto police hauled him inside. That little bluff did not avail him long. There were very lengthy extradition proceedings. Shoebox maintained that escaping from prison was not an offense for which he could be sent back to a foreign country, but the United States Government meant to have him. Lawyers specially came from Washington to fight him and in the end he returned to Allegheny to complete the twenty years which constituted a sentence for life.

The readers of this story of mine will no doubt have come to the conclusion that I had already succeeded in crowding quite an amount of incident into my life at the time I made my first real get-away from prison. As a matter of fact, I was only twenty-three, and if somebody had taken me in hand and put me into a decent job I might have gone straight for evermore.

I don't want to whine, but it is only the bare truth to say that I had no one except myself to lend a helping hand. Trade I had none. Brought up from boyhood days to nothing but odd jobs, the most I could hope for was something menial. I couldn't stand that. Also, I would always sooner steal than starve.

But having got out of the United States and with it the opportunity of turning over a new leaf, it rested with myself to keep away from trouble in the future. And what a lot of suffering

I would have saved myself if I had done it! But, there again, I had no one to really care two hoots in hell what happened to me. I dared not write to my mother in Chicago, or any of my relatives, for fear the police would get hold of the letters, and therefore I remained in Toronto for about a year, running a faro bank and following the races. I became what I was always intended for—an out-and out gambler. If I did not stake my money I would stake my liberty. You lose either way, so it does not very much matter.

Toronto of the early 'eighties was a nice, old-fashioned English city. There were no saloons open night and day as there were in Chicago and Pittsburgh. Saturday nights everything closed down and all you had to do on Sunday was to go to church and listen to the sermons.

I lived a quiet life and stayed in a good boardinghouse with nice people who hadn't the faintest idea that I was badly wanted in the United States. Every Sunday for a year I went to hear a famous preacher, Doctor Wild, a man whose magnetic personality made an impression on my mind which has never been erased. His church on Sunday resembled a theater. The people crowded it out while he talked to them in a way that no actor could ever do.

I tried my hardest to acquire a new outlook on life and I must say that the people of Toronto gave me every opportunity. They were unsuspicious, law-abiding, who never spoke an ill word of you, and if I could only have summed up sufficient determination to have taken some humdrum job and worked my way up in the world this story of mine would never have been written. Well, man proposes and God disposes.

The Riel Rebellion in the North-West of Canada broke out at about this time, headed by a young French-Canadian named Louis Riel. He raised some thousands of followers in Manitoba, armed with guns and rifles, with the idea of ousting the British rule. I offered my services for a volunteer regiment being raised in Toronto, but there were so many men available that they wouldn't have me, so still another link with respectability went phut.

The rebellion did not last long. They caught Riel and hanged him, dispersed his misguided followers, and effectually put an end to any further thoughts of French dominion in Canada. Nevertheless, while I am not unduly given to moralizing, I shall be greatly surprised if the French and the English ever settle down in peace and quietness. The French people look upon themselves as the rightful owners of the country and I am too much of an Irishman to believe that they are not in the right. Still, that has got nothing to do with this story.

I lost another chance of making good through sheer bad luck. A man whose acquaintance I made in Toronto, promised me a job at a factory four or five miles outside the town. The very next morning walking down the main street I saw a crowd of people rushing towards the Union Station. I went with them and learnt that there had been a terrible smash-up on the line, among the killed being the man who had promised to employ me. Probably it did not make much difference to me in the long run. After all, life is what you make it, and whether you mean to go straight, or whether circumstances force you to become crooked, your end is more or less ordained.

Toronto soon began to pall upon me. Two or three months longer I remained about the town hanging on by the skin of my teeth. Always there hung over my head a fear of being recognized, but in those days there was nothing particularly distinctive about my appearance and there was nobody to give me away. Tommy Hall had long since disappeared; he said he could not stand Toronto at any price.

But I could not get my mentality right. "Once a gambler, always a gambler." When you have made big money easily you can't go back to hard work for next door to nothing. Remember, I had done no work worth speaking of since the age of fifteen. I had done a bit in prison, true, but the idea of doing any outside never really appealed to me in the slightest. I am sorry to say I have always looked at it in the same light since. My first experience of jail life goes back over fifty years and all that time my wits have provided me with a living.

But what wits! When you have been in and out of jail for the best years that God gave you, you realize, when it is far too late, what an infernal fool you have been. There's nothing clever in going to prison; the real clever men keep out of it. Dissect the psychology of the average criminal and you will find there is little in him but a blind intuition to get the necessities of life with the least possible trouble. He doesn't really think of what he is doing—or he wouldn't do it., I can claim—for what it is worth—acquaintance with practically all the famous crooks of England and America. Some of them are men who have made a lot of money in their time, but they have all died broke. If I, for example, had put into an ordinary business half the courage and determination I wasted on crime I would have been a rich man. And the worst of it, from my point of view, is that the longest terms of imprisonment I have served were for robberies which brought me practically nothing. I got ten years' penal servitude in France for the Crédit Lyonnais affair, and the money wasn't in my possession more than a week before the police pounced upon me and took the lot. Then I received a life sentence of transportation for being concerned in blowing up the safe in the offices of the American Express Company in Paris. I got my whack of the £50,000 all right—but not for long. Two days only elapsed before the French police nabbed me on the way to England, and thrust me into a prison cell to ponder deeply on the indubitable truth that as a man sows, so will he surely reap.

Anyhow, I grew heartily sick and tired of the quiet life in Toronto. It could be only a matter of time before I broke out again. A couple of New York crooks, Red Carter and Billy Murphy, made their appearance in the faro joints I used to patronize and soon discovered in me a kindred spirit.

"Ed," they said, "you're wasting your time in this dowdy old burg. You'd better come along with us to New York. We'll get some money together."

"Good enough for me," I replied heartily. "If I don't break out soon I'll murder somebody."

If it hadn't been for the want of a decent pal I'd have busted a bank in Toronto long before. But Canada wasn't like the United States. Across the Border they took such things as all in a day's work and bore you no animosity when they caught you.

The Canadian bulls were a different type altogether; you couldn't play any tricks on them and they wouldn't listen to graft.

I had never been to New York, but I took the risk and went. Red Carter soon initiated me into the Tenderloin district[15] where I found the sporting fraternity, the crooks, the hop joints, red-light houses, faro banks and drinking dens where you could get poisoned to death in five minutes. Red, whose specialty was high-class thieving, knew everybody and everybody knew him. He introduced me as one of the boys—I was "all right."

I made the acquaintance of the man notorious throughout America as the king of New York's underworld—the famous Shang Draper[16]. He ran a big saloon on Sixth Avenue where there occurred on October 16, 1883, a sensational murder which set all America aflame with excitement. Johnny Irving[17] and John Walsh ("John the Mick")[18], both of them notorious burglars, quarreled, while in Cherry Hill Prison, over John the Mick's daughter, a beautiful girl whom he had educated at a convent school regardless of expense. It was John the Mick's one passion in life, and as far as I could ascertain Johnny Irving did something to offend him over his daughter. Although they were supposed to be in solitary at Cherry Hill, they regularly communicated with each other. Something Johnny said made Walsh swear to kill him the first chance he got and he was as good as his word. They were both discharged about the same time and went to New York to Shang Draper's saloon. Both of them carried revolvers. A regular duel ensued while all the patrons of the establishment dived underneath the tables. But John the Mick killed his man, only to be instantly shot dead in his turn by a man named Billy O'Brien, a famous safe-breaker and one of Johnny's closest friends. The police came in, arrested Billy, and put him up for murder. Billy procured the services of the cleverest criminal lawyer in America, the famous Abe Hummel, who got him acquitted. Shortly afterward, Billy came to England in company with Sheeny Mike[19], a Jewish burglar.

The pair of them came back with a small fortune but soon dissipated it and went back to a long term of imprisonment. Billy was well known in the criminal world as a man who never hesitated to shoot. In 1878 he was suspected of the murder of a fellow-burglar named George Leslie, who was found shot through the head in Westchester County, N.Y. It was surmised, although it could never be proved, that there had been a quarrel over the division of some plunder and that Billy had killed his confederate.

Another famous character I came across in those days was Little Joe Elliott[20], forger and bank robber. It was a long time before anyone suspected Joe's connection with crime. In the middle 'seventies he made the acquaintance of a very charming actress well known in the States under the name of Kate Castleton[21]. Joe courted the lady with lightning speed and married her within three days. When Kate went back to the stage Joe grew tired of trying to lead a respectable life. In the early part of 1883 he forged a draft upon a New York insurance company for 64,000 dollars, but while on his way to the Tombs Prison made his escape.

His wife still stuck to him when he was recaptured and sentenced to four years, and after he was released Joe faithfully promised her never to involve himself in trouble again. He became his wife's manager, but grew so jealous of her that he ultimately divorced her. However, they were re-married within a year, but instead of it being a lesson to Joe his jealousy grew worse than ever. In all probability Kate added fuel to the flame. There was a fight on Broadway in which Joe slugged one of his wife's admirers three times bigger than himself and a final parting which appears to have made Joe absolutely reckless. Somewhere about 1888[22] he fell into the hands of the police for a sensational forgery case which resulted in his being sent to penal servitude for fifteen years. It was surely the irony of fate that the first day he arrived at Auburn Prison to begin his term his beautiful wife should be starring at the local theater. The knowledge of it absolutely broke Joe's heart; he never came out of jail alive.

Chapter Four
THE WAY OF THE CROOK

I wish I could give my readers something like a decent picture of the New York of the 'eighties, and especially of its underworld. What a red-hot game it was!

Most of the saloons never closed, or if they did for just long enough to be cleaned out and then to begin afresh drinking, fighting, cursing, gambling and the Lord only knows what. Periodically the bulls would come in, usually four-handed, clubs swinging, ready to smash you over the head the moment you looked sideways.

Superintendent Thomas Byrnes[23], the head of the New York detective department, was the hottest customer I ever knew. The minute he got an idea you were crooked he would keep his men after you until he had you inside. At the time I am referring to Boss Croker[24] was in his glory at Tammany Hall. Byrnes, who didn't care a damn for anyone, went after one of the Boss's Aldermen, made friends with him, and then planted some of his men in the Alderman's office. A few hours later Byrnes' men pinched the Alderman for taking graft and got him twelve months in the Pen.

Luckily for me, I succeeded in keeping out of his way. I have no doubt that New York police knew all about my escape from Allegheny and I daresay they also had my photograph. But in those days photography wasn't nearly so good as it is now. Finger-prints were unknown and if you happened to be wanted you had a very much better chance—unless somebody snitched on you—of keeping out of jail than you have nowadays.

Life was fierce! Faro banks and poker joints by night, bed at five o'clock in the morning, up for the night's work at five o'clock in the evening, sometimes winning, more often losing. If I had anything to learn about the ways that are dark and the tricks that are vain I learnt them during the time that Red Carter and Billy Murphy were showing me the high lights of "li'l old New York." You could find in the Tenderloin the biggest toughs in creation, murderers, burglars, con men, boxmen, and the ordinary common or garden gunman on hire like the Italian bravo.

I soon got tired of the game. My natural pugnacity of character—I was never afraid of anybody—so frequently got me into trouble that I began to look for a get-out. A fight in a poker saloon one night when the knives came out got me badly injured.

"You'll have to quit this game, kid," said Red when he got me back to our lodgings. "Once Byrnes gets a line on you he'll slug you for sure."

Some weeks elapsed before I could get out and about again. Money was scarce and Red suggested a trip down South to see if we could get a bit. Three good yeggmen who had been laying up in New York for some months, Johnny Moran, Joe Hillier and Big Ed Rice, a celebrated bank sneak, had gone off to St. Louis in Missouri to do a bank. Red thought it would be a fine idea to follow; they were bound to have something pretty good in view.

Off we went, skinned in pocket but full of confidence. Lily Langtry, the famous English actress, happened to be staying at the hotel where we put up—the Southern. She had a madly infatuated New York millionaire named Freddie Gebhardt[25], following her around. An enterprising local newspaper man went to the hotel and published the diagram showing the position of Freddie's room and that of Mrs. Langtry. The lady was naturally furious; so was Freddie. He got hold of the editor on the verandah of the hotel and gave him a first-class beating up. I witnessed the occurrence; it tickled me to death.

Also staying in the hotel were the three yeggmen, top-sawyers all of them at the bank robbery game. They knew me by sight and I daresay they wondered what my game was. Johnny Moran came over to my table at breakfast one morning, sat down with me, and proceeded to inquire what I wanted.

"Say, you," he drawled menacingly, "what's your little game?"

"Nothing at all, Johnny, nothing at all. 'Red' and I are just down here on a trip."

"If I thought you were 'snitches,'" hissed Johnny, bending over the table to me, "I'd fill you that full of lead that nobody would be able to carry your body away. You beat it, see, or it'll be bad for you."

He got a bit excited towards the end. A waiter hanging round pretending to clear away dirty dishes gave us a look out of the corner of his eye.

"Easy up, Johnny," I said warningly.

"Aw," he growled, "what d'you think I am? It ain't the first time I've pulled a stiff like you. Get out of here quick or you'll be sorry for yourself."

He got up from the table and went off, leaving me in a rather thoughtful mood.

"'Red,'" I remarked to my particular companion, "this town isn't healthy. I've been having a few words with Johnny Moran," and I told him of what had happened.

"Him, huh!" said Red contemptuously. "What do I care about him? He's all wind."

Things began to hum. That very same morning three men followed a bank messenger to an office in the town. No sooner had the man got inside the place than some one asked him a question. He turned round to answer it; a flash, and his bag was gone.

Of all this Red and I knew nothing. We were in blissful ignorance of our danger when we hired a horse and trap and drove off to another bank where we expected to get something for ourselves. No sooner had we pulled up than four bulls jumped out on us, pistols drawn ready to shoot.

"Hey, you!" said a sergeant, "we've been looking for you. What d'you think you're doing here?"

I nearly dropped dead with astonishment. Fancy taking St. Louis for an easy town! Red, a cool old hand, civilly replied that we had just come out for a ride and were waiting for a friend.

"Tell that to the fairies," rudely retorted the sergeant. "We've had our optics on you for a long while. You'll come along and see the Chief. There's too many of you New York stiffs about for my liking."

"Hell," I thought. "Fancy coming all the way to St. Louis to be done like this!" However, the four bulls gave us no opportunity for meditation. The sergeant climbed into the buggy alongside me.

"Drive to the station," he ordered. "I'll show you the way and mind you don't try any funny business or I'll slug you as sure as God made little apples."

Two of his men ran Red up the street, while another stayed behind in case anyone else turned up.

I, for my part, had no intention of going easily. Turning round a corner I pulled the horse into the pavement to try and overturn the buggy. But the sergeant was up to all those little games. Promptly did he pull the reins and gave me a crack over the arm.

"I'll teach you something," he said.

Sure enough he did. The moment he got me inside the station he set about me. Then a couple of his men flung me into a cell and left me for a couple of hours until they took me out to interview the Chief.

"This is him," explained my friend the sergeant. "He's one of those bums from New York we've been watching."

The Chief looked even more formidable than the sergeant. He was an Irishman, and it didn't take me more than a minute or two to realize that I was in for trouble.

"Now then, you," began the Chief. "What are you after here?"

"I don't understand what you mean," I replied very civilly. "I am visiting St. Louis on a pleasure trip."

"Oh, are you?" sneered the Chief. "Well, I've just interviewed your pal and he's coughed up a different story to that. See if you can't think of a better tale."

I tried to. I said that Red and I had come to St. Louis on business, but the Chief wouldn't have it.

"Sling him back," he said to a couple of his men, "and charge him with being a suspect. We'll wire to New York and soon find out all about him."

I did a little hard thinking when they had locked the cell door on me again. Unless I got out within twenty-four hours my description would have gone on to the Pinkertons, who were bound to know I was on the run. The Pinkertons then had the protection of all the banks in America and they knew every man in the game. I walked up and down the cell for ten minutes or so, then I called out to a bull who was passing the door.

"Here," I said, "I want to see the Chief."

"What for? He doesn't want to see you."

"No," I replied, "but I've got something to tell him."

The Chief came along, glowered at me, and demanded to know why I had sent for him.

"It's like this, sir," I explained. "I don't know what you've got me here for. I've done nothing."

"Haven't you?" he said. "You'll soon find out about that."

"I'm not afraid of anything," I told him. "I haven't been in the town more than five minutes and my conscience is quite clear."

The Chief went away. Half an hour later I was taken out of the cell to his office. There I found some one I had not seen.

"Do you know him?" the Chief asked the stranger, nodding at me.

"No, that isn't the fellow," was the reply.

Then they brought in the waiter from the Southern Hotel who said he had seen me having breakfast that morning with a man. Remember, I knew nothing whatever about the real robbery and I felt more than a little puzzled as to what was going on.

The Chief was bluffing; I knew that. He began to ask me who were the three men who had breakfast with me at the hotel that morning.

"I don't know anything about them," I said. "I never met them before then."

"Didn't you!" the Chief snapped. "Well, if you can't tell us a better tale than that you'll stay here until you do."

"Look here, Chief," I said, "you're making a big mistake about this. I've got friends in this town who'll answer for me."

"Oh, and who are they?"

"Well," I said thinking hard, "there's Nick Roche."

Nick was one of the biggest gamblers in the South. I only knew him by name, but we had many mutual friends.

"I'll send for him," promised the Chief. "I don't know that it'll do you any good, but at any rate it can't do much harm."

Back to the cell, where I waited another couple of hours before Nick came along. He didn't know me from Adam, but when I told him who I was and mentioned to him the names of some of the men I knew he made no fuss about promising to help me.

"You're going to be charged on suspicion," he informed me. "In any case they'll 'vag'[26] you and give you six months."

Six months! That meant going back to Allegheny because my description would be circulated.

"Isn't there any means of fixing the Chief?" I asked.

"It'll cost money," said Nick. "You haven't got any, have you?"

"Only about seventy dollars."

"That's no use," Nick replied. "Can't you get hold of any?"

I asked him to wire to two friends of mine in New York, Pat Sheedy[27] and Alf Smith, both of whom he knew. But even then I didn't fancy the position. The longer I remained in that cell the more dangerous it became. They hadn't got anything definite on me and it suddenly dawned upon me that I could only get away by using a little diplomacy.

"Go and see the Chief, Nick, will you?" I asked. "I think I can tell him something that'll do him more good than keeping me here."

Nick went off. A quarter of an hour later I once more made my appearance in the Chief's room.

"What are you up to now?" he demanded. "Any more of your damn lies and I'll break every bone in your body."

I faithfully promised to tell the truth and this time I did. I said that Red and I had been waiting outside the bank to see a railway messenger whose money we hoped to get. Then, to my great astonishment, I learnt all about the robbery that Johnny Moran and his pals had pulled off. But they couldn't hold us for that. It had taken place about the same time that the bulls had dragged us in.

"If I find out that you are speaking the truth about the railway messenger," said the Chief—his eyes seemed to bore holes in me—"I might let you go. It'll be useful to know how to stop any more hold-ups in this town."

The cell again, where I remained until the following morning. Then I was let out, but I had my photograph taken before they pushed me out of the station and was relieved of twenty-five dollars for the trouble I had given them. The Chief also advised me, in a rather rude fashion, to quit St. Louis while I was safe. Nick Roche also gave me the same good advice.

"It's only a matter of a day or two before the Pinkertons put the Chief wise," he informed me. "You clear right out and don't come back."

Red joined me outside, like myself mighty scared. I had told the Chief we were going to the station to take a train to New York. But we didn't do that, having a pretty fair idea that there might be one or two Pinkerton men to greet us on our arrival. Instead, we walked over the St. Louis bridge into the State of Illinois and eventually took a train to Cincinnati.

I didn't fancy Cincinnati much, being rather too well known there. After a few days we chanced our luck and went back to New York.

"This is no good, 'Red,'" I said. "We can't live on nothing."

A look round suggested that a Brooklyn fur shop might be done. I was then staying at an hotel in Washington Market, while Red put up at another place. We didn't know how far the St. Louis bulls had gone. Singly we might escape attention; together it would be fatal.

The night we thought of trying the fur shop Red went on ahead to watch the staff out of the building. I kept him in sight, saw him standing at the corner of the street and went across to speak to him. Suddenly, without the slightest warning, five men from nowhere jumped on us and dragged us to the nearest police station. They fanned us, found nothing on me, but a gun on Red. Then the five of them set about us properly. We had a regular battle royal and at the end of it, with a couple of black eyes, a few teeth missing, and bleeding all over, we were thrown into separate cells.

"By God," I thought, "this is ten times worse than St. Louis." They hadn't charged us with anything and I didn't know how things stood.

The following morning I raised Cain about the savage treatment to which I had been subjected. Anyhow, they let me send for my pal Bob Norman who kept a big gambling house in New York at the time.

"Eddie," said Bob when he came along, "you'll have to get out of this quick. They'll surely have you back at Allegheny."

Bob knew all about that little affair and he promptly secured me the services of the best lawyer in Brooklyn, a very well-known man named Jerry Werthenberg. I discovered the police were charging me as a suspicious character, but when the case came into court Werthenberg protested that the bulls had merely seen me speak to a man and then arrested me. Nothing incriminating had been found in my possession—I knew too much about the game to be guilty of such foolishness as that. The upshot of the matter was that the magistrate discharged me with a caution and fined Red fifty dollars for having a pistol in his possession.

I got out of that court determined to give Brooklyn the go-by post-haste. But Bob Norman would insist on dragging me over to Werthenberg's place for a drink to celebrate my release. I knew nothing at all of what was transpiring or I wouldn't have gone. afterward I discovered that when they had taken my photograph in St Louis, Pinkertons had wired the police for my description. They soon found out I was wanted for escaping from Allegheny. The St. Louis photograph went into the *Police Gazette* and by one of these million-to-one chances which are continually happening in crime a policeman who happened to be in the court at Brooklyn when I was put up as a suspect recognized me from my photograph. He rushed over to the police office, and within a matter of ten minutes three bulls arrived and once more deposited me in a cell. They telephoned to Pittsburgh and before I knew where I was, Roger O'Mara, the Chief bull of that town, came to Brooklyn and without waste of time identified me. However, I will give him the credit of saying he did not bear me any malice.

"Hullo, Ed," he greeted me, "you've been a bit unlucky. You'll have to come back with me. Will you return without extradition?"

"Not me," I replied promptly. "I'll give you all the trouble I can. It'll take you at least a month to get me back."

Roger smiled.

"Well, that won't do you any good," he said, "you'll have to come back some time and I can promise you that if you don't make any trouble you won't be punished for escaping."

This made me think hard. Shut up for a month in a Brooklyn police station wouldn't be very pleasant, besides which I knew that Roger was right. I thought if he gave me his word of honor that I wouldn't be made to suffer for getting away it would be best to give no further trouble.

"I lose four months' good time," I remarked to Roger. "Is there any chance of getting that?"

He wouldn't promise anything except that he would do his best for me and I made the best of a bad job. To give Roger his due he treated me well enough. He took me over to a neighboring hotel, bought me a real good lunch, a bottle of claret and a couple of cigars. But there was no hanky-panky business about him. The moment we were finished he put the bracelets on, one of them on my wrist, the other on his. So our journey back was not exactly a State procession. Still, I didn't complain.

When we arrived at the prison I was promptly taken before the Warden, who did not seem at all pleased to see me.

"Well," he barked, "you've caused a lot of trouble."

"If you open the door of the cage the bird will fly out," I replied rather too impudently. "It's your business to see I did not escape."

"You've got too much to say for yourself," said the Warden. "By the time I'm done with you you'll be the sort of bird that will eat out of anyone's hand. Take him away," he ordered to the guards.

They put me into a small cell about four feet by eight, with only a small truckle bed in it and a lavatory in the corner. If Roger O'Mara kept his promise that I shouldn't be punished for getting away I was certainly made to suffer something much worse. I got nothing whatever to do. They let me out once a day to walk to the kitchen to get my dinner and then hustled me back to the cell. For nine long weary months I underwent this terrible torture. I don't suppose anyone would blame me for saying that I ought to have been given some work or at least allowed a little exercise. I was the only man in the prison so treated.

There used to be a musical hour every evening between seven and eight o'clock when the men were allowed to play whatever instruments they liked. I could hear the niggers in the jail singing their plantation songs to the strumming of the banjoes and the twanging of guitars played by the foreigners. But they never gave me a single thing to alleviate the awful monotony of my solitary confinement.

Occasionally the Warden condescended to come and see me. I asked him why I didn't get any work to do.

"You stay where you are," he replied. "If you start making trouble you'll be sorry for yourself."

"I don't suppose you're trying to croak me, are you?" I asked. "You seem to be doing your best with this 'solitary.' I have nothing to do all day but read."

In those days you were given a library book and also allowed to read a daily paper. I whiled away the whole nine months doing nothing but this. The monotony of it, the want of proper exercise, nearly drove me mad.

One day the Warden came round accompanied by his wife and a party of visitors. He was continually showing off his prison—God knows what for. I could never understand why such places should be open to sightseers. Perhaps the Warden said something to his wife about me. She came back to my cell.

"What a poor unfortunate boy you are," she remarked. "I'm dreadfully sorry for you."

I quite agreed and took advantage of the opportunity to tell her how I was treated. She seemed to think it was disgraceful and told me not to lose courage, but to hope for the best.

"I have a book I would like you to read," she said. "It is called *Within the Maze*[28], by Mrs. Henry Wood, and I'll send it round to you."

It was certainly interesting to me, being the tale of a man who had escaped from prison and the many thrilling adventures he underwent afterward. But it didn't help me to get out of Allegheny, which was principally what I wanted, nor did I get any opportunities.

The prison garb of those days was a dress of black and white hoops; we used to look like zebras. No prison is worth living in, but in Allegheny they certainly gave you good food. You could have as much bread as you wanted, while for breakfast of a morning you got fish or hash and coffee. There was more hash for dinner, while in the evening you got bread and butter and tea. You were also given a quart tin of syrup, molasses or sugar which had to last you a month.

They did not put me on trial again for escaping, and as time went on I began to hope that I would serve my sentence in the ordinary way and get out of Pittsburgh at once. I asked the civilian engineer attached to the prison who often passed my cell how I stood about the matter.

"Well, I've got a brother in Pittsburgh who is a lawyer," he said. "If you like I'll find out the position."

When the actual time of my sentence was up I expected to get out in the world again. Nothing happened. I got hold of my water-can and banged it on the bars of the door until one of the guards came along.

"Say, what's the matter, Eddie?"

"I want to see the Warden and I'll knock this can until I do," I said. "I ought to have been discharged to-day and I want to know why I'm being kept here."

The engineer had told me from his brother that legally my sentence was up and that all the time I was away from prison had to be counted in. I had also managed to get a letter to Bob Norman in New York acquainting him of what was happening.

The Warden came along to see me.

"Let you out, hey?" laughing loudly. "I think not. You're here for some time yet. You stop in that cell and don't make trouble."

For a couple of days I went almost mad. Then Bob Norman, like a real straight sport, came to see me. I told him to engage a lawyer and institute proceedings to have me brought into court and either charged with escaping or else get an order for my release. The Warden stood by during the conversation.

"Don't you waste your time about that," he advised Bob. "I'm going to charge him all right."

A couple of hours afterward the Warden sent for me again.

"I'm going to charge you with escaping from jail," he informed me, looking at me in a vicious way that almost tempted me to try and murder him. "The Mayor of Allegheny is now on the telephone and he wants to talk to you."

I thought it a funny way of doing things, but I picked up the receiver.

"Are you Guerin?"

"Yes."

"You are to be charged with escaping—what do you plead?"

"I don't acknowledge that I escaped at all."

"But you did."

"Well," I replied, "that will have to be thrashed out in court."

"Do you plead guilty or not guilty?" asked the man at the other end of the line.

"I'll do neither over the telephone."

They put me back in my cell, but the following day Bob Norman got hold of a famous Irish lawyer, Michael Reardon, a brilliant man at his game but always drunk. Bob brought him over to the prison and I was once more taken to the Warden's room. And I actually asked the Warden to go out of the room while Reardon and I talked the matter over!

I got no particular comfort from what the lawyer told me. He said that even if I was not put on trial for escaping I would most inevitably be charged for stealing prison clothes. Ultimately I appeared before a Supreme Court Judge in Pittsburgh who told me that the Writ of Habeas Corpus would have to be dismissed and that I must serve the thirteen months I had been at large from the prison. I told Reardon that I wouldn't come out of the jail alive.

"Don't you worry about that," he said. "I'll speak to the Warden for you."

He was as good as his word. When I got back to Allegheny the Warden sent for me, carefully explained that I didn't deserve anything, but that I would have a job dusting the cell doors and sweeping out the corridors.

"And mind you," he warned me, "if I catch you speaking to anyone or trying to make any more getaways, back you'll go."

I felt too pleased at having such a cinch job to play any more tricks on the Warden. Faithfully did I promise to behave myself. I was given a cell next to the dungeon in which I took immense pride. I had pictures on the walls and a mat on the floor. There was a guard attached to the prison to show the visitors around. They used to be charged twenty-five cents apiece, the money being devoted to buying books for the library. Some days there were as many as thirty people at a time and my cell was always shown to them as a model of what the State did for its criminals. Everybody used to compliment me on its neatness and I guess I never felt so proud in all my life.

Poor pride if you like! I don't suppose I had much intelligence then or I might have concluded that it would be an infinitely prouder thing to have your liberty and to be an honored and respected citizen. But there you are! Self-analysis isn't particularly conspicuous in any prison; most of the people who get there are utterly devoid of either foresight or sensible appreciation of what is worth while. It is usually late in life, when the past is utterly irretrievable, that you begin to realize what you have lost.

The dungeon cells at Allegheny were *not* shown to the visitors, or the Warden might not have received the bouquets that used to be thrown at him. He used to put men there for petty little offenses such as stealing cigars out of the factory. During the time I was at Allegheny the famous nigger preacher named Jasper had a son who got into trouble and received three years in a Western Pennsylvania penitentiary. They afterward sent him on to Allegheny. This poor devil was as black as the ace of spades and about as crazy as a man could be. Instead of treating him as a lunatic the guards beat him up and made him worse. One day he said he felt sick and a doctor came to see him.

"There's nothing the matter with you," said the M.O. "You're malingering."

The nigger immediately gave him a punch, a regular scrap followed, ending up by the coon being yanked off to the punishment cells. But before they took him away he managed to secrete a knife and the guards knew it.

The nigger became stark staring raving mad and threatened to knife anyone who came near him. Myself, I couldn't see much the matter with the poor fellow and he seemed harmless enough if treated in the right way. One of the guards came up and told me that all the prisoners were going to be locked in their cells while they got the nigger out dead or alive.

"You don't want to kill him," I said. "Let me have a talk to him. I'll make him give up his knife."

"What could you do?" demanded the guards incredulously.

"If you promise not to punish him I think I can get the knife away," I replied.

It took them sometime to agree to my idea, but eventually they let me do as I wished. I knew he wouldn't hurt me. Often had I talked with him and I knew his behavior was due more to the maddening spells of solitary he had received, plus innumerable beatings, that had sent him off his head.

He was sitting in the corner of his cell, morose and savage, when I went to the trap door.

"I shall sho' kill anyone that comes in here," cried the nigger.

"Now then, Jack," I said, "let me give you a bit of good advice. Hand over that knife and I'll see they don't hurt you. If they do put you in the 'cooler' and give you bread and water I'll manage to get you some food put under the door."

The guards were interestedly watching me from down the other end of the passage and it took a long time before I could make the nigger change his mind. But ultimately I managed to make him see that he had no chance. He gave me the knife, after which they put him in the dungeon for thirty days on bread and water. I kept my promise about the food. The guards knew I was giving him some meat and I daresay they were glad enough to get out of the bother so easily without troubling their heads much about breaking prison regulations. Anyhow, I stopped that coon from being killed, so at least I can claim the credit for having done one good turn in my life.

The rest of my time in Allegheny was filled in with my duties of keeping the cell doors clean and sweeping out the corridors and halls. It was during this period that I came in contact with Shoebox Miller who had been brought back from Canada. He was working in the prison as a painter and one day while passing him in a corridor he wanted to know why I hadn't put him in the get-away with Tommy Hall.

"We weren't going to take everybody with us," I said.

"Do you think I am a 'snitch'?"

"You damn well look like one," I replied.

Shoebox dropped his paint and brushes and came for me like a madman. It was crash! bang! and we were on the floor, punching and pulling at each other, the center of a most interested audience. Things were just coming my way when half a dozen guards came running up, wrenched us apart and shoved us back into our cells. Next morning we were interviewed by the Warden and got the usual thirty days' bread and water.

That pretty well ended my full period in Allegheny and I don't mind saying I wasn't sorry to see the last of the place. The Warden bade me good-bye with a sour smile, prophesying that it would not be long before he saw me again. I didn't give him that satisfaction. I certainly saw the inside of a good many prisons afterward, but not in America. What I have to relate now—I shall keep it until the next chapter—is one of the most unfortunate episodes of my life and one which resulted in my leaving America and coming to England.

Chapter Five
THE TURNING POINT

Leaving Allegheny in the fall of 1886 I went back home to Chicago, this time strongly determined to leave crime and prison alone. I was just beginning to appreciate that it couldn't possibly pay to spend all the best years of your life behind the walls of a jail.

The biggest liar that ever lived was the man who wrote that poem about:

> "Stone walls do not a prison make,
> Nor iron bars a cage."[29]

He lived about three hundred years ago, so he knew nothing about the penitentiaries they used to have in America in the days when I was serving my trade apprenticeship.

It felt good to be back in the old home town. Twenty-six years of age, with all the world before me and plenty of friends with money—if not altogether of the kind that a Sunday-school teacher would approve—there was no reason why I shouldn't make good. I went and saw my poor old mother. She wept over me, wanted to know what I had been doing, and no doubt believed the string of lies I told her.

But, alas, I soon got into trouble again. I found a café on Blue Island Avenue owned by a French woman[30] named Le Febre[31] with two pretty daughters who used to act as barmaids for their mother. I was dressing well at that time and had got hold of a bit of money from one or two friends I had known years before. And I daresay I was not a bad-looking fellow in those days. Anyhow, one of the girls, Sarah, the best-looking of the two, grew rather fond of me, and if all had gone well I might have married her and settled down in Chicago and thus saved myself the terrible experiences of later years.

But one morning going in the bar for an early livener I saw poor Sarah in a state of great agitation. She told me that on the previous day two detectives had been in inquiring about me. Sarah knew nothing about my past life in Chicago. I felt impelled to show a little astonishment at the police asking for *me*.

"I'm sure I don't know what they wanted me for," I said. And to be quite truthful I didn't.

That same evening I was again in the bar talking to Sarah, but keeping my weather eye open for trouble. For the life of me I couldn't imagine why the bulls were on my track, but of course they might want to take me inside just to find out what I was doing. I just picked up a glass of whisky when in the mirror at the back of Sarah I saw two men come in the door. Sarah whispered they were the same two who had been asking her about me the day before, but the moment I clapped eyes on them I knew they were coppers. You can always tell a policeman by the cut of his jib—at least I can. There is nothing like experience in these matters. Nevertheless, my conscience, if only for once, was quite clear. The trouble that was coming had really nothing to do with the law. A pal and I had been having a bit of a game with a couple of women down town, one of whom had the misfortune to be married. She also happened to be the wife of the bull coming in.

I had no time to explain things, or to tell the aggrieved husband that it was not I who had been making up to his missus, but my pal. As a matter of fact I never knew she was the wife of a policeman or I would not have gone within a million miles of her. I had met her out drinking while her husband was on duty and from rumors flying about I got the warning to carry a pistol.

The bar was crowded with people, most of whom I knew. I stood stock-still, slowly dropping my hand down on my pistol. Suddenly one of the new-comers, a great burly hooligan-like fellow with tough written all over him, came up and put his hand on my shoulder.

"Here, you," he growled, "I want you."

"You do, hey?" I replied, stepping back. I saw him put his hand into his inside pocket and I also saw sticking out the butt end of a big pistol. I didn't stop to do much thinking then. Like a flash of lightning I jumped back, pulled out my pistol and fired at him twice. God only knows what impelled him to say it, but as he fell on the ground with the blue smoke of the shot curling upwards he cried out:

"My mother!"

"You damned dog!" I yelled at him, "who are you to call out about your mother? You didn't think of *my* mother."

A complete hush had come over the crowded bar, as there always does in the presence of tragedy. The policeman who had come in with my opponent was cowering in a corner with his hands up. It was no time to stop and explain. The noise of the shot would bring in the man on the beat. Poor little Sarah looked at me with frightened eyes and at the pistol still in my hand.

"Get out of the way everybody," I shouted and gradually backed out of the door covering every one in the place. But not a soul attempted to follow me. I went half way round Chicago to hide my tracks and late that night scrambled through the back window of my mother's house expecting any moment to be pinched for murder.

May Heaven forgive any man for causing his mother trouble. What suffering I caused mine nobody will ever know, but that night, weighed down with the consciousness that I might go to the gallows for what I had done, I told the old lady everything. Panting, filled with an awful dread, I told her that the police would surely come for me soon and that she must try and put them off the track. As it turned out, I never saw my mother again after that night. With the tears pouring down her face she faithfully promised me that she would do what she could to save me.

I went out again the back way, over the fence, to a pal who hid me in his place while the great hue and cry went on for something like a fortnight. There were bills posted all over Chicago offering five hundred dollars reward for me alive or dead. Occasionally I sneaked out at night and saw them. I learnt from my brother that the people who had been in the bar at the time of the shooting were all in my favor and that if I were caught they were prepared to give evidence that I had only pulled out my pistol in self-defense. They all advised me to give myself up, and said they would go bail for me. But not for me. I knew too much about the police to take any chances in that direction. The justice they meted out in Chicago in those times had nothing much to do with the actual rights and wrongs of the affair. If you were foolish enough to jump on the police you could expect them to give you the same treatment with a little bit extra thrown in by way of interest.

An uncle of mine was Captain of the police in the district where my mother lived. He took a party of men over, knocked at the door and said to my mother: "Is Eddie in?"

"No, he isn't."

"I'm afraid we must search the house," replied my loving uncle, a first-class brute named Ward. He would just as cheerfully have shot me as anything else.

"But this house is my property," cried poor mother determinedly, "and no one is going to search it unless they do it legally. Eddie hasn't lived here for years and you know very well I don't hold with any of his doings."

Brave as a lion, the old lady picked up a rifle that lay in a corner of the hall.

"Get out," she shouted at Ward. "Relation or not, if you come into this house I'll blow your brains out."

Like all the Irish, mother liked something at hand to keep the landlords at bay. Evidently Ward didn't fancy the look of her; he cleared out and left her in peace. But years afterward, when I was arrested in London for the sensational robbery at the Crédit Lyonnais in Lyons, they never bothered extraditing me when they might have done so. As a matter of fact, the man I shot did not die of his wounds. I shall have a little story to tell about that later.

Friends smuggled me over to Ontario in Canada, where I remained for about three months. My brother sent me some money to keep me going but, of course, such an existence could not go on for ever. To go back to the States was utterly impossible and I could only thank my lucky stars that the Canadian police knew nothing about me. Eventually I made up my mind to go to England, and trust to luck as to what happened in the future.

What I intended to do was more or less in the lap of the gods. I had no trade at all; the only way I could get a living was by my wits. I knew all there was to know about the crooked ways of life, and practically the only people I knew were men precariously existing on crime. I had nothing in my mental make-up to tell me that I must be heading for a big crash. But then, the average crook rarely thinks of the future or gives himself the time to cogitate on what will be the ultimate effects of spending the best years of his life sinning against society. He never stops to think that the time will come when the years will find him with fingers less nimble and brains no longer agile. If prison authorities would put in each cell a series of pictures showing what crime does for a man at different stages of his life, ending up with the poor-house, or perhaps dying in a jail, friendless and forlorn, it would do more to cure crime than all the savage sentences ever imposed. I know; it is when you are approaching the three-score years and ten allotted to man that you realize the fatuity of it all.

I have known thousands of men who have lived for years on nothing but crime. None of them have ever made any money at it and certainly not one has ever died a rich man. What they have earned they have dissipated in riotous living. Women and wine have claimed the lot until, of course, the time comes to get some more.

The psychology of the average crook is easy enough to understand. He lives for to-day, reckless of the morrow. Egotistical by nature, oblivious of the fact that once he has become known to the police he must always be known—and made to suffer accordingly—he blindly goes on his way hoping for just one more big touch which will put him beyond the reach of want. He is just like the gambler who goes on backing horses expecting a smashing win that will enable him to finish with the bookmakers for ever. Fools every one of them! I know what I am writing about, because I have staked both my liberty and my lucre more often, I should think, than any other man on this earth.

Oscar Wilde, one of the cleverest men that ever lived, summed it up at its true worth in "The Ballad of Reading Gaol"[32]:

> The vilest deeds, like poison weeds,
>   Bloom well in prison air;
> It is only what is good in Man
>   That wastes and withers there:
> Pale Anguish keeps the heavy gate,
>   And the guard is Despair.

True, every word of it. Not one man in a hundred is reformed by a long term of imprisonment. I will unhesitatingly admit that the world must do something with its criminals, but I don't think jail is the solution. Anyhow, other and better brains than mine have tried to solve the problem and I can only suggest, as in my case, that the principal damage is done when you send a child to prison at a time of life when he or she is incapable of properly distinguishing between right and wrong. Think over that, you reformers!

London! City of my dreams! The place where I had been born! I had always looked upon it as my natural home and I longed to see it as a wanderer on the face of the earth yearns for a sight of the place where he spent his boyhood days.

They were having busy times in London the year I arrived. It was 1887, just about the time of Queen Victoria's Jubilee[33]. I had come over with about £200[34] in my possession, and, for a time at least, unheedful of the future, enjoyed myself immensely. But I had no friends worth speaking of, and when I made my way into the old Criterion bar, which was then the principal haunt of the boys, I had to pay my way like a new-comer. I ran across Adam Worth[35], more commonly known as Harry Raymond, the man who afterward stole the famous Gainsborough picture of the Duchess of Devonshire[36] from Agnew's Art Gallery in Bond Street. If ever a man in this world could be pointed out as an exception to the rule that no crook ever makes money, it was Adam Worth. He owned an expensive flat in Piccadilly, he entertained some of the best people in London, who never knew him for anything but an apparently rich man of a Bohemian nature. And yet he died in poverty.

I soon got into the swim. Some of the heads had heard about me and took me off to Newmarket racing. For a time things went well, but they soon busted me backing horses. One of my newly made friends put up a job to get into the Cannon Street Post Office and for that purpose took a room overhead. I had always been told that the London City Police were the slowest bulls on earth. In fact, I didn't even know that they kept detectives in the City area. But I was very soon disillusioned. About half-past eight at night, just when we were thinking of beginning operations on the Post Office below, there came a sharp rat-tat-tat at the door.

I don't mind admitting that my heart took a bit of a jump. A look at the window to see if I could get out that way brought me no consolation. My pal and I looked at each other. "Open it, Ed," he said. "It's no good. It may be nothing."

One sight of the three men who filled the doorway soon disabused me. They had detective written all over them. They didn't wait for an invitation to come in; they just walked in.

"What's your little game?" asked one of them.

"Game!" I exclaimed. "There's no game here. We've rented this office and we're here to do some business."

"I daresay you are, but it isn't the sort of business you're wanted to do in London. We've been watching you for quite a long time. You've been in and out of the Post Office a little too often. Come on."

They hauled us over to Cloak Lane Police Station—nice and handy—and then came back to see if we had left any tools behind. But they didn't find any. We were charged as suspects; they couldn't put it against us that we were on enclosed premises with intent to commit a felony because we had rented the office. I must give the City of London police their due by admitting that there wasn't the slightest attempt at ill-treatment. They just put you in a cell and left you there; they didn't even try to make you confess anything by hazing you, which is a favorite game in the States.

The morning came and with it the usual shyster lawyer who gets his living touting the detective force. I got hold of one who took all my money and faithfully promised to get me off, but I didn't tell him—or the police—my real name. If they had sent over to America for a few particulars about me it might have been slightly disastrous. The name I gave was Albert Woolf, and when they got me up at the Mansion House, after I had first of all been remanded for seven days to see if Scotland Yard knew anything about me, I was sentenced to three months' imprisonment, my pal getting the same.

I will be perfectly truthful and at once admit that my first experience of an English prison didn't in the least make me long for another dose. They took us off in the Black Maria to Holloway, then a male prison, mostly used, I believe, for short-term men and remands. But hell, what a place! The American jails were palaces compared to it. Enormous hungry-looking rats ran about the place like rabbits; you did not require much imagination to believe that they would eat you if they got the chance. The prison itself stunk; there was no proper sanitation and the poor devils awaiting trial had nothing to do but lounge about all day passing the time as best they could. They weren't allowed to smoke; the only privilege they received was to have a dirty, repulsive-looking meal sent in from outside. I remember the Governor well. Milman [37] was his name, and I believe, although I could not ascertain for sure, that he had charge of both Holloway and Newgate, the latter the place where all the prisoners in the London area condemned to death were hanged. Governor Milman was a big full-bodied fellow who looked as though he would take a savage delight in seeing you hanged. I didn't fancy the cut of him at all—and I knew something about prison Governors.

The food at Holloway was a million times worse than that of America. I never felt anything but hungry all the time I was there. I used to see men in the exercise yard falling out of the ranks to pick up a crust from the ground. I don't know what it cost the English Government to keep their prisoners, but it must have been very little. I should put the amount at about sixpence a day.

However, they didn't keep me long at Holloway. After a week or two I found myself transferred to the old Millbank Prison which stood on the site now occupied by the Tate Library. If I had been condemned to serve a long term of imprisonment there I would have gone out of my mind, because of all the foul, dirty, filthy holes I have ever come across it was easily the worst. Millbank, of course, was one of the oldest prisons in the country and had undergone an extraordinarily checkered career. Once upon a time it was the principal London depot prison for young criminals, military offenders, and also for convicts *en route* to Botany Bay, Van Diemen's Land, and Western Australia. They told me when I went there that thousands of men had died within its walls and I could well believe it. Sanitation there was none. The water supply was pestiferous; even the very air of the prison seemed to poison you.

Just previous to my arrival it had been temporarily utilized for women, but Holloway was then being emptied and most of the male prisoners were being sent to the new jail at Wormwood Scrubs, Holloway becoming, as it is now, the only female prison in London. I found Millbank a dirty, common, noisome hole, where nobody took much notice of you. The guards set me to work picking oakum in my cell. I could not do this very well owing to an injury to my hand, whereupon the screws—as they call the guards in England—promptly reported me. Hauled before the Governor the following morning, accused of shirking, I could only ask for a medical examination. The doctor soon saw I could do no work and exempted me. But that didn't end my troubles. They wanted to take my photograph, and experience had taught me the wisdom of dodging this honor as far as possible. I said I would not have it done, which resulted in another interview with the Governor. I remember the ordeal vividly. The screws took me into a room which strongly resembled a court and certainly brought back memories of a none too happy nature. I want to be quite fair and so I will admit that the Governor did not attempt to ill-treat me.

"Now, look here," he said to me quite pleasantly, "the Home Office has instructed us to get your photograph and you refuse to have it taken. What have you got to say about the matter?"

I did not let on. I merely said I had never had my photograph taken and that I didn't want it done.

"All right," replied the Governor resignedly, "you'll have to be punished."

Nothing more was said. A couple of men took me away and informed me I would be photographed whether I liked it or not. But for all the good it did them they might just as well have saved themselves the trouble. At the time they took it I was wearing a couple of months' beard. Also, on my way to the photographer I picked up a couple of pebbles from the ground, put them in my mouth, and screwed up my face until even my own mother would not have recognized me. I don't even remember how the Governor punished me. It could not have been anything very serious because it has long since passed out of my memory.

They were a poor lot of cheap stiffs in Millbank, sneak thieves most of them, serving short sentences, with not a decent man amongst them.

Recently, I believe, the English prison authorities have awakened to the fact that it isn't altogether advisable to keep the big crooks in one prison, because they get together and make arrangements for the future. I could have told them that forty years ago. There are more big jobs planned inside prison walls than outside.

The clothing at Millbank was shocking and the boots as bad as they could be. They never fitted, you just went out into the yard and picked out a pair and you were lucky if you got anything near your size. The place itself was as cold as charity and I don't mind saying that I did not feel at all sorry when the time came for me to be discharged. The Deputy-Governor handed me half-a-crown and his blessing and I went out into the world fervently of the opinion that English prisons were no good to me.

Fortunately for me, I did not come out of jail entirely friendless. An acquaintance picked up in the West End of London met me at the gates and accompanied me to Cloak Lane Police Station, where I picked up £15 which I had been carrying the night I was arrested. I spent part of that money as nearly every discharged prisoner does—on a real good feed and damn the expense!

Now here, of course, had arrived another period of my life when I might have paused and said to myself: "Eddie, what are you going to do now?" I ought to have realized, if I had possessed any sense at all, which I didn't, that it must be only a matter of time before I went the same way as I had done in America, with the infinitely more serious handicap that my record in the States would sooner or later be known and would tell heavily against me if I came up for sentence.

I certainly possessed enough intelligence to conclude that it would be better to get out of England for awhile, and so, for over six months, a gang of us travelled the Continent, visiting Paris, Berlin, Brussels, Monte Carlo, and innumerable other places where you could pick up money in various ways which need not be enumerated here. It was while I was in Paris in 1888 that I met the notorious Sophie Lyons and her equally famous pal Flash Billy Burke.

I needed no introduction to Sophie Lyons[38]. As the wife of Ned Lyons[39], one of the greatest burglars and bank robbers ever known in America, she had achieved quite a considerable notoriety a long time before I made her acquaintance. Ned Lyons was the man who in 1869 took part in the robbery of the Ocean Bank[40] in New York when over a million dollars were stolen by one of the most daring schemes ever hatched.

Some years before this affair Lyons had married a young Jewess named Sophie Elkins, a protégée in crime of the celebrated Mrs. Mandelbaum[41]. Evidently the fair Sophie was a born thief, because she used to steal, unknown to her husband. She gave birth to a child, and Ned bought a farm on Long Island, hoping it would cure her of her passion for crime. However, Sophie placed her child out to nurse and went out on the warpath again, being subsequently sentenced to a term of six months. That marked the beginning of a career which made her well known to every policeman in the States.

She was arrested in New York and given five years in Sing-Sing for larceny. With the aid of her husband she got away from the prison by a daring ruse when Ned, with a couple of companions, drove up to deliver some fruit for his wife. Sophie, by means which could never be ascertained, was waiting behind the prison gates. The moment they were open she dashed out, jumped in the waiting carriage, and for a time disappeared. The police got her again, in company with Ned, picking pockets at a Long Island fair, and eventually had her sent back to finish her sentence.

After this little episode, Sophie blossomed out as one of the greatest blackmailers in America. She lured a man into her room in a Boston hotel and with the aid of another notorious female crook stole his clothes. She then demanded a huge sum of money and received it in the form of a check. Unfortunately for her, the victim's banking account did not contain enough money to meet it. A policeman was sent to the hotel and the two women were arrested. However, the man in the case refused to prosecute, with the result that the charge was dismissed.

Sophie had also acquired the reputation of double-crossing the people with whom she worked. I had never met her before, but lots of men who knew her well told me that they thought her to be a secret agent of the Pinkertons. At one time in her life she lived in Detroit and fenced all sorts of stolen property. No doubt she got a lot of money out of the game, but I suppose it gradually got about that she ran with the hare and hunted with the hounds—hence her presence in Europe.

It takes a pretty determined sort of woman to get a living out of crookedness and I will be quite fair to Sophie Lyons when I candidly admit that she had plenty of character. When I first met her in 1888 she must have been about forty years of age, not a particularly good-looking woman, but one who certainly possessed a personality of her own.

She had need of it in the company she kept. When I made her acquaintance she was over in Paris with Flash Billy, Dago Frank Denin, and Bill Stetson, the latter known far and wide as Bill the Brute. Bill Stetson and I came to know each other rather well, in a way that I will tell later. All three of Sophie's pals were American yeggmen and every one of them had done a lot of time in the States. Dago Frank had served twenty years for safe-breaking, while Flash Billy could also claim to have been over the wall pretty often. And I expect they were in the same position as Sophie—that of making their native land a bit too hot to hold them. There comes a time in the careers of all crooks when it pays to get out and make a fresh start in another country.

Somehow or other, I didn't fancy Sophie. I looked upon her as a pimp and a dangerous one at that. She wanted to rule the roost. She must have made money at the game, because she used to live at the best hotels and go about the world like a woman of position. Her headquarters used to be in London and when business on the Continent did not claim her she could be found almost every night in the old Café Royal and the Monico, then the meeting places of all the sports in London. Sophie loved to pose as the master mind of crime. Privately, I looked upon her as a low-down snitch and I kept a wary eye on her.

Flash Billy was her fancy man just then. Perhaps she thought that I might make a desirable second string, or that I would pull off some big jobs and hand her a share of the proceeds. But in those days I had a bit of a personality myself and I had no intention of taking orders from any woman.

"Say, Eddie," she said to me one day over a drink at a café on the Boulevard des Capucines, "you're all right, but it'll take you time to learn the game over here. You stick to me and we'll get some money."

Sophie's idea of making money was to get you to do all the work, take all the risk, and coolly hand her the lot to divide as she thought fit. Like all fences, she thought that a quarter share was about all you were entitled to. Another reason I didn't care about her was that in America she was known to snitch the moment the police came on the scene. She was no good to me and I told Flash Billy so.

"That sanguinary bovine" (which were not my exact words), I said to Bill, "is about as useful to us as a fur coat in hell. What's the sense in having her around?"

"I'll tell you," replied Bill. "She's got money and she's useful if you fall. Besides, she hears of things and finds out if they are likely to be worth while."

"Well," I said, "I haven't yet got to that time of life when I want a woman to order me about. Besides, I'm quite capable of looking after myself and I'm also able to take care of whatever I can get without having a woman to pimp on me."

Bill and I talked matters over for quite a long time and in the end I brought him round to my way of thinking.

But I discovered then that it doesn't pay to play with women. When Sophie found herself deserted she began to write us threatening letters—to me in particular—saying that we would rue the day we left her in the lurch. Poor Bill got fairly worried over them.

"Here," he said to me one day, "what do you think of this?" showing me a note from Sophie calling him all the skunks she could think of. "We'll have to go a bit careful, Ed. You know what she is."

"Tell her to go to hell. What can she do to us?"

Sophie, of course, knew all about things. To do a job in Paris was simply inviting trouble, and I proposed to Bill that we should look further afield.

All my life I have gone up against banks and suchlike places where you can get hard cash. I don't believe in going after jewelry. When you hock it with a fence he never gives you anything for it because, as he truly says, he has to take all the risk in getting rid of it. Furthermore, it is easily recognized and the only thing to be said in its favor is that it is not so closely guarded as money.

Bill and I had a good scheme on foot. We were going to show the Frenchmen one or two good American tricks, but Paris wasn't the place to do it. Dago Frank came into the game and the three of us split out to try and find a town where we might do a bank with the minimum of risk. And we wanted a fairly big town where we would be likely to get some money.

Bill stopped in Paris watching Sophie. I went north to Lille and had a look round there while Dago Frank went south to Lyons. The two of us got back a few days later, reported the result of our investigations to Billy, and eventually decided to have a go at Lyons. I hadn't seen much money about at Lille. The French people in the north, like those in the north of England, seemed a bit too canny with their cash for my liking.

We had no intention of taking any more risks than were absolutely necessary. What I had seen in St. Louis a few years before when Johnny Moran, Joe Hillier and Ed Rice were doing a job taught me the less you were seen about together the better it would be for you. Besides, we were foreigners and I concluded the French folk would have no difficulty in recognizing us as such. So we went off from the Gare de Lyon by three different trains and put up in Lyons at three different hotels, all of us in assumed names. Dago Frank had already fixed on the bank where something might happen. We arranged to meet in Lyons two days later, talk everything over again, and make proper plans for getting away if everything came up to expectations.

Chapter Six
THE FAMOUS LYONS ROBBERY

When I set out for Lyons in 1888, leaving behind me in Paris a vindictive woman who would go to any length to get her revenge, there was no thought in my mind that I was taking the most fatal step of my career. I don't even know whether Flash Billy or Dago Frank gave the matter one single moment's consideration. They, like me, lived for the day and not the morrow.

We had no settled plan of campaign. Our intentions were to try one of the big banks and work the old game of attracting a messenger's attention, trusting to luck to make a get-away. All the planning in the world won't save you from the risk of capture. The three of us talked the matter over and had come to the conclusion that if forewarned is forearmed we would be more likely to succeed because the French people would not expect an attack in the way we were going to deliver it.

Billy, Frank and I went into the Crédit Lyonnais. It was a busy morning. Dozens of people were going in and out of the bank and nobody paid any attention to us. A messenger came in, went up to the counter, and put a *sacoche*[42] in front of him. I also happened to be at the counter changing some money, right alongside the messenger. He opened his *sacoche* and drew from the cashier a big packet of mille-franc notes. It was the opportunity we were waiting for! Flash Bill came up on the other side of him, asked him something in English which he obviously didn't understand. Like a flash of lightning I put a newspaper over the *sacoche* and whizzed out of the bank. It all happened in a matter of seconds. When the messenger turned round again his money had disappeared and so had I.

If he had thought for a second, he might have come to the conclusion that the man who had spoken to him knew something about the matter. But he didn't; he was one of those excitable Frenchmen who lose their heads the moment anything happens. Screaming out that he had been robbed, he made a bolt for the door where Dago Frank judiciously got in his way and held him up for a valuable second or two while I cleared off down the street, as I thought unrecognized. Bill had also stood not upon the order of his going but had gone. It had all happened in less time than it takes me to tell.

I saw nothing and heard nothing. I slipped down a side street and kept the hounds at bay. Nobody took any notice of me. The wad of notes had been stuffed into my pocket and I didn't know then that anybody had seen them in my possession.

For four or five miles I went walking, away to a wood where the plunder was to be hidden. I kept on and on until I had reached absolute loneliness. Then I took a piece of mackintosh out of my pocket, in it wrapped the notes, and dug a hole in the ground where I buried them. If I had thought for a second I might have wrapped them in an envelope and posted them straight off to London, which is infinitely the safer way of getting rid of your plunder. In this instance we had arranged to bury the notes and get them later. Coming back I marked the trees in the way that the pioneers of old blazed their trail in the American forests. It sounds melodramatic, I know, but it was the plan we had evolved. Common sense might have told us the risk of going back to Lyons after the robbery, but I, for one, uncompromisingly declined to take the chance of making my way back to Paris with the notes in my possession. And they represented a nice little sum of money. I counted them as I went towards the hiding-place, two hundred and fifty notes of a thousand francs each, worth at that time about $50,000[43].

I did not return to Lyons. From an outlying station I returned to Paris unsuspected and stayed there two days, intending to go on to England in a day or two. The French newspapers came out with screaming great headlines about the robbery, something like this:

SENSATIONAL ROBBERY AT LYONS.
BANK MESSENGER LOSES 250,000 FRANCS.

The next day they came out with another big black streamer:

THREE ITALIANS ARRESTED FOR LYONS ROBBERY.
IDENTIFIED BY WOMAN WHO WITNESSED THE
CRIME.

That made me laugh a bit. I never knew I looked like a Dago, so I shook hands with myself and rather rashly came to the conclusion that I had nothing to fear. But instead of keeping quiet in Paris, as I ought to have done, I went out on the booze and ran into Billy Murdin, one of the hangers-on of the American crowd. I suppose the fact that I was flush soon brought the carrion crow; at any rate, within a very short space of time Bill Stetson came on the scene and demanded his cut.

"I don't know what you're talking about," I said.

"The Lyons job," replied Bill softly. He was an old man, nearly double my age, with white hair and the most peaceful expression you ever saw. But for all that he had a nasty record. He had shot two or three men in America, and was known to pull a pistol whenever anyone suggested double-crossing him. By trade he was a pawnbroker, but he soon gave up the unprofitable profession of taking in hock the everyday articles of the pawnbroking business, becoming instead one of the greatest fences in America. Bill Stetson and Sophie Lyons had been pals together for many years. They were both at the same game— living on the jobs that other men did.

Anyhow, Bill seemed to think he should have been in with Flash Bill, Dago Frank, and myself. Sophie Lyons also thought the same thing—according to Bill Stetson—so it seemed as though the cut-up wasn't going to be anything like as good as it promised.

One thing led to another. I definitely refused to pay Bill a cent, whereupon he promptly informed me that I was several degrees of a low-down shyster who ought to be dead.

"And you," I said, "are a dirty old skunk not worth calling a man."

We were both pretty drunk at the time. Bill and I were facing each other in a sitting-room he had at the St. Petersburg Hotel in Paris. Bill made a covert threat of blowing. I picked up a chair to brain him, when like a flash he produced a pistol. I made a blind jump at him hoping to get him before he fired. Instantaneously there was a tremendous flash before my eyes, a crack like the roar of a rifle, and a terrible stinging pain in my right shoulder. But the momentum of the leap sent Bill flying with me on top of him.

The marvel was that nobody seemed to take any notice. Lying on the floor half-fainting from pain, I fully expected the servants to come rushing in, and semi-conscious as I was I realized the danger. But nothing happened. Bill pushed me from him, slowly struggled to his feet, mumbling: "Good God, Eddie, what have I done?"

He put the pistol in his pocket and knelt down beside me, asked me where I was hurt and then, on my instructions, turned the key in the lock in case anyone attempted to come in. I won't repeat what I called him. It will be sufficient to say that I designated him in the choicest American I could muster a dirty, common, murderous, lying, thieving swine, embellished by a few adjectives which no doubt made him feel sorry for the trick he had served me. I could feel the blood pouring out of my shoulder and a red-hot pain as though the bullet was made of molten lead.

"You unmentionable —— —— dog," I cried to him. "Wait until I can deal with you. This'll be the worst night's work you've ever done."

The shot had sobered Bill; he kept on mumbling apologies. My shoulder had now gone numb with the pain and I didn't care much what happened to me. Bill gave me a big jolt of brandy, laid me down on a couch and went out to get a surgeon. I don't mind saying we weren't at all anxious for the matter to get to the ears of the police, I, for one, realizing that inquiries of any sort must inevitably result in my being detained for the robbery in Lyons. Bill, for his part, was full of remorse.

Heaven knows how he did it, but within a quarter of an hour he came back to the hotel with a little French surgeon who pulled off my clothing, had a look at the wound, and then promptly produced a pair of calipers with which he extracted the bullet.

Holy Moses! I nearly jumped to the ceiling when it came out. I have sampled one or two choice specimens of pain in my time. I have also given and taken quite a number of tampings. The police of many countries have gone out of their way to maim me—and very nearly succeeded, but I never experienced such acute agony as the night in Paris when that little Frenchman, without administering any anesthetic, yanked the bullet out of my shoulder. Then he cauterized the wound, after washing it out, and put a wad of cotton wool soaked in raw carbolic in it, making it burn like blazes and sending me almost dizzy with the pain. After that he produced a roll of bandage and bound up my shoulder so tightly that it went numb again.

He was a tactful little fellow; he asked no questions, told me in broken English to get the wound properly attended to as soon as I could, and took his departure with five hundred francs in his pocket tendered by the repentant Bill.

"Now," I said to Bill, "you've got to get me out of this. I want to get over to London as soon as I can."

It hurt more than the shot in my shoulder to think that lying outside Lyons was a small fortune waiting to be dug out of the ground. I couldn't see Flash Bill and Dago Frank waiting very long for me. They would have the money up and be away if I was a day over the fortnight we had arranged.

Bill Stetson, a little more sober now, promised to do everything he could to help me. He went and borrowed a big Inverness cape, gave me another tot of brandy, and then took me off to another hotel where we spent a restless night wondering what was going to happen to us. But nothing occurred, and at ten o'clock in the morning, with my shoulder aching like the devil, we drove off to the Gare du Nord, where we took the train for England. Bill was so sorry for what he had done that he looked after me like a mother with her first child. Nobody seemed to be following us. I half expected to be held up at Calais, but we just walked on board the boat and made our way up to London as though we were one of the everyday crowd that crosses the Straits of Dover three hundred and sixty-five days in the year. He took me up to an hotel in Great Portland Street, saw me comfortable, and went off promising me, almost with tears in his eyes, to do anything he could to compensate me for the shooting. I told him in London to forget everything I had called him. He was mad drunk at the time, while I was in little better plight. Most of the trouble in this world comes through drink or drugs. I have done things under the influence of booze that I would never have dreamed of in my full senses. It makes me reckless, pugnacious, and utterly blind to danger. Ask the coppers—they know!

A good many years afterward, when I was back in London for good, I happened to go into the American bar at the Waldorf Hotel and was having a drink there when Gray, the hotel detective, came up to me and said: "Eddie, why don't you go and get that money?"

I naturally asked him what money. He then told me a long and curious story about Bill Stetson having died in Boston, leaving behind him a considerable sum of money. The Crédit Lyonnais in France heard about it—probably from the Pinkertons—and instituted a legal action against the executors of Bill's will to recover the money they believed he had obtained as his share of the Lyons robbery. Apparently Bill had left his money to his niece.

The matter had come into the hands of Smale, a Pinkerton detective, who represented the business in London. Gray wanted me to go across to him, make a statement on oath that Bill Stetson had received a big share of the Lyons' job, which would enable the Crédit Lyonnais to recover the money from his estate. They probably thought, in view of what Bill had done to me, that I would be ready and willing to snitch. The bank was actually prepared to pay me £1,000 if I would do what they wanted.

Well, I have done a good many desperate things in my time, but I was never the man to play a dirty game like that. However, I went with Gray to see Smale, who probably thought I was willing to do anything for money.

"You can make a statement here if you wish," he said. "Bill is dead now and can't possibly do you any harm. You'll get a nice big reward which will put you on your feet again."

"What do you want me to say?" I asked, anxious to earn a bit if I could.

"I want you to tell me all about the bank robbery, what part Bill took in it, and how much money he had out of it."

"So that's what you want?"

"Yes, that's it," said Smale, who never believed in wasting any words with you.

"Well," I replied, giving him a look straight in the eye, "I can't tell you what you want because it wouldn't be true. If you want me to tell you any tales I am quite ready to do so, but Bill was not with us at Lyons and never got a single cent out of the job."

I don't think Smale believed me, but at any rate, beyond informing me that he didn't want that sort of yarn he said nothing more and I walked out of his office as rich as when I had gone in.

It was July 1 that Flash Billy, Dago Frank and myself met by arrangement at a West End cafe and fixed up to go back to Lyons for the money. I had made a good recovery from my wound and I insisted upon going because I was the only one of us who actually knew where the money lay. Dago Frank wanted to go in my stead.

"Not if I know it," I replied. "You won't be able to find the place and somebody might see you walking about looking for it."

Privately, I didn't trust him overmuch. Flash Bill had brought him into the scheme against my wishes. He was to get a third share for doing practically nothing.

"You'll stop in London," I said to Dago Frank, "till Billy and I get back with the stuff."

We got back to Paris without incident, but Billy foolishly refused to keep himself quiet as I wanted. Drinking around the American bars the news soon got out that he was again in Paris and I have no doubt that Sophie Lyons heard about the matter. I never saw her myself and I didn't know then that she had already communicated with the French police to inform them who had done the job at the Crédit Lyonnais. She was only guessing, of course, as far as I learnt, but no doubt she had a pretty good idea. You couldn't kid Sophie very much. She knew the American yeggman's box of tricks as well as we did.

(In passing, let me say that the *coup* we pulled off at the Crédit Lyonnais in Lyons was responsible for all bank messengers having their wallets chained to them. They don't go about with them loose now. Every time a big bank robbery takes place the method of it is closely investigated and precautions are then taken to guard against a repetition of it.)

For a night and a day Flash Bill and I stupidly enjoyed ourselves in Paris when we should have kept quiet. What we really wanted was to find out whether we were suspected. But nothing happened; we didn't see Sophie and for the time being we went on our way ignorant of the fact that she had already snitched.

We went down to Lyons by a morning train. Nobody took the slightest notice of us. We half expected the gendarmes to be on the station awaiting us, instead of which we walked out of the place like a couple of respectable silk merchants. Over a fortnight had elapsed since we were there before and probably the hue and cry had died down. Billy and I shook hands with ourselves, and as we went out of the town towards the woods where the hoard lay hidden, I soon found the cuts I had made on the trees to point the way. The hole I had scooped with a few bushes to hide it had not been disturbed.

"Bully for you, Ed!" exclaimed Flash Bill. "We'll sure have this money away like a Methodist preacher taking home his collection."

Some time later on I discovered that Dago Frank had tried to twist us. He had sent over to some one in Paris to say that a big sum of money in thousand-franc notes was secreted in the woods, but evidently the messenger he sent to get it never succeeded in finding the place. I know I lifted it out, carefully put the mackintosh back in the hole, filled it in, and walked back to Lyons with the money in my pocket.

We didn't bother changing the notes in Lyons. The first train out of the town did us. No one asked any questions, no detectives searched the train as they would have done in the States, or, at any rate, if they did they took no heed of us. We reached Paris about midnight and without waiting to make another stay we hiked ourselves across the city to the Gare du Nord and took the night mail to England.

I suppose I must take the credit of having taught the French police a good deal in the way of catching criminals. The second time I had a go at them they did not let me get away as easily as they did in 1888. Probably it dawned upon them then that foreigners were interfering with the native-born crook. I think I am right in saying that they rubbed it into us with a vengeance for showing them a few tricks they hadn't seen before. I don't like the French and I never did. If you rob them of anything they squeal worse than a penful of pigs in a Chicago meat-yard waiting to be stuck.

"Here's to it, Billy," I said, raising my glass to him in the dining-car as we sped on our way to England, home and beauty. The $50,000 worth of notes made a comfortable tight feeling inside my waistcoat and the only thing that worried me was whether we would land at Dover unmolested. Remember, I knew nothing at all of what Sophie had done, or I might not have felt so easy as I did. That old poet who wrote of heaven having no rage like love to hatred turned, nor hell a fury like a woman scorned, knew what he was writing about. I spent many good years of my life in prison pondering on the inscrutable nature of womankind, wondering what the devil ever induced me to have anything to do with them.

Nothing happened just then. At Dover we saw a detective watching the people off the boat, but he didn't appear to be looking for us. We got up to London safely and that very same afternoon shared out the swag.

It is a bit of a problem, even when you are dealing with bank notes, to get rid of them without exciting suspicion. Dago Frank had arranged all that. There was a fence in Percy Street, off Tottenham Court Road, London, who did a big trade in such things. Old Jack Carr he was called. He had been at the game for forty years and what he didn't know about dealing in snide notes wasn't worth knowing. Every thief in Europe knew him; his reputation was international and he must have died a very rich man. Of course, you get a funny crowd of people in these money-changing bureau. At any rate, Old Jack knew all the people in the business and put down the notes I brought at a place in Leicester Square where I daresay he had had many transactions before.

He was what I would call a straight fence, that is, he took a fair share of the risk and received a fair profit for doing it. If the police had caught him he would have said that he had received the notes in the ordinary course of business and had no knowledge of their being stolen. As a matter of fact, I don't think the numbers of the notes were ever known, so that they could not be published. It would not have worried Old Jack if they had. I know my share came to about $12,500 which I received in English bank notes, American Express checks and small French money. And I daresay most of it had been stolen. There is a regular trade in paper money that never goes back to the banks.

Now here I come to a period which shows the arrant idiocy of a crook's life. If Nature had endowed me with just the tiniest morsel of foresight I might have said to myself: "Eddie, my boy, you've just had a nice little touch and it's up to you to make the best of it. Go and buy yourself a business and cut this game out for evermore."

Did I do it? Not a bit of it. What I did was to go off on a first-class jag, spending my money like water, buying drinks for everybody I knew, and generally making a damn fool of myself. I never received the slightest hint that Sophie Lyons had written not only to the Prefect of the Police in Paris but also to Scotland Yard, telling them that Dago Frank and I had done the robbery at Lyons. She carefully left out Flash Billy's name.

I had been back in London a week when I received a letter
from Sophie which, as near as I can remember, ran like this:

"If you don't send me my share you'll be sorry. I have
been waiting over here (Paris) ever since you did it. I
know all about it and I will give you just three days to
play the game. Don't think I'm bluffing."

S.

I took no notice of the letter. I certainly mentioned the
matter to Dago Frank, but we were both boozed at the time and
we mutually agreed to let Sophie and her threats go unanswered.
I didn't think for a moment that she would snitch, if only for the
sake of Flash Billy, which shows you how mistaken you can be in
a woman. It certainly put me on the *qui vive,* but I didn't clear
out of London as I might have done. I simply didn't feel afraid of
anything happening.

Sophie, I afterward discovered, had read all about the
robbery in the Paris edition of the New York *Herald.* With her
lover safely out of the way for the time being she determined to
have her revenge on me. It was certainly a remarkable fact that
Flash Billy was never caught, and in my own mind I have no
doubt that he got the warning from Sophie. It was me she
wanted.

I thought I would be safer in London because Scotland Yard
did not know me very well. The only time I had against me was
the three months I had previously mentioned for the Cannon
Street Post Office affair. I had been convicted in a false name,
while the photograph they had taken of me at Millbank was so
bad as to be almost unrecognizable. I reckoned that Sophie,
whatever she thought about me, would not go to the length of
actually telling Scotland Yard who had been in the job. There
again I made a fatal mistake.

The Yard men instructed to deal with the matter, Detective-
Inspector Leach (one of the old-timers and the father of the man
who used to deal with all the confidence tricksters) and
Detective-Inspector White, were two clever birds. They picked up
Dago Frank right enough, but they couldn't find me. But acting

on the old principle that all animals seek their mates they didn't bother to knock off Frank then and there. Instead, they waited and followed him around confident that sooner or later he would lead them to me.

The first inkling I got of detectives being on my track came at the hotel in Great Portland Street. I had been staying at the place for over a week, spending £7 to £8 a day on booze and cigars. One afternoon, to my intense surprise, the manager brought up my bill.

"What's the matter with you?" I demanded. "Don't you think I'm good enough for the money?"

"Oh, yes, saire, but we like to have our money as they do on the Continent. M'sieu knows the French custom, does he not?"

King Booze again! If I hadn't been drinking bottles of champagne that day I might have taken a tumble when he began talking about France. Anyhow, I paid the bill, about £40. The thief took it, made me a mocking bow, and then said to me: "Now, M'sieu, will you please get out of this hotel at once."

"Get out! What for?" I asked.

"Because, M'sieu, I do not want bank robbers in my place. Downstairs there are two detectives waiting for you. I asked them that I should obtain my money before they took you away."

Chapter Seven
A MEMORABLE BATTLE

I have always been a quick thinker. When the little hotel proprietor told me that Scotland Yard detectives were waiting for me down below I wasted no time. A look outside the corridor effectually disabused me of any idea of escaping that way. Clustered in a group near-by my door were a couple of chamber-maids, a waiter and a porter, wanting, I suppose, to be in at the death.

Unfortunately, I wasn't exactly dressed for going out. The wound in my shoulder was still troubling me and I had been loafing about the hotel in a shirt, trousers and slippers, drinking a good deal more than I should have done until I could move about more comfortably.

The only way out I could think of was through the window overlooking a dirty lane at the back of the hotel. Like a shot out of a gun I went, took a twenty-feet drop, and went through a house with a maidservant yelling "Stop thief!" at the top of her voice. Out into the open street, with the servant-girl still screaming, other people took up the chase. A soldier in a red uniform began to run after me, and the harder he ran the quicker I went. My slippers went flying, but nobody attempted to stop me. And, mind you, this in a busy street of London, the biggest city in the world!

I slipped up one of the side streets, panting hard, wondering where the devil I should go. Suddenly I espied a hansom cab, the driver of which was nodding in his seat half asleep.

"Here," I called, "drive me down the Euston Road, will you?" and I jumped into his cab. But I couldn't stall him as easily as that.

"What are you up to?" demanded Cabby, looking down at me through his trap-door. "Are the police after you?"

"Not they," I panted. "A fellow has just caught me with his wife and I've had to make a run for it."

I don't suppose he believed me, but he whipped up his horse and started off. But instead of taking me towards the Euston Road he turned right and began making in the very direction I had left!

"Hi!" I yelled, "you're going the wrong way."

He didn't seem to understand. I could see people running all over the place evidently looking for me and I had no intention of being caught like a rat in a trap. Out of the cab I sprang and in my stockinged feet ran up the road to the Portland Road tube station.

But by this time the whole neighborhood was in a ferment. "Stop thief!" was being shouted after me, while half a dozen people tried to trip me up. I ran into the station expecting that I would be able to get out by another entrance. Hell, the gate was locked! I couldn't scale it: it had long iron spikes on the top. By now I was indeed like a cornered rat. A hundred people had taken up the chase. Desperately I ran into the station buffet hoping that I had not been seen. There I stuck for ten minutes, fool-like not thinking that the station would be surrounded.

They didn't let me remain in hiding long. I had not yet recovered my breath when a couple of policemen came in, unceremoniously hauled me out, put me into a cab and took me off to the Tottenham Court Road Police Station. There I was taken into the charge room and stood between the two men who had arrested me until Leach and White, who had gone to the hotel for me, came back.

"Got you at last, eh?" remarked Leach. "You've given us a lot of trouble."

They searched me, took out of my pockets £600 in English money, and then shoved me into a cell where I spent the remainder of the day and the long night in a most unpleasant state of meditation. I said good-bye to the £600, but I worried myself all night long about another big sum I had planted in French and American money on the top of a cupboard in my room at the hotel. I discovered later that a maid dusting the room found it and handed it over to the police, which only goes to show that even a crook should find a safe hiding-place for his money. I might have taken mine to a safe deposit if I had known of somewhere to keep the key in security.

Although the police had arrested me and charged me as a suspect, it did not necessarily follow that they had a case against me. Leach came into my cell and said to me: "Now, look here, Eddie, you'd better tell us all about it. We've got Dago Frank inside and he's given the whole game away. Tell us the real truth and you'll probably have an easier time."

I wasn't standing for any stool pigeon tricks. I knew they had Dago Frank, but it didn't follow that they had me for keeps. He might have told them something—and he might not.

"It's no good your coming to me," I replied. "I don't know anything about the matter. I've never been in Lyons in my life. The money you found on me I won at the races."

"You did!" Leach exclaimed. "You'll have to think of a better story than that, Eddie." He didn't worry me after that.

I was brought up at the police court the following day and remanded. They then drove me off to Holloway to await developments, which soon took place. They brought over from France a woman who had been in the Crédit Lyonnais in Lyons when the robbery occurred. She came to the prison with Leach and professed to be able to identify me after I had been placed in a row with some other men. For all I know, the police may have shown her my photograph beforehand, or they may have given her my description. It was not one that could be easily mistaken. At any rate, she came up to me and said to Leach: "Yes, that is the man." She was also shown Dago Frank, but in his case she did not seem at all certain. After returning to France she wrote over to Scotland Yard making the statement that on second thoughts she could also recognize Frank as having been in the bank at the time of the robbery. I doubt very much whether she ever saw him, or if she did for more than half a second. Still, her word was accepted and on the strength of it Frank was extradited and sent over to France to stand his trial.

But I had no intention of going under as easily as that. I knew very well, short of Dago Frank snitching on me, that it would be very difficult for any court to convict me on the identification of a woman whose evidence would not stand much cross-examination. And I also had another shot in my locker. The solicitor I engaged to defend me told me that I would have a good chance of resisting extradition on the ground that I was a British subject. To plead the case he briefed one of the greatest criminal lawyers England has ever known, the famous Charles Gill[44], a man who never had a superior in the defense of prisoners. Gill was only a rising young barrister at the time and I think he saw in my case a wonderful opportunity to make a name for himself.

I was taken into custody on July 24, 1888, but the extradition proceedings at Bow Street, the chief police court in England where all cases of this description are dealt with, were so tenaciously fought by Gill that a couple of months elapsed before the magistrate, the late Sir John Bridge, made the order to send me to France. That did not finish Gill. He appealed to a higher court on the ground that I was a British subject, and therefore not liable to extradition as the laws relating to that matter between England and France then stood.

Gill so far succeeded that the court ordered evidence to be brought from America as to my nationality. Pinkertons, employed by the Crédit Lyonnais to hunt up facts that would get me convicted, found an Irish policeman in Chicago by the name of MacMahon who came over to England and swore that he had known me from my childhood days and that I had always been looked upon as an American subject. The detectives brought him to my cell in Holloway and thus they got me identified.

"That's Eddie, isn't it?" they asked the copper.

"Sure thing. I know him by his broken nose. 'Twas smashed by a truncheon in a downtown saloon one night."

That didn't frighten me. My indefatigable attorney had me examined by a Harley Street surgeon who swore that my nose, judging from the growth of it, must have been broken at a very, very early age. Other damaging evidence against me was that I could not prove my birth in London. Nor, for the matter of that, could the police prove it in Chicago. So we remained quits on that issue.

Dago Frank lay in prison in France all the time my case remained before the British courts. Another two months went by, when Gill took out a writ of Habeas Corpus and had me brought into the High Court where a judge and jury could finally decide whether or not I was liable for extradition. It proved to be an epoch-making case and if it was any consolation to me I could take pride in the fact that the trial of Regina *v.* the Governor of Holloway Prison (*ex parte* Guerin) constituted a precedent which is still quoted in Great Britain. Gill advised my solicitor that he had better bring in Sir Harry Poland, Q.C.,[45] then the leading criminal barrister in England, with the idea that Poland's great name and the magnetic influence he exercised over a jury would sway the verdict in my favor.

The Chicago policeman, MacMahon, swore that he had seen my parents week by week during the days of my boyhood, though he didn't attempt to perjure himself by saying that he definitely knew I was born in Chicago. Sir Harry Poland countered this by calling a Mrs. Walker who said that she had been present at the house in Hoxton (in the East End of London) when I first saw the light of day. This evidence was nullified by other people testifying that the only child in the house at the time put forward by my counsel was Dutch, and therefore could not be me.

So it went on for many days until the time came for the summing up. Then the judge, Baron Huddlestone, left it to the jury whether or not I could justly claim British nationality. They came back into court and said I could not, with the result that the judge made the order for me to go back to France and there, with Dago Frank, stand my trial.

Flash Billy had evidently not been caught. The police would give me no information about him, hoping, no doubt, to extract some news as to his whereabouts. But from other sources I ascertained that he had completely disappeared, as I also discovered that Sophie Lyons was responsible for my capture. Perhaps it was just as well for her that I did not get my liberty then and there. If I had done so I don't think her life would have been worth very much.

You can commit all the crimes in creation, be as bad as it is possible for any man to be, and yet have a certain amount of respect for the conventions.

Even in the criminal world there are certain standards which must be observed. You may be a robber by trade, but you must not steal from the poor. The sneak-thief who robs his landlady is utterly outside the pale of humanity, because she will be a poor widow woman dependent on the rents she gets for her rooms to keep a roof over her head. The burglar who breaks into a house and out of the proceeds pays his way for his board and lodgings is a proper man in the eyes of his fellow-crooks. He may have to pay another—and a heavier—price for his crime; so long as he has not bilked a poor woman he has nothing to be ashamed of. But Sophie Lyons! The lowest thing that any human being can be, a pimp, a blackmailer, a female Judas if ever there was one in this world. All the long months I lay in Holloway Gaol awaiting the result of my struggle I bitterly cursed myself for having anything to do with her and vowed that when the time came she would pay the price for what she had done. When you are locked up in a cell day after day and night after night, with nothing better to do than chew on the sour cud of what might have been, you can readily lash yourself into a fury which only murder could appease. It matters not whether you are innocent or guilty.

But even when the judge made the order for my extradition there was still plenty of fight left in me. I didn't mean to go back to France if it could possibly be prevented. I had friends outside—good friends, waiting to give me one more last chance to escape the long term of penal servitude I knew to be inevitable. When I got back to my cell in Holloway that evening, with the knowledge that I would have to go to France in a day or two, there was a pleasant surprise awaiting me. A good fairy had visited the cell, leaving behind her a brace and bit and an extending jemmy.

Who could have put them there? Not Sophie Lyons; the only thing she would have supplied me with free of charge was a good strong dose of prussic acid. Some kind friends must have been interested in getting me out of prison, and as they hadn't been able to do it legally no doubt they thought they would try to get it done illegally. I suppose they hated to see a poor fellow like me being sent away to a prison in France. But I shan't give any names; the arm of the law is long, and although it is nearly forty years ago since it happened I am not going to get anyone into trouble. Anyhow, the day all hope was lost in the court, I thought, when I saw those useful tools, "Well, if I can't get out one way I'll have a damn good try for another."

Night fell and the noises of the prison gradually grew less. Outside the sound of the traffic went on unceasingly, giving me the chance of doing what I wanted to do in comparative safety. Holloway Gaol is in one of the busiest parts of London. It is situated in a busy road leading from Camden Town which is one of the main arteries out of the city, and in those days there were innumerable 'buses, cabs and carts rumbling over the rough road until the early hours of the morning. When the prison had quieted down I set to work on the wall with the brace and bit, widening the hole I made with the jemmy. I had to stop at regular intervals as the warder on duty came by; the moment I heard the sound of his footsteps I jumped into bed and began snoring. Nothing happened as I continued at the work throughout the night with the sweat pouring down my face, while the hole in the wall gradually grew bigger and I began to see visions of freedom. A man in the cell underneath evidently thought the rats—for which the prison was famous—were hard at work. I could hear him calling out: "Get away, you swine. Shoo! Shoo!" Occasionally I had to stop and laugh at him.

I was in a corner cell adjoining the wash-house, and if I could have got out a six-feet drop would have enabled me to land on the roof and out into the street. For hours I kept on, but God! weren't those walls thick! I got to the full length of the jemmy without seeing daylight on the other side, and when the morning came, and with it the impossibility of doing anything more for the time, I covered up my traces as best I could, hiding the tools in the mattress and placing the washstand over the hole I had made.

I remained in the cell all day, expecting any moment to be taken away. But the long hours passed without any incident. Once more did the shades of night descend over the foul-smelling prison and with it the opportunity to continue my bid for freedom. But I could make no impression on the wall. It must have been something like three feet thick. When morning came I was still as far away from my liberty as ever.

The good fairy I have already mentioned continued her activities—this time, unfortunately, not so successfully. A warder going his rounds found a big piece of wire hanging over the wall. He pulled it up and hey, presto! what should he catch but a rope ladder! Obviously something was afoot. There were two murderers in the prison awaiting trial. Suspicion fell upon them. They were each put in another cell while those they had occupied were turned inside out, but nothing could be found to incriminate them. Apparently they did not think of looking in my cell; I must have appeared too unsophisticated.

But alas for my calculations! A woman friend came to see me and a warder came upstairs to take me down to the visitors' room.

"Hullo," I thought, "they have found me out."

As I left my cell I saw a star warder go in and I concluded, rightly, that developments would take place before very long. I didn't say anything much to my friend because I knew my conversation would be listened to. They soon sent my visitor away as quickly as it dawned on them that I wasn't going to compromise myself. The moment I got upstairs again a pretty sight met my eyes. All the furniture had been pulled out of my cell. Standing outside was Cook, the star warder, with a couple of other screws.

"Well, this is a nice little game you've been having, Eddie," said Cook. "So it was you the rope ladder was for?"

I didn't attempt to prevaricate; there was a nice big hole in the wall to tell a story much more convincing that anything I could invent.

"That's so," I replied cheerfully. "A bird wants to fly, and I want my liberty. I couldn't get it one way so I tried another."

"We'll soon stop that," Cook assured me. "Come on, you'll go into another cell, where you won't be able to play any of your little tricks while I see the Governor."

The Governor, my old friend Milman, whom I had met before, soon disposed of the matter. He had me downstairs in front of him, heard a more or less truthful account of what had taken place, and then ordered a strong iron chain, big enough to hold an elephant, to be riveted on to my legs.

"I shan't be troubled with you much longer," he growled, "and if I were I should put you in a place where you wouldn't even think of escaping. But you'll be leaving here soon. The papers for your extradition have been signed and you'll be on your way to France before you know where you are."

I was taken out of the office and put into a cell, the chain clanging along the stone floor with a discordant jangle that matched my drooping spirits. I didn't know what was before me in France, but I had a pretty good idea that there would be nothing very much to my liking. Two hours after seeing the Governor, Leach and three other detectives came for me. They didn't seem at all hostile and it is only fair of me to admit that they did not attempt to ill-treat me. The warders took Leach upstairs and showed him the hole in the wall.

"Oh, oh!" he remarked to me when he saw me again, "I'll have to keep my eye on you, my lad. You're a pretty slippery customer."

With four detectives to escort me—quite a nice little compliment to pay any prisoner—I was put into a cab and taken to Cannon Row Police Station, which is situated within the precincts of Scotland Yard. It is not used very frequently—practically only for people arrested by Central Office—and is more a depot than anything else. Anyhow, they kept me at Cannon Row all night, fed me very well, and generally gave me the impression that I was a hell of a fellow. Somehow or other they seemed to have the idea that I was an opponent worthy of their steel, and that, after all, brings you a certain amount of decent treatment. A policeman is only a human being, and he despises the sneak-thief and the snitch as much as anybody else. They all knew Sophie Lyons was responsible for my downfall and I have no doubt they were rather sorry for me. Leach especially made himself very agreeable, with an object which I discovered before I took my departure for La Belle France. He came to my cell late at night, in friendly fashion, and sat down.

"Now, look here, Eddie," he began. "I'm talking to you as man to man and I'm going to give you the opportunity of doing yourself a bit of good. You're going to get a long sentence when you are convicted, and it rests with you whether you make it a bit less."

Before I answered him I got up and peered through the trap-door to see if anybody was listening.

"It's all right," said Leach. "There's nobody there and I'm not double-crossing you. I'm giving you a chance that a hundred men would jump at."

"Tell me what you mean," I replied, looking at him suspiciously.

"It's like this," he explained. "There are a lot of forged Bank of France notes in circulation all over Paris. We've had information from the Sûreté that you can tell us something about them."

"I've read about it in the papers," I said.

"I daresay, but I thought you could tell us a bit more," Leach said confidentially. "They say that some of you Yankee fellows have been putting them down."

"Oh, yes!" incredulously.

"You know who did it," continued Leach.

"I know nothing of the kind," I protested.

"Now, Eddie," my visitor added—and I could see he didn't believe me—"if you will tell us where the 'plates' are we'll get you a short sentence."

If I had known anything about the matter I wouldn't have told him. I could only reply that I was completely ignorant of the whole affair, and he went away shaking his head, firmly convinced that I was lying. The next morning I went off on what was destined to be indeed a long trip to France, with the same four officers escorting me. They even reserved a first-class carriage for my benefit—but kept the chain on me. But they weren't in the least unsympathetic, and I will say this of the average English police officer—that with a few notable exceptions they are scrupulously fair in the way they treat their prisoners. Those four men who had to take me to Calais to hand me over to the French Government seemed to be sorry I had not succeeded in making my escape. As we sped through the pleasant countryside they commiserated with me, gave me a handful of cigars to smoke, and told me how they admired the way in which I had attempted to regain my liberty. More than that, short of letting me go altogether, they could not do.

There were two thousand people on the pier waiting to see me off when I crossed over from Dover to Calais in a special cabin, the chain still dangling around my legs. The Scotland Yard men bade me goodbye and wished me the best of luck. And Heaven only knows I wanted it!

I received quite a flattering reception from the French detectives.

"Ah, Eddie! So we have you at last! It has been a long time."

"Yes," I said, "and I daresay it would have been a damn sight longer if that dirty—" (mentioning my friend Sophie in a way that will not bear repetition in these pages) "had not put you wise."

"Ah, Madame Lyons," they replied, looking very artful; "yes, she is the bad woman."

The long and bitter years I have spent in prison have driven most of the humor out of my body, but I can still raise a laugh over my journey from Calais to Paris with those French policemen. They had taken over from Leach a bag containing £1,500 which, including the sum found hidden in the hotel, had been in my possession at the time I was arrested. Instead of guarding it closely they put it on the window-sill, where it would have been the easiest thing in the world for anyone to have grabbed it. Unfortunately, I couldn't see anyone to whom I could have tipped the wink. I would have shammed a fit and while they were attending to me the money would have disappeared. But the only people who came past our carriage door looked too meek and mild to be worth the trouble. I had to sit there mournfully watching quite a nice little nest-egg go begging.

Paris again! Things began to look black when I arrived at the Gare du Nord and found myself taken to a depot prison in charge of the famous Debischof, the foremost detective in France. He also greeted me warmly and was decent enough to have the chain knocked off my legs.

"I do not think you will escape from me, my little Eddie," he informed me. "And it will be well for you that you do not try."

"Oh, go to hell," I replied. He didn't understand what I said, which perhaps was just as well. I used to get a lot of satisfaction cursing the French coppers in my native tongue.

Debischof fully kept his word about looking after me. He put a couple of gendarmes in the cell with me all night, so that if one of them fell asleep the other would be awake. They were both there when I woke in the morning, and at ten o'clock, after a typical French breakfast of coffee and bread, which made me feel hungrier than ever, we drove off to the Gare de Lyon for the long journey south. But even then I hadn't given up all hope. I pretended to be taking no notice of anything, and if anybody had seen me they might have thought what a poor simpleton I was.

With just a little bit of luck I would have got away just before I arrived at Lyons. I asked to go to the lavatory, and one of the gendarmes, a decent old fellow who seemed a bit sorry for me, accompanied me. When I passed the door I took one step back; if I had taken two I should have been out of the train like a shot. The gendarme caught hold of me like a vice.

"Ah, so you would go!" he cried. He hustled me back to the carriage, put a pair of handcuffs on my wrists, and guarded me for the rest of the journey as though I were made of gold. No further chances presented themselves. A cab was waiting for us at the station in Lyons and in it I drove to the local jail, where I was put into a cell for the night, waiting, with a dread in my heart which no words can express, the coming ordeal. I knew, of course, from what Leach had told me, that I would be very lucky if I escaped a long term of penal servitude. The French police seemed to think that I was a member of the gang that had been flooding their country with forged bank-notes. They were quite wrong, nevertheless I am sure they took that matter into consideration when I stood my trial for the robbery at the Crédit Lyonnais.

Chapter Eight
A CONVICT'S LIFE IN FRANCE

I am an old man now and my blood has cooled.

It is with a moderate amount of philosophy that I can sit down and in cold blood recapitulate the dramatic events of forty years ago. The natural venom I felt against the woman who had betrayed me has long since disappeared, but I can still acutely remember the feelings I underwent while lying in the prison at Lyons awaiting my trial.

I don't ask for sympathy. What I had done would in the eyes of most people deserve condign punishment. But it was gall and wormwood to think I had been grossly betrayed by a woman to whom I had done no harm. I wouldn't have minded so much had she been a law-abiding citizen herself. But Sophie Lyons was a pimp; she battened on crooks, sucked their life's blood, and then bartered away their liberty to the police.

She is dead now, and it is while I am at this stage of my story that I might take the opportunity of relating the last adventure

Sophie and I had. I was walking down Oxford Street, London, one day, a good many years afterward, in company with the Harry Raymond whom I have mentioned in the early part of this book. Whom should we run into but the fellow whom Sophie Lyons had married quite recently, none other than my old friend Billy Burke. Sophie, like a good many more women getting into the *passé* stage, wanted a young man, so she picked upon Burke. He knew perfectly well that his wife had snitched on me.

Anyhow, when Harry Raymond and I met him he seemed quite friendly towards me and I suppose I should not have borne him any grudge. We went to have a drink together, and over it Harry, always a good sort, said to us: "Now, you boys, you don't want to start quarreling. Shake hands and be good friends. We'll have dinner to-night and see if we can't do a bit of business together."

"All right," I replied, "I don't mind," and I left them.

After I had gone Burke must have tried to insinuate himself into Harry Raymond's good graces. He suggested that Harry should invite Sophie to the dinner, thinking, no doubt, it would be a good thing to patch up our quarrel. He was only a youngster and I expect he imagined that if I turned up at the dinner and found Sophie there we would kiss and be friends, or some other foolishness like that. Cut her throat I might have done. Burke didn't know me. I can forgive a lot of things in this world, but I could never forget the years I had spent in a French convict prison through her treachery.

That evening while on my way to keep the dinner appointment I ran across a man named Willett who had also been invited. I daresay if the police had looked in at the gathering they would have found quite an interesting little party. I asked Willett where he was going. He told me and added that our mutual friend Sophie would also be present. He liked her about as much as I did. I could hardly believe him and said I would go round to see if it were true.

"Now don't go and make a dashed fool of yourself," Willett said warningly. "You'll only get pinched, and it isn't worth while."

I knew he was right. That dinner might have been like an Irish wake by the time I had finished with it if I had found Sophie there. But I took Willett's advice and never went. Some time later I met Burke in America. He owed me some money and I asked him for it. He started talking to me about the dinner and wanted to know why I had made all the fuss about not going.

"Sophie's as good as you," he remarked. "I don't know who the hell you are, to go picking and choosing."

I didn't say anything in reply—I just slugged him, which nearly got me a bit more time. But I could never understand how he had ever come to marry the woman; she seemed to have some mysterious hold on him. For a long time he tried hard to get her back into the circle, but at one period or another she had twisted everybody and nobody would look at her. She certainly must have made a fair amount of money out of the game because when she died a few years ago she left quite a snug little fortune. And I won't be doing the lady any injustice when I suggest that the pangs of conscience must have got hold of her, because she left a big sum of money for the benefit of discharged prisoners. It was about the only reparation she could make for the damage she had done. But she didn't mention me in her will.

If you should happen to be caught for a bank robbery you will have the doubtful satisfaction of knowing that you will be prosecuted to the uttermost limits of the law. I know; I have gone up against banks in America, France and England. I could soon see when they lodged me in the St. Paul prison in Lyons that my trial wasn't going to be over for a long time. Dago Frank had been extradited from England some months before I made my appearance. I hadn't seen him for three or four months, and then on one occasion only at Bow Street in London, when we happened to come up together on remand.

He looked very much down in the mouth when I saw him again before the *juge d'instruction* in Lyons. The two of us were put in a line with other people and identified by the woman who had been in the bank at the time of the robbery. The police brought her in and gave her all the opportunity she could want to pick us out, thus repeating the farce which had already taken place in England. I tried to have a few words with Dago Frank, pretending I didn't know the rule about keeping silent, but I soon got stopped.

The strangest part of the whole affair was that Flash Billy had disappeared off the face of the earth. Quite obviously the Frenchmen then knew something of the part he had taken in the robbery, because they showed me his photograph and asked me if it was a picture of my confederate. I am no snitch, whatever else I may be.

"No," I said, "I have never seen such a man in my life."

"Ah, yes, you have. That is Flash Beely."

But I utterly declined to recognize the gentleman. Then they had a go at me over the forged bank-notes and swore that I must know the people who had made them. They were even more in earnest about this than over Flash Bill, but here I was telling no more than the truth when I protested I knew nothing about the matter.

Two months elapsed before Dago Frank and I were put on our trial, a dreary time enlivened by nothing but long and fierce duels with the *juge d'instruction*, who had us up before him once a week trying to make us confess. When you get into a French police court you are not interrogated by the counsel or the lawyer for the prosecution as you are in England and America. The *juge d'instruction* is both magistrate and prosecutor. He has done his work if he succeeds in dragging out of you evidence which will get you convicted when you go to an Assize Court. The principle on which French "justice" is administered is the quintessence of simplicity; you are deemed to be guilty unless you can incontrovertibly prove yourself to be innocent. It isn't the duty of the magistrate to balance the scales of justice; he himself sticks a lump of lead on the side of the prosecution and goes in great danger of losing his job if he doesn't get you a stretch.

However, I don't think he got much change out of Dago Frank and me. Although I was only twenty-eight years of age I had already undergone plenty of experience, and I knew, apart from the money found in my possession, there was no incriminating evidence against me except that of the woman who professed to be able to recognize me. So I sat tight, fiercely determined to make a fight for it. The time passed drearily enough in all conscience. All my money had been taken away from me with the exception of about two hundred francs, out of which I bought myself a bit of food to make life more bearable. They weren't taking any risks with me. I was locked up all day long with the exception of half an hour for exercise chained to one of the warders. They thought—and quite rightly—that the bird might fly again. Dago Frank remained outside all day long; nobody seemed to have any fear of him escaping. My clothes were taken away from me at night and put outside the door. If I had attempted to get away it would have been in my shirt. And I don't mind saying I would have done that if I had had half a chance.

Friends in London corresponded with me and sent me a big box of food, but I didn't find any brace and bits in it. I couldn't speak the language, and long before the time came for our trial I heartily reviled the evil day that had induced me to visit Lyons.

Dago Frank, who had been allowed plenty of money, engaged one of the most famous barristers in France, Maître Demarge. He also got one for me, so that when we were put into the dock together we could not plead the want of a good lawyer. But I did not require to be able to speak French to understand that we had no chance. The judge, a sour-faced old gentleman who seemed to harbor a great dislike to us, never even listened to what Frank and I had to say when we gave evidence on our own behalf. He made a speech to the jury which would have got the conviction quashed in any country in the world where the elementary principles of justice exist. He said that Frank and I had undoubtedly been in the bank when the robbery was committed, that we had been identified—particularly me; that we had immediately fled to England, where we had been arrested with the proceeds of the robbery in our possession, and that both of us were American criminals of the worst possible character. He even went to the length, this model of judicial impartiality, of saying that Dago Frank was a notorious safe-breaker who had been robbing banks all his life.

Our trial, which attracted a crowded court for two days, might just as well have lasted two minutes. We were doomed from the very beginning, not so much for the offense with which we were charged, but because of the statement openly made that we had also been engaged in circulating forged notes. My lawyer had told me I would not get more than five years' imprisonment. He proved to be sadly mistaken. I got ten years—on a charge of simple larceny! There were no damaging circumstances about the robbery—such as violence—which might have justified such a severe sentence. In either England or America a term of three years' penal servitude would have been imposed. But I was told before being taken to the court on the second day that they were going to make it hot because I would not tell them who was forging the bank-notes!

Dago Frank received the same sentence, the judge ordering that we should serve our ten years in the prison of Rion, near Vichy. I wanted to appeal, but I had no money and so I reconciled myself as best I could to the awful prospect of spending what should have been ten of the best years of my life in a foreign jail, practically unable to make myself understood. Think of that, any of you who may be on the verge of crime, and ask yourself whether you will be prepared to sacrifice the happiness of freedom for the paltriness of money.

If ever I wanted a lesson in the utter fatuity of a crook's life I received it at Lyons in 1889. I could sit down in my cell, with nothing better to do than miserably ruminate on the foolishness of my life, asking myself what profit I had to show for all that I had done. I had received from the robbery close on £2,500[46]— quite a useful little sum of money. But how long had I had it? Precisely a week. And here I was in a French convict prison compelled to reconcile myself to ten years' incarceration so that I could pay the price the law required. I did not want anybody to tell me then that you can't win; I knew it, and I made up my mind again that when I got out of France I would never touch a single crooked thing for the remainder of my life. If I had only kept to that resolution I might not have done so badly.

I very soon discovered that the prison of Rion was no kindergarten school. It must have been one of the biggest jails in France; when I arrived there, there were fully six hundred men in the place, and of all nationalities, French, Corsican, Italian, English, plus a good sprinkling of Soudanese, Arab and Moors, poor devils who had broken laws they never understood. It had originally been an old chateau and there were no cells in it such as are usual in the penitentiaries of England and America. It was supposed to be a seclusion prison, but they did not strictly adhere to that and we were allowed to mix together in a way that I had never seen before or since. All the prisoners slept in big dormitories; provided you behaved yourself the life wasn't unduly hard. Be sure I had a good look round for the possibility of getting away.

But all around the prison was a sheer stone wall forty feet high, and on the top of it paced, night and day, relays of warders armed with rifles. They watched us like cats, and while I never gave up hope of the chance coming my way I soon realized that I would as likely get a bullet in my back as my freedom. In a way, the prison was something like Edinburgh Castle. The jail itself was a palace compared to some of those I had known in America. We rose at daybreak, paraded in the prison yard for half an hour's exercise in charge of a warder, who ran us round at the double shouting: "*Gauche! Droit! Gauche! Droit!*" after which, thoroughly warmed up, we washed ourselves in a big pool and were then given our bread ration for the day. If you were lucky enough to possess any money you could buy yourself a cup of coffee. Then we were marched off to the different shops where we worked. For the nonce I had perforce to become a tailor, though I don't pretend that I would be eligible for a job in Savile Row. They certainly treated you much better there than in America. You were allowed to work at your trade and were paid fifty centimes a day. One-fourth of this amount you could spend on little luxuries such as coffee and tobacco; the remainder they put by until you were discharged. I would certainly like to take this opportunity of saying—for what it is worth—that the French prison authorities are not guilty of the barbarous behavior which characterizes the prison system of England and the United States. When you have completed a sentence in either of these countries you are turned out into the world with next door to nothing. And then, when you go back to the old crooked ways and in due course find yourself standing at what is humorously termed the "Bar of Justice," the presiding deity reads you a long homily on the iniquity of having lapsed into crime again so soon. As if a man could do anything else! Unless he has friends to help him he hasn't got a dog's chance of salvation.

I know that when I left Rion after serving my term I went out with £50 in my possession, which, when all is said and done, is quite sufficient for any man who honestly intends to turn over a new leaf. In America they would sling you out into the world with about five dollars, which would go in one good square feed.

The prison dress consisted of a khaki uniform and you were allowed to buy yourself warm underclothing. I know it was mighty cold when I arrived. Every morning I shivered as though I had the ague. Nevertheless, one couldn't deny the healthiness of the life and I have no doubt the years I spent there did much to atone for the dissipation of times gone by. You couldn't feel anything else but fit in a bracing climate where the air was like champagne and you led a life of early to bed and early to rise. It certainly made you healthy, if not particularly wealthy and wise. At ten o'clock in the morning, when you had acquired an appetite like a horse, you stopped for a sort of breakfast or *petit déjeuner*. If you were fortunate enough to possess any money you could buy sausages, cheese and such-like things.

The French penal system gives you plenty of opportunity to behave yourself. First offenders receive more money for their work than the old-timers, so that whatever inducement prison life may have had it could not be charged against the authorities that they made crime a paying proposition. A man with a dozen convictions against him received no money whatever and unless he could cadge something all he would get for his breakfast would be a bowl of thin soup. For the time being I had money enough to keep myself going in the little luxuries that you prize so highly when you are cut off from them, although I don't think it ever dawned on me that the greatest luxury of all—liberty—was the one I valued least. It is rather amazing how a man can settle down to a long term of imprisonment contented if he can obtain something to eke out the scanty fare provided by his jailers. It may be a chew or a whiff of tobacco, a bit of food which he has not tasted for months. Whatever it is, he thinks more of it than he does of the freedom of which he has deprived himself.

The French people are wise in allowing their prisoners a few little odds and ends to make their life more bearable. It puts a definite check on smuggling and keeps the warders straight, as it also prevents a great deal of trouble. I had been at Rion for some months—unable, of course, to speak French—before I began to appreciate the undeniable fact that it would pay me to play no tricks. Not long after I had begun work in the tailoring shop I became friendly with an Italian serving a sentence of five years for burgling a jeweler's shop. He "spoka da Inglese" and took advantage of the opportunity to inform me that he would like to "smoka da cigarette." There were two barriers to overcome. He had no tobacco and no money.

"That'll be all right," I told him. "I've got a bit." And I had—a hundred francs smuggled in when I was brought from Lyons. I knew, of course, that it was dead against prison rules, but that didn't worry me. I always like to carry a bit of cash around with me; you never know when it will be useful, even in jail.

Unfortunately, the Dago must needs get himself into trouble. He bought some tobacco and then got involved in a dispute with the man who sold it to him. Words led to blows, the two of them were locked up, and the following morning I found myself hailed before Monsieur le Commandant, a fiery little Corsican fellow clad in a most elegant pair of red pantaloons, smartly cut blue tunic, and peaked cap plentifully bespattered with gold braid. Also, he had a large-sized spiked moustache, a pair of beady black eyes, and an irascible manner. When I went into his office he didn't exactly embrace me in the fervent manner so popular in France. In fact, his greeting was terse to the point of sheer rudeness.

"Guerin, where is that money?"

"Money!" I replied. "I have no money."

"Oh, yes, you have," with a most ferocious scowl. "You have given this man," and he nodded towards the Italian, "money with which he has bought tobacco."

Well, I have never believed in being bluffed. I like to go the limit and then have a look at the other fellow's hand. But the Dago swine, like all his breed, wouldn't play the game. I turned to him and said: "I've never given you any money, have I?"

Judge of my astonishment when he burst out: "Yes, yes, you giva da moni." I called him a few names which luckily for him—and me—nobody but myself understood, and after this little outburst the Commandant promptly ordered me thirty days in the dungeon and a diet of bread and water.

They stripped me of my warm underclothing, gave me an old suit of clothes to wear, and threw me into a cold, damp cell underneath the chateau. Each day warders came down to search me, thinking I must have money concealed somewhere. They went over my body with a fine-tooth comb, but they never got the slightest satisfaction. Almost daily the Commandant visited me, brought an interpreter with him, and questioned me for an hour on end. I knew nothing, and at last he gave me up in despair. I don't suppose for one minute that there is anything particularly clever in getting yourself locked up in a dungeon. The only thing you can do is to bear this awful punishment without squealing. I will not harrow the feelings of my readers by trying to describe the dreadful monotony of waiting for the hours to go by and of how each day seems like a year. No words can adequately depict the brutalizing after-effects of solitary confinement. It makes a man a beast, fills his heart with nothing but hatred of his fellow-beings, and only succeeds in sending him out into the world determined to have his revenge on the society that could permit such barbarous treatment.

What had I done? To be quite precise, I had given an unfortunate fellow-prisoner one single solitary franc to buy himself the tobacco for which his body craved. Being a Latin, he didn't understand that great Anglo-Saxon code of playing the game. In the vernacular of the underworld, which describes these things far better than all the dictionaries, he promptly snitched. For doing a kindness to a man who should at least have kept his mouth shut I was condemned to solitary confinement for a month. And then people sometimes wonder why criminals murder each other!

I finished my time in the dungeon, when the Commandant again had me up in the office.

"Now, Guerin, you've got a long while to go here, so you might as well try and make things as easy as possible for yourself. Give me the money you have and you shall go back to your shop."

Incredibly foolish of me, no doubt, but I still asseverated that I had no money.

"Très bien, then you must go back into confinement for another fortnight."

Who can argue with people who administer justice in this sort of fashion? Of course, it is only the system which obtains in the French courts.

"Come along," they say when they have got you. "We know you are guilty and we want you to give us all the evidence so that we shall be able to send you to prison."

That sort of thing never did for me. I have always been a fighter, and a fighter I will remain to my dying day. I don't believe in knuckling under the moment the police appear on the scene. Nine times out of ten the coppers are bluffing; it is only when they induce you to talk that they can get the evidence they want. So, bullet-headed as usual, I did another two weeks in what is humorously termed the cooler. And still they didn't find out where I had my money.

When I made my reappearance in the tailor's shop, whom should I find there but my friend the Italian? He wanted to kiss and be friends. I retaliated with one of my best efforts in the way of lurid language. I called him more unmentionable sons of loose-living ladies than any other man has ever heard before and wound up my peroration by a first-class uppercut which sent him sprawling over his bench. That necessitated another interview with the gentleman from Napoleon's isle, to be followed by a further dose down below.

I was always getting into trouble in that prison. The French element had no time at all for the English and the Americans.

Sneers and insults—most of them behind my back—perpetually kept me in a fury. Being pretty useful with my fists I didn't hesitate to have a fight, with the result that I was continually in front of the Commandant. Altogether I spent two years of my time at Rion in the punishment cell, and I remember that it was during one of my numerous spells there that I first saw a motor-car. By stretching on my toes I could look through the bars of my cell into the market-place below. One day, to my intense astonishment, I saw a crowd of people following behind a curious contraption which chug-chugged its way across the square, riotously cheered by the excited country-folk. I didn't know then that it was one of the first motor-cars in the world, long before they were ever seen in England or America.

All sorts of punishments came my way. I got a month for knocking down one of the prisoners who threatened to report me for saying something about some one else. They were like a lot of children, these foreigners, bickering and backbiting, for ever provoking petty little quarrels about nothing. The mistake I fell into was that of making myself a marked man. I was easily the most regular attendant at the Commandant's office and I knew my way to the cooler blindfolded.

I never saw that greatest iniquity of all, the straitjacket, used in France, nor did I ever hear of a prisoner being flogged. When all is said and done, the French people are about the most civilized race in the world and their penal code religiously abstained from punishments which were for so long a disgrace to both England and America. I am not saying that the transportation of convict prisoners to the fever-stricken swamps of Guiana, which still takes place, is in any way justifiable. France, I believe, is the only country that continues to use its overseas possessions in the way that England used Australia for so many years. So far as I know the penal settlement in French Guiana is the only one that remains throughout the whole world. The one in New Caledonia, where men were treated like wild beasts, has been abolished.

I doubt very much whether the transportation of criminals ever achieved any good results in the long run. Everybody is aware that New South Wales, Tasmania and Western Australia began their existence with convict settlers working under the supervision of a big staff of officials, and also that many of the oldest families in Australia are descended from those self-same convicts. The mistake the French Government has made has been in sending out poor unfortunate devils to barren islands doing work that could only be unproductive. None of their prisoners was given the opportunity to begin a new life, as was the case in Australia. There is something radically wrong in a prison system that only stops at the point of actually exterminating the criminal.

At Rion I found them making the same error that had been responsible for my wasted life. There were numbers of young boys in the prison, peasant lads who had committed minor offenses for which they should have been released on probation. Apparently the authorities made no distinction in their favor. They were put into Rion, to find themselves in the company of assassins, burglars, forgers and about as fine a collection of cosmopolitan crookedness as you could see anywhere in the world. What could happen to these boys after being released? It would be nothing short of a miracle if they did not take to crime.

However, Rion was free enough from physical brutality such as was common in America. The place was run on military lines; the warders were all old soldiers and the Commandant had been an officer of the French army, as is usually the case in England. He made an inspection of the prison twice a week, when everybody, warders included, rigidly stood to attention.

I never tried to escape. I certainly gave the matter some very hard thought, but each time concluded that it would be next door to impossible. The men on the walls were ceaseless in their vigilance, and besides, I had no friends in the country to whom I could turn. Occasionally I came into contact with Dago Frank, but not in the spirit of comrades in adversity. I mistrusted him, as I did all Dagos, and we finished our relationship by coming to blows, which resulted in one of my frequent visits to the nether regions. However, if my long sojourn at Rion did nothing else it taught me the French language. Inside a year or two the Commandant and I could dispense with the services of an interpreter on the occasions—all too numerous—that I fell afoul of regulations. I got no remission whatever. The unending trouble I had caused compelled me to serve the full ten years.

It is rather interesting to record, in the light of what happened afterward, that the French authorities looked upon me as a British subject and proposed to send me back to England on my discharge. They were not so anxious to regard me as an Englishman some two or three years later. Dago Frank was in a terrible quandary; he had £1,500 waiting for him in England, only to be told by the Commandant that he was of American nationality and would therefore be deported to the United States. For some reason or other he seemed to think I was to blame for his being sent to America, and that I had been writing letters about him to England. He threatened to knife me when he got free. The matter came before the Commandant, who went out of his way to prove to him that I had not even mentioned his name in any letter I had written. If I had done so, the letter would never have been sent.

The undercurrents of prison life are unfathomable. It stands to reason, when you herd six hundred men together—and criminals at that—that there will be all sorts of individual quarrels and petty disputes likely to lead to blows. At any rate, when the time came for Dago Frank and me to be discharged we were still at daggers drawn. The Commandant threatened to shackle the pair of us if we could not behave ourselves, so eventually we gave our words that we would go in peace.

I left Rion in a prison van after ten of the longest and weariest years any man has ever spent—accompanied by my companion of the Lyons robbery—*en route* to Havre. But when I reached the depot prison in that place they wanted to keep me over my time. That didn't suit me at all. I banged the cell door down until I saw Monsieur le Directeur. He said he had no instructions about me and that I must wait until he heard from Paris as to the country I should be sent to.

"You're not going to keep me here a day longer than you are entitled to," I replied forcibly. "If I don't get out of here to-morrow morning I'll have the British Consul up."

Good old British Consul! How often has that little bluff been pulled off! It certainly worked all right this time. The Directeur hurriedly asked where I wanted to go.

"I don't care where you send me," I said, "so long as you do it quick. England is quite good enough for me."

I knew what they were holding me for; they were waiting for some one to shadow me all the way over to England. On my arrival at Southampton my return would be reported to the English police and I would undoubtedly be tagged wherever I went. But I succeeded in making myself such a nuisance that at nine o'clock the following morning they gave me the money I had earned in Rion and let me loose in Havre. I was fully aware I would be watched on to the boat, but I think I circumvented that. First of all I went and had my beard shaved off, made myself look a little respectable with a collar and tie, and then hurried into a restaurant to feel how good food tasted once more.

The joy of that first meal and the bottle of wine with which you wash it down! It is almost worth the years you spend in prison. And to get a cigar in your mouth, and to walk about the streets able to do as you like. God, what a fool a man is to barter away his freedom! Look what had happened to me. All I could show for ten years spent in a French convict prison was a sum of money I could have earned in less than a month by honest work. I had spent two years of that time in solitary confinement, undergoing a misery of mind which must be experienced to be understood. The money I had obtained from the robbery which cost me my liberty had been returned to its owners. I had to go back to England hoping to pick up the threads of a broken life handicapped by the fact that most of my friends of times gone by would have disappeared.

Of all the curious feelings you can experience let me recommend a return to civilization after being locked up for ten years in a foreign jail. I arrived back in London in the early part of 1899, having practically forgotten my own language. If I spoke to people it was in a curious mixture of French and English and I never felt quite certain of what I said. But nevertheless I felt wonderfully free and happy walking about armed with the knowledge that I could do as I liked with no one to say me nay.

Dago Frank had been shipped off to America and I saw nothing at all of him after leaving the prison at Havre. I had offered to get his money in London and send it on to him, but beyond a brief "No, I guess not," he declined to say anything about the matter. Probably he thought I would pinch the lot. He wasn't far wrong; I would certainly have taken my share out of it. I never even discovered where he had hidden it. I expect he had planted the money in a safe deposit and given the key to some one to mind. It is a favorite hiding-place for the crooks, because no questions are asked and you can get your valuables, money, jewels, papers, or whatever may be there, years afterward. But it doesn't do to have the key in your possession if the police get you. They will soon find out where you have stowed away the swag.

I would like to tell here the romantic story of a famous man with whom I had been on the most intimate terms of friendship since the days of my boyhood. The name with which he came into the world was Mike Kenna[47]—Irish, of course, like myself— but he was known all over the United States of America as Hinky Dink. In his way he was one of the greatest characters America has ever produced, and if he has not succeeded in amassing the wealth that Carnegie, Rockefeller, Pierpont Morgan and other men have done, I am quite sure he has acquired something that will afford him infinitely greater consolation—the personal esteem and affection of everybody with whom he has come in contact.

Hinky Dink! There isn't a down-and-outer in the States—and particularly in Chicago—who hasn't been to him for help and always come away with something. Hinky started right down at the bottom of the ladder and he never forgot it. I had known him in Chicago as a boy right from the time I was working for the Western Union Telegraph Company. He had a newspaper stand at one of the street corners, where even in his boyhood days he used to make about fifty dollars a week. The time came when the *Chicago Tribune* began to be distributed far and wide and Hinky got a job from the old manager of the paper supervising the circulation. Somewhere about 1887 he got out of the newspaper business, having saved a good many thousands of dollars, and opened a little public-house and sample room which used to attract the ordinary casual trade. But it wasn't long before Hinky's compelling personality began to draw a lot of people. The sporting fraternity took him up and of a night time you could see all the regular gamblers of Chicago congregated in his saloon. Hinky certainly worked hard; you could always find him behind his bar with a nod and a smile for every one, the essence of tactfulness, the savior of many a thirsty soul without a nickel to buy a drink. Also, like a wise man, he kept right with the police.

His next venture was to rent a big building in which he installed a hundred beds and let them for ten cents a night to anybody who came along. Most of his customers, of course, were the hobos and the down-and-outs, but the place made money because everybody liked Hinky and trusted him. I don't suppose I am exaggerating when I say that he knew more about the criminal classes of Chicago than all the police of that city together. The great thing about Hinky was that he didn't let down on them. Whatever they told him went into his head and stopped there.

As the years went on Hinky continued to increase in popularity until finally he ran for alderman of his district and came home an easy winner. Such influence did he wield that he became the mayor's right-hand man, a true democrat who never failed to carry out his municipal duties with an eye to the interests of the people who had elected him. He remained in his office of alderman for over thirty years, and if he is still alive I hope he will read these lines and accept them as a tribute to his honest and sterling nature.

Hinky and I had kept up a regular correspondence ever since I left America in 1887. He knew all about me, knew what I had done, and the only grievance he had against me was that I would not give over the bad life and take to a business where I could get some money. Well, I know it now. Anyone who lived in Chicago in the 'eighties could have made a fortune by sticking to hard graft for twenty years, just the same as you can in any new country. Somebody is bound to make money; it might just as well be you.

All the time I had been locked up in Rion, Hinky had corresponded with me and when the time came for my discharge he sent me 250 dollars[48] and a new suit of clothes, with instructions to write for more money if I wanted it. Truth to tell, I hadn't the faintest idea of what I was going to do. I realized it would be practically impossible to get any work in England where I might earn a decent living. The English are a funny people in many ways. They are naturally good-hearted, but they will ostracize you the moment they know you have been in jail and their police will go out of their way to keep you on the run. Once they get the idea in their head that you are a crook your life is hardly worth living. And I know what I say is true. You get an appalling number of men and women in England who spend the greater part of their lives in and out of jail, and one of the reasons, I think, is the difficulty these poor devils find in obtaining regular employment. I am going to have something to say about the matter later, giving my own case as an instance of the pernicious system that enables an officious detective to send a man wrong in spite of himself.

With Hinky Dink's help, plus the nice little sum given to me by the French prison authorities, there was no immediate need for me to worry about the future. I couldn't plead starvation if I took a jump back into crime. Hinky had written saying that Pat Sheedy, an American sportsman both of us knew—I have mentioned him in the earlier part of this story as the man who used to manage John L. Sullivan—was in London and would be glad to see me. Pat had practically finished with the fighting game. I think he got a fortune out of John L. and promptly invested it in a Chicago gambling house in Hinky Dink's district. Hinky, I fancy, used to protect him from the police; at any rate they were the warmest of friends.

Pat was living in great style at the Hotel Metropole, London. He appeared very glad to see me, but he told me point-blank: "Now, look here, Eddie, I can't afford to be involved in any trouble. You've got to go straight and steer clear of the old crowd."

"That's good enough for me," I replied. "I'm finished with jail." And I meant it. When you have done ten years in the society of foreign convicts you don't exactly hanker for another dose. At least I didn't.

Pat Sheedy could never be mistaken for anything but an American sport. A big, burly fellow, radiating energy and confidence, he was one of the sights of the town with his big wide-awake hat, huge cigar, and a diamond ring worth a small fortune. He really belonged to the old race of showmen who are now almost extinct.

He took me around London, introduced me to a lot of well-known American people, and also recommended me to a tailor in the West End of London who supplied me with a brand-new and very badly needed outfit. I tell you, it was the best time I ever experienced. The idea of having half a dozen suits of clothes made to my measure, with all the shirts and collars and ties I wanted, gave me as much pleasure as a woman let loose in the establishment of a Paris *couturier*. You want to wear a stinking prison uniform for ten years to appreciate properly the joy of getting into clean, new clothes. All jails stink, and everything in them.

"Now, Ed," said Pat after he had fitted me out, "you'd better go down to Brighton, put up at a decent hotel and keep yourself quiet for a month or so until you get your bearings. You're out of touch with everything and everybody. I'll probably take you back with me to America."

He wanted to go out to Cairo, where he had another gambling house, but he promised to return before long and take me under his wing. But before that happened I ran across another friend of days gone by, a very prominent man known as Blind Condon. He had formerly been a hairdresser in a small town outside Chicago until he began to launch out and eventually became the owner of the Hawthorn race track at Haarlem, where things so prospered with him that he became a millionaire. Another instance of a friend of mine who had made good.

He was not actually blind at the time I saw him in London, but his sight was certainly going and he had come over to England in the hope of finding a specialist who could cure him. He knew all about my last fall from grace and after greeting me said:

"Well, Eddie, I think the best thing you can do is to go back to Chicago. The police won't give you much of a chance here. You've had enough trouble and you must surely want to turn over a new leaf. Go back home and I'll put you in the swim again."

Condon was certainly right about the London police. While they didn't put me to any real trouble they kept me under pretty close surveillance and frequently asked me what I was doing for a living. They were a good deal stricter in their methods then than they are to-day. They had a system whereby all the prisoners in the remand jail, Brixton, were put in a row every morning while a procession of policemen from different districts went by and had a good look at them. In this way the coppers got to know almost every crook in London.

The ten years I had just served had quite cured me of any desire to try any further conclusions with the police, but naturally I saw plenty of Scotland Yard men about and they saw me. But beyond "Well, what are you doing now?" to which I would give an evasive reply, nothing much passed between us. These Scotland Yard men have a funny way of doing their work. They will invite you to take a drink at their expense and then casually ask you, "Seen So-and-so lately?" If you are a damned fool and reply, "Yes, I saw him over at the Cafe Royal yesterday," you will probably be shopping somebody who has never done you a moment's harm. It is just the difference between the

English and the French systems. In England all the evidence for the prosecution is collected by the police and usually presented by the prosecuting lawyer with scrupulous fairness. But in France the police work in the dark. They wait until they get you inside before they set about you, and then the *juge d'instruction* becomes policeman, prosecutor, and magistrate rolled into one. If I had to make my choice I would choose the English method as giving the prisoner a better chance. The average stipendiary magistrate before whom you appear is almost always impartial. But then they are very carefully chosen for their posts, more or less regardless of political influence. They are not well paid. Their salary is £1,500 a year, which, when all is said and done, isn't opulence.

I did not go back to Chicago for six months. Fortune chose to be kind to me, both on the racecourse and at the card table. Nevertheless, it was good to smell the old town after being away for something like twelve or thirteen years. It had grown out of all recognition. Great new buildings had sprung up everywhere and I had to take a good look round before I could finally satisfy myself that it was indeed Chicago. But, alas! there were very few of my old friends about. The majority of them seemed to have gone wrong. Judicious inquiry brought the information that most of them were doing time in various prisons all over the States—which, I suppose, doesn't say much for the company I used to keep. But my old pal Hinky Dink was flourishing amazingly. His official designation was Alderman Kenna. I found that he owned two enormous public-houses, one of which must have cost him a small fortune to build. It was the meeting-place of all the local politicians, sportsmen, gamblers, and the people who got their living by their wits. In fact, it was more or less a miniature Tammany Hall, with Hinky Dink pulling the wires. I think he must have been desirous of emulating Boss Croker, who had then taken up his residence in England.

Hinky Dink's other place, also a very big one, was for another class of customer entirely. There you would find the hobos, the yeggmen, and practically all the crooks passing through Chicago. The name of Hinky Dink's hotel was famous throughout the country. He gave them all a good square deal and never turned a man away.

We had a long talk together at his office, when I told him everything, that I wanted to make a fresh start in life, and leave crime alone for evermore.

"It's the only way," said Hinky. "You're getting on a bit now, Ed" (I was then thirty-nine), "and if you don't settle down now you never will. You'd better look around for a little public-house." In those days you could sell liquor with practically no restriction whatever. There were thousands of little joints similar to the off-license in England. The only fly in the ointment was that you had to take out a license from the police, and to be quite candid my reputation in that quarter wasn't all it might have been. They still remembered the shooting of 1887, although they never took the trouble to apply for my extradition after I had been released from prison in France. But I had not yet finished with the matter, as I will relate shortly.

Hinky gave me a couple of hundred dollars to go on with and I took a look round the city to see if I could get hold of some small business to keep me out of trouble. But there you are; when a man has spent behind prison walls the years of his life which ought to be devoted to learning a trade he can hardly wonder that it is well-nigh impossible to settle down to some humdrum occupation such as washing up dishes or sweeping floors, which was about all I was fit for. My commercial value was precisely nil, a fact I have discovered many times since.

I found that the Chicago police were hotter than ever and also, unfortunately, they had not forgotten me. The news of my return soon got about and I had not been back more than a month before they ran me inside for being concerned in a burglary of which I was as sublimely innocent as a new-born babe. They kept me in the House for three days, put me through the Third Degree, a sort of variation of the French examining-magistrate system, but infinitely more brutal. They didn't get anything out of me for the simple reason that I had nothing to tell. A week later they had another go. I was driving a buggy out of the town when one of the detectives from Central jumped out, trying to stop me. They must have wanted me for something, but

I didn't bother to wait and inquire. Instead I whipped up the horse, whereupon they pulled out their pistols and began shooting at me.

I know that these sort of things will sound almost incredible to English readers, but they are nothing more than the bare truth. Anybody who has read Upton Sinclair's famous novel *The Jungle* will be able to gain some slight conception of what Chicago was like in 1900. The big meat yards had imported all sorts of people to work in the factories, Russian and Polish Jews, Austrians, Germans, Italians, Lithuanians and God alone knows how many other different breeds. The police of the city were almost entirely Irish, and in my humble opinion the Irishman makes the worst policeman of all. To start with, he is a born prevaricator and much too officious when it comes to a matter of the liberty of the subject. Once upon a time Scotland Yard used to be full of Irishmen, but the authorities are gradually working them out. Much the same change has taken place in America. It is a curious thing that the Irish are usually to be found as priests, politicians, policemen and publicans. The average Irishman always likes to be in a job where he can have an argument.

To be quite fair to the Chicago police, I must admit when I got back there in 1899 the city was full of thieves—worse, I should think, than any other part of America. There would be at least twenty robberies a day, and I daresay the coppers found it a difficult job to deal with the complaints that poured in. So you couldn't very well blame them if they pinched you first and asked you questions afterward, particularly if your reputation had gone before you, as mine had done. But they did things which in any other city would have caused a lot of trouble. There was an old pal of my boyhood days named Tom O'Brien who had married a girl with a bit of money, opened a public-house, and seemed well on the way to making a fortune. We were racing each other along the boulevards one day behind a smart pair of trotters. After a time I went home and I did not learn until afterward that a policeman had stopped Tom and wanted to arrest him for fencing some stolen property. I hadn't the faintest idea of the rights or wrongs of the affair, but Tom resisted arrest and in the struggle that followed was shot dead. The matter created a tremendous sensation and the policeman was put on his trial for manslaughter. However, he was found not guilty, probably because Tom had been mixed up in crime, although I knew that he was getting an honest living at the time he was killed.

They certainly had no intention of leaving me alone for long. I discovered I was being shadowed all over the city, which brings to my mind an amusing little adventure I had with Ryan and Lonergan, two Chicago detectives who were very well known at that time. Ryan, by the way, afterward became a politician and a millionaire. Just fancy the average London policeman making a million! Anyhow, these two followed a pal and me downtown into one of the big department stores, expecting, no doubt, that we were on business bent. We got up to the third story, when we came to the conclusion that it might be rather difficult to get out of the building without running into the two detectives. A way out of the trouble presented itself. I opened the lift door and we climbed down the center rope while Ryan and Lonergan were chasing about for us downstairs. To this day they never discovered how we dodged them. They were going to pinch us as suspects, but although I got away on this occasion Lonergan subsequently found me and charged me with vagrancy. He got no satisfaction out of that because he had no evidence to call, while I had the assistance of my friend Hinky Dink to prove that I was not engaged in crime.

I have related this little incident, not because it is of any particular importance, but because it proves the impossibility of getting an honest living in a town where you are well known to the police. The average Chicago cop of those days only wanted to see me on the streets. He would say to himself: "Hullo, there's Eddie Guerin. What's he up to?" Then they would follow me round and in their minds construe the most innocent of actions into a potential robbery. Of course, this sort of thing isn't confined to America. It is bad enough in England, as I shall relate when I am coming towards the end of my story. It gradually dawned upon me that it would be useless to think of remaining in Chicago. All Hinky Dink's friendship could not save me from the police and, besides, I had no chance whatever of keeping any employment for any length of time. Without in the least desiring it, I seemed to have acquired the reputation of being a desperado of the most dangerous type. The shooting affray with which I had been concerned in 1887 was still well remembered. As a matter of fact, the widow of the policeman I had shot—he did not die until some years afterward—went to my brother to try and obtain compensation from him. I don't think she succeeded, but what she did manage to do was to make life in Chicago very uncomfortable for me. My brother said I had better clear out for good, and I took his advice. Hinky Dink also agreed that it would be best to get out of the country and handed me 250 dollars to see me on my way.

So there I was, once more a wanderer on the face of the earth. Unless a man is an out-and-out blackguard, completely devoid of any pretense to decency, he could not feel anything but a wrench at being compelled to take up the role of Wandering Jew, restlessly traveling from one country to another, unable to lay his head in peace anywhere.

What price prison! How much would any man in his sane senses give for a life of larceny and the knowledge that wherever he went he would be hunted down? Forty years of age, no home ties, no wife and family to welcome me, nothing to look forward to but one long, unending battle with law and order. Most of the men I had known in my youthful days were already broken and battered. I had none of the decent friends most people make in early life. The men I knew were crooks, gamblers and the hangers-on of the underworld.

In 1900 I once more set out for England *via* Toronto and Nova Scotia. I might just as well confess that I crossed the Atlantic under a false name. I had no wish to be identified the moment I landed in England, because I honestly and truly intended to make a fresh start and cut loose from the ramp and robbery game for the rest of my life. There were relations of my father in Liverpool who were going to lend a helping hand and it just rested with myself whether I would succeed in making good. My poor mother had died in 1897 while I was still in prison in

Rion, broken-hearted, I have no doubt, by the trouble I had caused.

I daresay the readers of this story will wonder why I never made a serious attempt to obtain regular work and settle down in life. Ten years in jail should be enough for any man. I don't think I looked at it in that light. Being caged up as I had been for so many years had embittered my nature to such an extent that I was not altogether in a position to sum up what was worth while in this world, and what was not. Any man who is compelled to spend the greater part of his time locked up in a prison cell naturally comes out into the world like a savage beast looking for something to prey upon. And what the world won't give him he will just as naturally take.

Chapter Ten
THE GREAT AMERICAN EXPRESS JOB

I now come to the most eventful period of my checkered life, beginning with the sensational robbery of the American Express Company in Paris, my capture, followed by transportation for life to the penal settlement of French Guiana. Thence, with more incident than could ever be crowded into any film, there came my escape, my return to England via New York and Chicago, my betrayal at the hands of Chicago May, a long and agonizing period of suspense while I lay in Brixton prison awaiting the result of the extradition proceedings brought by the French Government, the release for which I have to thank that fighting Scots lawyer, the late Sir Richard Muir, and then, to the grand finale, when Chicago May and her newly acquired lover, Cubine Jackson, alias Charles Smith, attempted to assassinate me, culminating with the celebrated trial at the Old Bailey before the famous Judge Darling, when Smith was sentenced to penal servitude for life and Chicago May to fifteen years.

What I am about to narrate now is nothing but the plain, unadulterated truth. The time has come when I can tell it, if only for the purpose of finally killing the preposterous stories that were put into circulation when I made my escape from the penal settlement in French Guiana. The wild lying that went on! It was alleged that three of us had got away from Devil's Island in a boat and that one of the party had been killed and eaten to keep the remaining two of us alive! I know I have been many things in my time, but I have not yet been reduced to the straits when I could be compelled to turn cannibal. Anyhow, with my active career in crime at an end I might just as well tell the true story of everything that happened, right from the very beginning up to the time in the Central Criminal Court in London, popularly known as the Old Bailey, when the gunman who had tried to do me was reviling, in the foulest language ever heard, the Judge who had sentenced him. Smith couldn't have possessed the slightest sense of the eternal fitness of things, otherwise he might have reserved his maledictions for the vindictive creature who had lured him to the length of murder.

For some time after my return to England in 1900 I succeeded in leading a fairly respectable life. I had relations in Liverpool with whom I stayed for a few months while I worked for an uncle who made a book on the racecourse. But I always found myself short of money. What I earned in the way of salary I lost backing horses, with the result that I set off to London with the feeling that I must do something to get some money.

London was much the same as I had left it. At the old Provence in Leicester Square, a famous place extensively patronized by the foreign *demi-mondaines* who were then so common in London, I found dozens of Americans I knew, kindred souls most of them, ready to take on anything. I made the acquaintance of the notorious Kid McManus, one of the best boxmen in America, who had crossed over to London to keep out of the way of the Pinkertons. He had heard of me and I knew all about him, with the result that we palled-up and for a time went about as two brothers.

I was in the company of Kid McManus when I first made the acquaintance of Chicago May, the woman who subsequently played such a dramatic part in my life. Don't think I am going to paint any romantic pictures of this lady. As I am writing this story for the purpose of proving that you can't win at the crooked game, I am going to do nothing but keep to the truth. So I might just as well say straight out what Chicago May was.

She was already famous—or shall I say infamous?—in London. When Kid McManus first introduced me to her she would be about twenty-eight or thirty years of age, painted up to the eyes, with peroxided hair, pretty enough in a way, and no doubt quite fascinating in the manner she spoke to you. At any rate, I fell for her, so nothing more need be said about her charms. May's profession was the oldest one in the world, but the way in which she carried it on would have got her lynched in any decent society. She used to patrol Northumberland Avenue, a London street where there are several big hotels used by well-to-do provincial visitors. I saw her there myself many times, and I was informed, long before I knew her, that she worked in conjunction with Tim Oats, a panel man, and his wife. So that the uninitiated may understand what a panel man is I will explain that he works with ladies of easy virtue who take men to their rooms with the intention of robbing them. There is a panel in the room which is slid to one side while the victim's clothes are stolen. Then the female blackmailers get to work and demand anything for the return of the clothes. Ninety-nine times out of a hundred they used to succeed, and Chicago May played this game for quite a long time without getting into the serious trouble she deserved.

Times without number had she been taken to the police station on the complaints of her clients, and on each occasion had she told a tale which resulted in her being discharged. As I have already said, May had a bit of a way with her. McManus introduced her to me at a flat in Tottenham Court Road.

"May," he said, "this is a doctor friend of mine from the States."

May took a good look at me. She was naturally a shrewd judge of a man and it didn't take her long to size me up.

"Doctor!" she laughed, "you're no doctor. I know who you are." And she did; she told me I was Eddie Guerin and, right from the jump, seemed to take quite a liking to me. The whisky bottle went round and round, with the result that May and I got very drunk. We decided to get together.

Kid McManus took me on one side to warn me. "You leave that dame alone. She's dangerous. She'll rob you of everything you've got."

"Don't worry about me, Kid," I replied. "She can't get much because I've got nothing to lose"—which was the absolute truth. So, indifferent to the warning I had received, I took Chicago May under my wing and generally let it be known in the underworld of London that she and I were as one. I daresay it suited her book pretty well. She knew that I could get money, and if there was one thing in this world her soul craved for it was that. Money to her meant plenty of booze, as many dresses as she wanted, while it also freed her from the necessity of going out on the streets to rob men.

Originally, May had come from Chicago, like most of us. One way and another the old city turned out—and I mean in the most literal sense—some of the finest crooks in creation. If Chicago May wasn't exactly what I would call a good criminal she certainly knew how to batten on the blood of the men who got their living by various means outside the pale of the law. Her real name, I believe, was May Latimer, while she was also known as May Churchill—no relation of other and more distinguished families of that name. In her thirtieth year she was undoubtedly a smart piece of goods, calculated to attract the eye of any man. As she wasn't at all backward in pressing her claims upon you she did fairly well for herself while her looks lasted.

Kid McManus and I remained together in London for some two or three months waiting the opportunity for a big smash. I meant it to be something good because while you are about it you might just as well get a few years for a job that is worth while as be caught in a paltry little theft which brings you practically nothing more than the price of a meal. The Kid thoroughly agreed with me. Irish-American by birth, safe-breaker by trade and desperado by nature, there was nothing in the world he would not dare to do. He, also, had a lot of time behind him in America. We were what the poet calls "birds of a feather." With Chicago May as a consort I daresay we constituted a trio ripe for any mischief.

It must have been about January or February, 1901, that there arrived in London from Paris a man whom I knew slightly, a highly educated German-American known as Dutch Gus. His real name was Gustav Muller, but like most of the criminal fraternity he soon achieved the distinction of a nickname. Tall, fair, handsome, and the possessor of a refinement of manner which often made me wonder what had induced him to take to robbery, he was known to me by repute as one of the greatest dan men in the States. From being an engineer with a first-class job in Pittsburgh he took to dynamiting safes all over the country. The thousands of little banks and post-offices that were scattered all over the States used to use safes that were easy to an expert like Dutch Gus. However, the Pinkertons got him in time and Gus came over to Europe to make a fresh start. He had been temporarily engaged purloining diamond and pearl scarf-pins, rings and any other small valuables he could pick up in a jeweler's shop. It is a trick called penny-weighting; you go in to buy something, get a few trayfuls of diamond pins and such-like in front of you, and palm one or two under the eyes of the jeweler. I will give Gus his due, whatever I have to say about him afterward. He loathed such petty tricks. He, like the Kid and I, was on the look-out for something that would keep him in affluence for a year or two. In Paris he had found it; the offices of the American Express Company in the Rue Scribe contained a safe which might be blown open if the black caretaker could be put out of the way.

Gus, it appears, had been having letters addressed to him at the office, and from continually going into the place he had come to be very well known. He also made friends with the nigger, and the next thing to be done was to find some one to work the job with him.

I did not hear of the matter until he had talked it over with Kid McManus, asking him if he knew of a third man who might be trusted.

"There's Eddie Guerin," said the Kid. "He's all right and he can speak French. You couldn't get a better man."

Gus gave me a very close scrutiny when the three of us met. He asked me a hundred questions, told me what it would mean if we were caught, and warned me at the peril of my life to keep my mouth shut. I told him I knew all about the danger and that as far as I was concerned he could count on me to the death. So then and there we settled the deal; the three of us should do the American Express Company and share and share alike.

Now, it just shows you how your good fairy may be lurking near at hand to save you from yourself. It was just about this time that I made the acquaintance of a wealthy Australian racing man who wanted to take me to the Antipodes to see a bit of the game down under. I foolishly told him I had important work to do in Paris before I could go, but nevertheless I would run down to Naples and see him there before he left on the steamer. I kept my promise to him to the extent of traveling to Naples from Paris while we were waiting to pull off the American Express job, but circumstances made it impossible for me to board the Orient liner *Ortona* as my Australian friend wanted. afterward didn't I wish I had! It would have saved me a few years' suffering.

I realized, of course, the considerable risk I was running in returning to Paris. When you have served ten years' penal servitude in a country like France you would be well advised to give it the go-by for evermore. In my case I was not only well known to the Sûreté, and therefore liable to be arrested on sight, but also in danger because I had been deported and forbidden to return to France after serving my ten years in Rion. Still, I never let little things like that deter me. I decided to go and to take Chicago May with me. She would be what we call a good square. If the police saw me in her company they would probably conclude I was perfectly harmless.

I told May nothing at all about the real object of the trip. Never having seen Paris, she was delighted with the idea of going, and never for one single moment suspected what I wanted her for. "Sufficient unto the day—" was always May's motto. Dutch Gus didn't mind her accompanying me; I fancy he was rather sweet on her himself and probably thought he might work me out. I wish he had.

All three of us got over to Paris, traveling separately, without arousing any suspicion, and we remained doggo in the city for three weeks before we attempted to make a move. I kept under cover more than the others because mine was the greater peril. Once the police discovered I was back it would be all up as far as I was concerned. The three weeks that went by were mostly occupied in keeping observation on the American Express offices, taking turn and turn about and reporting the result of our vigil as we went back. All the time this was going on Chicago May blissfully enjoyed herself. Neither the Kid nor Dutch Gus was inclined to trust any woman with their life and liberty, any more than they believed in allowing a woman, whatever her character, to be mixed up in the dangerous job of dynamiting a safe. May and I were staying at an hotel near the Madeleine where they asked no questions. I took her around to all the stock sights of Paris, the Bois de Boulogne, the Louvre, even the Morgue. She never dreamed that I was just waiting.

Sentry duty continued. Night after night, with the glare of the street lamps still full upon us, we kept watch. We discovered that the nigger caretaker left the offices about seven o'clock at night and went off to the cafés drinking. He would get back about half-past nine or ten. In turns, Dutch Gus, the Kid, and myself visited the offices almost every hour of the night, watching for anything that might undo us. We gave the place a look over at midnight, at two o'clock in the morning, at three o'clock and at six o'clock. Not a sign could we see of any watchman patrolling the premises. Evidently what happened was that the nigger went in and straight away went to bed. It seemed that nothing could possibly happen.

The clever Gus had got hold of a duplicate key of the office. It wasn't a difficult matter to get the nigger out drinking one night and obtain possession of his door key just long enough to make a wax impression. The key was slipped back with the nigger none the wiser. It must have been half-way through our vigil that we were guilty of a most foolish lapse. More to while away the time than anything else, but also to provide an alibi that we were American tourists, the three of us frequently went to the offices of the American banking firm Drexel & Company in the Boulevard Haussmann. Gus had the idea in his head that he might also pick up a mug there, which only shows the stupidity of being too clever.

Our almost daily visits there, added to the fact that we never attempted to transact any business at the bank, aroused the suspicions of one of the attendants. He thought the matter so curious that on his own responsibility he telephoned to the Sûreté. If I, for one, had known that my old friend Debischof, the self-same detective who had received me from the custody of Scotland Yard for the Crédit Lyonnais robbery, was following me about Paris at that time, I would have skinned off so quickly as to break all records in evacuating a battle-line. But Debischof did his work so cleverly and so quietly that none of us suspected anything wrong. The most extraordinary part of the affair was that neither he nor any of his men were ever successful in discovering the hotels where we were staying. The reason was that we always separated when we got out into the Boulevard Haussmann and, as it happened, did not go back to our hotels. The crowded Paris streets swallowed us up, with the result that Debischof had to keep continual observation at the banking office to pick us up again. Even then he did not suspect what we were in Paris for; he must have thought we were after some of the people who had business with Drexel & Company, not an unnatural assumption in view of our past records. As a matter of fact, Debischof would have done me a good turn had he pinched me then and there, but he was much too cunning for that. He knew there was something on the boards; what it was only time would reveal.

Everything had been planned out and to us there seemed no possibility of failure. We had even discussed how we should make the getaway. Kid McManus said: "I'm for Italy; it's a million to one on that we shan't be able to get back to England." Dutch Gus made up his mind to go to Marseilles and from there take a trip to Egypt.

"I'm with you," I said to the Kid. "We'll be nabbed in London for sure. Leach will soon know who's done this."

Unfortunately for me, I changed my mind—so did Dutch Gus, with results that will be disclosed later. The Kid was the only one who made up his mind and kept to it.

The time came for the job to be done. Think of it, you people who lie in your bed of a night, and ask yourself whether you would like to go out at midnight for the purpose of dynamiting a safe, a job fraught with half a dozen disastrous possibilities, in my case magnified tenfold by the fact that I had already served a long term and that I would as sure as fate get at least another ten years if the police nabbed me. It is no use saying that crime doesn't require pluck and plenty of it. I know it does; the man doesn't breathe who can break into a place in the early hours of the morning without feeling the qualms of fear. He may be shot dead the moment he becomes a burglar. The alarm may be given while he is inside doing the job. A dog may bark, and of all the horrible sensations any housebreaker can experience let me recommend waiting inside a house, afraid to move one way or the other, with a dog incessantly barking. Then you know what it is to die a thousand deaths. If you are wise you will get out at once and chance what happens; it is nothing short of suicide to try and silence the brute.

There was nothing particularly elaborate about the scheme we had evolved. With the key in our possession there was little or no difficulty about getting into the building. Once inside we intended to gag and bind the nigger, the Kid and I to keep guard over him and make him remain quiet while Gus blew the safe. The dynamiting was the great danger. Anything might happen. The windows might be blown out, the noise of the explosion might attract the attention of passers-by. Both Gus and the Kid were armed; if the worst came to the worst they would make a bid for life and liberty. I thought I might just as well follow suit. As time drew on it dawned upon me that we would have to be pretty lucky to get away clear.

We were certainly fortunate enough while the plans were going forward. The last time we visited the Drexel offices we were followed, entirely without our knowledge. The three of us made our way towards the Halles, McManus and I standing at the corner while Dutch Gus went into a chandler's shop to buy some rope which we intended to use in tying up the nigger. The market square was crowded with people and after Gus had left the shop the detective rushed in, showed his police card to the proprietor, and asked him what the man had bought. Rope, the detective was told.

"What for?" he asked.

"How should I know?" replied the chandler, probably disliking the police as much as we did. "To tie up a trunk, I expect."

By the time the detective had finished his questioning the three of us had disappeared, so for the moment we were safe enough.

The great night arrived. Two of us stood outside the American Express office, carefully watched the nigger go in and shut the door behind him, after which we went off, intending to return about half-past one, when the streets of Paris were quietening down. I took a trip back to my hotel to see what had happened to Chicago May. That evening she was blind drunk—I had seen to that. I wanted her to be sound asleep all night long, so that if I were arrested she could truthfully declare that I had been with her at ten o'clock and had not left her all night. When I left her about a quarter to twelve she was speechless; I had no fear of her waking up for at least another eight hours.

I managed to slip out of the hotel without the concierge seeing me, and went round to the rendezvous where Gus and the Kid were waiting. There we stopped until it was close on the time.

Kid McManus, who had made the key, went along and opened the door. There were very few people about. Watching him from the shadows of the other side Gus and I saw him slip in unnoticed. At intervals of five minutes we followed suit, shut the door behind us, and then looked about. Everything seemed dead quiet. Except for the noise of passing cabs there was not a sound. The bank was as silent as the grave and but for the flickering lights of the arc lamps outside we might have been in a graveyard.

The nigger blissfully sleeping upstairs received the shock of his life when the Kid and I crept into his room and seized him. He thought at first it was some of the clerks of the office playing a joke on him! "Now then, boys," he cried, struggling to get free, "stop yo' funny business. Dis ain't no time ob de night to wak' a man up."

"If you don't keep quiet," hissed the Kid, "I'll throttle the life out of you. This ain't no game, nigger. Shut your mouth and you'll be all right."

I have no doubt that the poor devil was petrified with fear.

"I'll sho' keep quiet, boss, if you don't hurt me," he said, quivering with fright.

I gagged him with a handkerchief, while the Kid tied his hands and feet. The two of us were masked, even if the nigger could see in the dark. He must have known, of course, that we were Americans, although he afterward swore that he thought we were Germans, which only goes to show what fear will do for a man.

Dutch Gus had been waiting to see if we got the nigger all right. Then he went downstairs to get his dynamite ready, leaving the Kid and me to look after the nigger. It seemed ages before there came a tremendous explosion which rocked the whole building. I stopped upstairs, expecting any second to hear the police rushing in. Nothing at all happened. The Kid went downstairs and then called me to have a look. Gus had done his work so well that the safe door stood open, with only a twisted and distorted lock to tell what had occurred. Hovering over the place was the acrid, pungent smell of the dynamite. When I got down below Gus was busily shoveling out stack after stack of checks and bank-notes.

Outside the day was beginning to break. We knew the staff did not get there before nine o'clock, leaving us plenty of time to divide the loot then and there. As near as we could estimate there was between $200,000 and $250,000[49] in the safe and about $20,000 in hard cash. Time was of no particular value. The explosion had gone by unheeded, the only danger for at least three hours was the poor nigger upstairs. So then and there we shared out in three equal parts, stuffing the money into our pockets and congratulating ourselves on having pulled off the job so easily.

Another hour went by. Then we opened the front door and one by one sneaked out. There were but a few people passing by.

We disappeared as we had entered—at intervals of a few minutes. Kid McManus, the last man out, coolly locked the door behind him without attracting the slightest attention and went off to his hotel, while I, creeping in once more unseen by the concierge, went into my bedroom to find the fair May still sound asleep.

Now for the *dénouement!*

Chapter Eleven
IMPRISONMENT FOR LIFE

I realized that the Paris papers would be screaming the news of the robbery before long.

You can't dynamite a bank safe in the heart of a big city without the story leaking out. In the beginning, the French police concluded that a son of one of the officials must have had something to do with the affair. A short time previously this boy had broken into the office one night, prised open a couple of desks, and purloined a tidy little sum of money. When the actual culprit was discovered the matter was hushed up.

The police thought that our job had also been done by the same boy. However, they speedily discovered their mistake and, aided by the knowledge that Dutch Gus, Kid McManus and myself had been acting suspiciously for some weeks past, went out hot on our trail.

When I got back to my hotel near the Madeleine in the early hours of the morning I had a fortune in my pockets. "Chicago May's" peroxided head peacefully reposed on the pillow. I was busy shaving myself when she woke up, blissfully ignorant of what had been happening.

That same morning I paid the bill and with May in my company moved over to the Hotel Regina in the Rue Rivoli. I carefully kept the newspapers out of May's way, and for a time at least she had no suspicion of anything wrong. She knew I had got some money from somewhere. In a foolish burst of generosity I told her to get some dresses for herself.

"What's the matter with you all of a sudden?" she demanded. "It isn't like you to be buying dresses."

"Go on," I replied, "I don't mind. What's the use of a woman coming to Paris if she doesn't get herself some clothes?"

Anyhow, a modiste came round and showed May a few dresses, but she fastidiously declined to have them and told me I had better wait until we got back to London.

My intention was to go to Italy. I had a pretty good idea in my head that the way to London might be dangerous. We stayed at the Regina for a couple of days and, of course, the papers were full of the robbery. But May never saw them; I carefully kept them out of her way, feeling it would be quite time enough to tell her the story when we reached another country. But one morning, when May and I had gone into a café in the Avenue de L'Opera to have *déjeuner,* who should come in but one of the cashiers from the American Express Offices. He knew me well enough by sight because I had repeatedly changed money in the bank.

"Morning," he said. "Heard what's happened?"

I professed entire ignorance.

"Well, the bank has been robbed. There's nearly 250,000 dollars gone."

"Good heavens!" I exclaimed shocked. "As much as that?"

"We don't know for certain yet. We're just checking off the amounts, but it won't be far short of a quarter of a million."

"Dear me! How dreadful! Have the police caught anybody yet?"

"No," said the cashier, "but they think it is a gang of Russians. They'll have them soon,"

He left me, went over to another table and ordered himself a drink. May shot a look at me.

"Oh," in a way that only a woman could say it, "so that's the reason why I haven't been able to see a paper for a couple of days!"

"Don't talk like a damned fool," I whispered to her, "and don't start shouting. I've had nothing to do with it."

I got her out of the place as soon as I could and took her for a walk into the Place de la Concorde, when I got another nasty surprise. Who should we see riding past in a *fiacre*[50] but Dutch Gus. He pulled up and made us go and have a drink with him. Gus was in rather a vain-glorious mood and anxious to show May what a hell of a fellow he was.

"Well, May," he began, "we'll be all right soon. Plenty of money for you to spend," giving her a dig in the ribs.

May, as fly as they make them, took it all in and said very little. But I could see her looking at me in a way that boded no good for me in the immediate future. However, she said nothing at the time and when we left Gus it was with the arrangement that we should meet in London a week later. The moment we got back to our hotel May let loose.

"Now, then, what's it all about? Where's the money? Either I get my share or else there'll be trouble."

When a man is between a she-devil and the deep blue sea it's no use hesitating. I produced what she wanted and her eyes glistened as only a woman's can when they see a big sum of money in front of them.

"Ah," she exclaimed, "so you thought you were going to do me, did you?" She picked up bundles of checks and notes and began stowing them away in various parts of her clothing. Some went down her stockings—a favorite hiding-place with ladies of her profession—a lot more she secreted in her bodice. She kindly left me a bundle of French notes for my own use.

"The best thing we can do," said May, when she had secreted the money to her liking, "is to get out of here at once. We'll be nabbed for sure if we stop much longer. I'm going back to London."

I didn't care about the idea at all. Kid McManus had disappeared and I concluded he had gone to Italy, where I also meant to go. Where Dutch Gus intended to make for first of all I didn't know. I certainly hadn't the slightest notion that he would have tried to reach England via the Gare du Nord and Calais.

The papers were still full of the robbery when May and I took our departure from Paris—as we hoped for good. We arrived at the station at the very last minute and I don't mind confessing that I was in a devil of a funk. The first thing the police of any country do when a big *coup* has been pulled off is to watch the main exits from the city, and I had no illusions about the danger of trying to get away from Paris unrecognized.

But everything seemed to be all right. May and I sat down in the compartment anxiously watching for developments. I knew, of course, that I could be trapped in the train like a rabbit in a hole. We sat talking for some time when suddenly I grew uneasy. Two or three people walking by the compartment looked to have police written all over them.

"Well," I thought, "it's no good stopping here if there's anything doing."

I lit a cigar and nonchalantly walked outside into the corridor. Two Frenchmen passed me and politely asked if there was a buffet at the end of the train. "I think so," I said. I walked on when suddenly they grabbed me by the neck and threw me into an empty compartment, slammed the door and forced me down on the seat.

"What's this b— game?" I panted.

"You will soon know," they replied.

They put a pair of handcuffs on me, drew the blinds of the compartment, and sat on either side of me until we reached Amiens. There they pulled me off the train and asked me, on reaching the police station, whether I would consent to being searched, if I was as innocent as I protested.

"No, you won't search me if I can help it," I replied. "You've taken me off the train, knocked me about, and treated me like a common crook. Now, tell me what it's all about?"

"You are wanted for a robbery in Paris," said one of the men. "Beyond that we can tell you nothing."

"You're making a big mistake," I exclaimed. "I'm a British citizen and you'll hear about this."

"Ah, that will be all right, Monsieur. We know who you are and we want you."

The only spark of comfort I had was that May held possession of the bulk of the money. She, wide as they make them, had heard the struggle on the train and had seen me hauled off to the police station. She didn't want me to tell her of the risk she ran.

Here was a pretty predicament! May gone with the money, Dutch Gus and Kid McManus out of sight. I resolved to keep a tight mouth; the bluff would begin as soon as I was taken back to Paris. The detectives in charge of me said very little, which made me realize that I was in grave danger. When the police ask you a lot of questions they know nothing; when they keep silent they know a lot.

I learnt a few things on the return journey to Paris. Dutch Gus, like a damned fool, had gone down to the Gare du Nord to catch a train *en route* to England. Detectives watching the station recognized him as the man who had bought the rope from the chandler's shop. They at once grabbed him and took him off to the Sûreté where a little judicious questioning and the usual promise of getting him off if he would snitch induced him to tell the story from beginning to end.

Apparently Gus made no bones about giving the show away. He had told the police that Kid McManus and I had been in the job, how McManus lived in a flat near St. Thomas's Hospital in London, and that in all probability they would find him there when he returned for his clothes. As a matter of fact, they never got the Kid. He cleared out of Europe altogether and never turned up again until some years later when he got a seven years' stretch in Canada for blowing a safe.

But they certainly had me tight enough. I spent the night in a cell with a man outside all the time. The following morning my old acquaintance Debischof came into the cell and told me I was to go before the *juge d'instruction* to be interrogated. He wanted to know whether I was going to confess.

"Confess!" I retorted. "What for? I don't know anything about it."

"Ah, ah, it is the same old Eddie," said Debischof. "What you call the American bluff, eh? We shall see."

The police court proceedings quickly demonstrated that things were pretty serious for me. The *juge d'instruction* somewhat unnecessarily informed me that I had been followed from the Drexel Bank in the Boulevard Haussmann, and that I had been in the company of Dutch Gus when he bought the rope. He also added that the chandler had identified the rope with which the caretaker of the American Express Company had been bound.

"What's all that to do with me?" I asked. "It doesn't prove I had anything to do with the robbery."

"Ah," the *juge* exclaimed shaking his head wisely. "We have got 'Dutch Gus.' He has confessed that you and he were confederates."

But I never believed in being bluffed myself. They might have got Dutch Gus in custody and again they might not. Anyhow, I wasn't owning up to anything.

"Take him away," ordered the *juge,* waving his hand, "and bring in the other man."

I was put into a cell below and while there Dutch Gus, escorted by two gendarmes, passed by. I took the opportunity to call him a b— traitor, but he hung his head and wouldn't look at me.

Gus didn't remain long before the *juge d'instruction.* Only five minutes elapsed before a couple of men opened my cell door and took me upstairs again. I saw Dutch Gus in one part of the room, while I was stood on the other side in between two gendarmes. Once more the *juge* started.

"Well, Guerin, you say you know nothing about this?"

"And I do not."

"It's no use your denying it," said the *juge* angrily. "We know all about you, and this man," pointing to Gus, "has told us you were with him."

I gave a look at Gus but he would take no notice of me.

"He is a liar," I said. "He wants revenge because I took the woman he was after."

So it went on for another quarter of an hour, but I admitted nothing. Downstairs I went again and eventually was taken away to a depot prison where they tried to get my photograph. I don't think they succeeded very well. They searched me, found something like a thousand francs on me, and demanded to know what I had done with my share of the money.

"I don't know what you're talking about," was my reply. At which there was much shaking of heads and muttering of threats.

"You have given it to the woman," Debischof informed me. "Never mind, she shall be brought back here before long."

It is more than twenty-six years ago since the events I am narrating took place and I have forgotten the number of times I was brought up before the *juge d'instruction* to see if I would not confess. I had been arrested on May 1st, 1901, but something like nine months elapsed before I was put on my trial. When the *juge d'instruction* finally came to the conclusion that he could get nothing out of me he ordered that I should not be allowed to have any more money. I was kept in solitary confinement in La Santé prison, idling away the time, grimly determined to confess nothing. There was always the chance of being acquitted. Some American friends of mine smuggled me in some money and with it I managed to buy odds and ends of food, cigars, and various other things to make the life bearable. The prison authorities winked at it, hoping I would let up and tell them what they wanted to know. But I didn't intend to do that.

I had been in custody for about five or six weeks when Chicago May did something incredibly foolish for a woman of her profession. She came over to Paris to see me and put her head right into the noose by calling at La Santé to ask whether she could see me! She could not have known, of course, that the police were looking for her, or if she suspected it she might have thought that she would take the risk and do what she could for me. Possibly she may have wanted to discover whether I had snitched, and if so whether she would be safe in having anything more to do with the money. She certainly saw me, but that was about all. While she was at the prison the Sûreté was telephoned to and May was arrested the same night. From my point of view her action was absolutely suicidal; the only evidence against me up to then was that of Dutch Gus. In all probability I would have been acquitted had May kept out of the way.

The French police found upon her evidence that the money had been put into a safe-deposit in Albany Street, London. Scotland Yard got the safe opened at once, but found nothing. The money had gone and only May could say where. Chief Inspector Froest, of Scotland Yard, had been following May about all over England without being able to discover the whereabouts of the missing money. When she had seen me taken off the train at Amiens she had gone on to London undetected and put up at a Bloomsbury hotel, and while staying there had rented a box at the safe-deposit. The watchman at the hotel said he had seen May put into her stocking a packet of checks, but from that time, until Scotland Yard discovered that the checks were being put down all over London, no trace of them could be found. Three or four men engaged in getting rid of them were arrested and held on suspicion.

I will give May the benefit of the doubt and say she was drunk most of the time, or she wouldn't have been so insane as to go over to Paris to see me. Her arrival in the Gay City coincided with a great drinking bout among the ex-jockeys and hangers-on who were to be found all round the cafés sponging on the people from the States. The fact that May had had a touch seemed to be no secret, and it was also generally known that the money she was throwing about came from the American Express Office. The crowd following May about were all under police surveillance, and when she took it upon herself to come and see me at La Santé the Sûreté then knew for certain where she had got her money.

Also, I believe, my old friend of years gone by, Sophie Lyons, had written to the French police telling them that Chicago May was in Paris and that it might be worth their while to follow her. The only wise thing May did was to keep her address a secret from the loungers with whom she was mixing. It was only when in a state of maudlin generosity she called at the prison that the Sûreté were able to pick her up.

They had no direct evidence, unless she liked to give it, that she had ever received any money from me. I continued to deny all knowledge of the matter, May also taking the same attitude. One day, I was sent for by the *juge d'instruction*.

"Now, then," he said to me sternly, waving a bundle of checks in front of my eyes, "here is the money you gave 'Chicago May.'"

Everybody in the room was looking at me, no doubt hoping for me to blab. They couldn't catch an old bird like me.

"I never gave her any money," I replied.

"Four people have been arrested in London passing these checks," the *juge* informed me.

"Why don't you bring them over here? They are probably the people who committed the burglary."

The months slipped by. May was shut up in the women's prison at La Rocquelle, and I only saw her about three times in nine months. I felt a bit afraid, not quite knowing what she would do. Dutch Gus had already snitched, but unless May did the same I had a good fighting chance. To keep her square I got a friend outside to engage a lawyer for her, but nevertheless it was an anxious time looking forward to the day when we would be brought up at the Seine Assizes. I had retained Henri Robert, one of the greatest French barristers of his time, and another lawyer who spoke English well. This man came to me one day and said: "What is the use of going on with the case? Why don't you plead guilty and throw yourself on the mercy of the court?"

"I'm not going to plead guilty for what I haven't done," I replied.

"Chicago May wants to plead guilty."

"She can do what she likes. They've got nothing against me except that I am supposed to have given Chicago May the money."

This was the occasion I discovered that Sophie Lyons, who was in London when May returned from Paris, and naturally came to hear that she had plenty of money, immediately informed the French police. Scotland Yard could do nothing to her while she was in England. I also found out that Sophie had written to the Sûreté. The letter was produced at my trial; it was the same sort of thing that she had done in 1888 when I was arrested for the robbery at Lyons.

And so the great day arrived. Kid McManus had got clear away. Dutch Gus and I were indicted for burglary with violence, May for receiving monies knowing them to be stolen. In the usual French fashion the police reconstructed the crime; they took a safe out on the ramparts and used dynamite upon it so that they could describe the operation in full. They might have invited me to take part in the scene, but they didn't even go to the length of asking me to participate. In fact, they never apologized for putting me on my trial. I wanted them to, but all I received was a contemptuous "Bah!"

It has been my doubtful fortune to take part in many criminal trials and this one at the Seine Assizes was certainly well done. In France, when you are charged with an offense, they get out your dossier, in which is written everything that is known about you. Your past is sifted out from childhood upwards. If your father or any of your relations were ever in trouble the facts are duly recorded against you. It is set out when, how, where and why you were born, what you have done for a living, and what your habits are. They call it the Code Napoleon, no doubt from the fact that Napoleon Bonaparte invented it as a means of keeping a check upon his enemies. My dossier certainly astonished me when it was handed to me to be read, so that I might have the opportunity of contradicting anything that was said about me.

I don't suppose there is any necessity for me to deal at length with the trial. Evidently there was considerable public interest in the case. A crowded court watched in breathless silence when Dutch Gus, Chicago May and myself, were put into the dock. Gus and I had a couple of gendarmes between us, while May was on the other side of Gus. The thought flashed through my mind that she was going to give me away. The nigger from the American Express Company contradicted the statements he had made when Dutch Gus and I were arrested. He had told the police in the beginning that he thought the robbers were Germans. When they showed him Gus he suddenly remembered him! When the nigger saw me before the *juge d'instruction,* who asked him: "Is that Eddie Guerin?" he promptly replied that it was. As a matter of fact, I doubt whether he had ever seen me!

On the second day of the trial there came a dramatic interlude. Dutch Gus was evidently stricken with the pangs of remorse, because I received a note he had written telling me that he was sorry for what he had done and that he had only snitched hoping to get away with a lighter sentence. He was good enough to add that if there was anything he could do to save me from a severe sentence he would do it. One of the warders saw me in possession of the note. We had a fight for it, until I was overpowered. Eventually it got into the possession of the Commandant of the prison, but I succeeded in extracting from him a promise that it would be produced before it was too late.

The President of the court read the note and remarked that it was undoubtedly a message from one guilty man to another.

"Yes," I shouted back, "put a knife in his (Dutch Gus's) hand and he'll cut the throat of anyone in the court."

The only defense I could put forward was that of an alibi. I went into the witness-box and swore that I was at an hotel with Chicago May and had not left my room all night. I went to bed at ten o'clock and did not go out. I added that Dutch Gus had tried to implicate me in the crime owing to jealousy, and that if the court liked to have read his police record it would show that he was an old and experienced bank robber who had been guilty of many similar crimes in the past. Chicago May went into the box and told exactly the same story, saying I had been in her company at the time the robbery took place and furthermore that I had not given her the large sum of money I was alleged to have received.

The unfortunate part of the whole affair was that Dutch Gus broke down and told everything. The copy of the indictment I had been furnished with contained all sorts of statements about English and American crooks in Paris, how Kid McManus was the man who robbed the Wagon-Lit office and got away with several thousand pounds, how the Kid and three other men had committed another big robbery at the Gare du Nord offices, embellished by all the names of the men concerned in it. There were hisses in court while these statements were being read.

Henri Robert made a passionate speech to the jury on my behalf, dramatically pointing out how terrible it was that a man should be betrayed by another so that he could escape the full consequences of his misdeeds. "Chicago May's" lawyer pleaded want of guilty knowledge on her behalf. The President of the court summed up and the jury went out. We were being taken below when I made a jump at Dutch Gus and landed him a smash on the jaw which sent him staggering down the steps. Three or four gendarmes jumped on me to prevent further mischief, but at any rate I got the satisfaction of giving him something he would remember for a week or two.

Half an hour elapsed before we were brought back into court. I am no coward, but my heart was thumping ominously when the jury returned and delivered their verdict—all three of us guilty, with "extenuating circumstances" in the case of Dutch Gus. One by one we came to the front of the dock to receive sentence—Dutch Gus and myself transportation for life, Chicago May penal servitude for five years. I more or less expected what I got, but I certainly did not think that Dutch Gus would get a lifer. In the savage satisfaction of realizing that he was to suffer the same as myself I completely forgot what it would mean to spend the remainder of my existence in a convict settlement. It was not until I had been taken back to the depot prison that night that I got the opportunity of appreciating the terrible time before me. And in this instance I think I could truthfully say that I had made the worst blunder of my misspent life. The money from the American Express Office had not been in my possession for more than three or four days, and I had spent practically none of it. Yet here I was, doomed for evermore, for committing a barren crime. What I called myself in the seclusion of my solitary cell, as it finally dawned upon me what it all meant, I need not repeat. All night long the maddening refrain drummed itself into my head that I was to be a prisoner for the rest of my natural life.

Chapter Twelve
THE ISLES OF THE DOOMED

Lying off the north-east coast of South America there is a group of three islands owned by the great Republic of France—the Îles du Salut. They are named Île Royale, Île St. Joseph and Île du Diable, the last-named one being the most famous of all, not only on account of its sinister name, but because of the fact that a few years previously it had achieved great notoriety as the place to which the ill-starred Captain Dreyfus had been sent for an offense of which he was afterward proved to be entirely innocent.

The Îles du Salut are situated but a few miles off the coast of French Guiana and the whole colony is nothing but one vast convict settlement, sparsely inhabited by French officials and their families, French convict prisoners, and the native population of Indians. It is not a land in which any man would choose to live of his own free will. The thought that I was going there chilled my heart with a dread of I knew not what.

For three months following the time when I had been sentenced to transportation for life I lay in the solitary prison of Fresnes, on the outskirts of Paris. Some of the older prison officers, who had been at Rion when I was there, recognized me and commiserated with me in my plight. There was no nonsense about the discipline at Fresnes. Every time we left our cell a mask was put over our faces so that no one should know us and each man exercised by himself.

The President of the Seine Assizes had ordered that I was to be sent to the islands straight away, but something like three months elapsed before I left France. During that time I lay at Fresnes sorting ostrich feathers, which struck me as rather a humorous occupation for a man supposed to be a desperate criminal. However, I took the work and said nothing, sufficiently thankful to have my mind occupied at all and to keep me from thinking of the dreadful years that lay ahead. I never saw a soul except the prison officials. My food was pushed in through a little door and at a certain hour every day I could go out into the exercise yard with a mask over my face. None of the prisoners were allowed to speak to each other, an abortive precaution because we never saw each other. With the exception of an hour's exercise each day we were locked up all the time. The Governor I never saw at all; occasionally the curé visited me and asked me if I would not confess my crime. I am afraid he got no satisfaction out of me. I had certainly been brought up a Roman Catholic, but religion had long ago ceased to make any appeal to a man leading a life like mine.

The prison itself was a tremendous affair; there must have been fully a thousand men within its walls, most of them doomed to long terms of penal servitude. We wore a sort of blue uniform with long trousers, and while we behaved ourselves we had nothing much to complain about. To all intents and purposes we were in a state of transition, awaiting the change from the light to the dark and dread of a convict's life with nothing in front of us but many years' imprisonment.

However, this period of waiting could not go on indefinitely, and one evening towards the end of 1901—the exact time has long ago slipped out of my memory—twenty of us were taken out of the prison and put into a train. Evidently it was a pretty frequent sort of occurrence, because we were locked up in what seemed to be a gigantic Black Maria, a special carriage with cells on either side of a narrow corridor.

I had succeeded in obtaining a certain amount of information—more or less comforting—while at Fresnes. I discovered that no prisoner is sent to the Islands with a sentence of less than five years. Such men are allowed to return to France. The news I got about the lifers did not sound so reassuring. For us there was no return. The only salvation we could look for was to behave ourselves for a term of twenty years when, by the grace of the Commandant, we would be allowed to live on the mainland of French Guiana and drag out the remainder of our existence as a convict on parole.

As we left the prison four of us were handcuffed together. One of my companions in adversity was a lively little Apache who had been sentenced at the Seine Assizes at the same time as myself. The poor devil had been mixed up in some shooting affray in the Montmartre district and for all I know was perfectly harmless. I would never have classed him as a hardened criminal. During the journey to the coast I made the interesting discovery that the party included Dutch Gus, and I thought then, as I still think, that I would have cheerfully given my life to have put him out of the way. At intervals during the long run, when the train had stopped and my voice could be heard, I took the opportunity of telling him what I thought about him. All the other prisoners took it up; shouts of execration sounded throughout the carriage, and when we reached the first stopping place the warders heard the noise and took Gus out of the way.

When we arrived at Marseilles we were lodged in the local jail and there I found myself punished for what I had done. The Commandant of the prison directed that I should live on bread and water for fifteen days for being a little too free with my tongue, and I did it without a murmur. Following this little episode, the officials were very careful to keep Gus and me apart. They thought I might kill him, and they weren't far wrong.

I watched every opportunity to escape, but never a chance came my way. The French prisons were not like the American; they shut you up so that you never saw anybody who could help you. I had no intention of serving my sentence if I could possibly help it, but I daresay a good many other thousands of men had gone to the Islands with the same determination. The days drifted on—it is astonishing how you lose count of time in prison—until I, in company with about three hundred other men, was taken on board the *S.S. Loire,* a ship of about six to seven thousand tons burden. Apparently she was engaged solely between France and French Guiana, carrying convicts, officials and their families, and supplies. From Marseilles we crossed the Mediterranean to Algiers, where we took aboard a big batch of Arabs, something like two or three hundred of them, who I daresay had been doomed to life-long punishment for offenses they did not know they were committing. It often struck me as I saw the poor wretches on their bended knees praying to their God that there, indeed, was the greatest condemnation civilization could receive. Why France, or any other country, should occupy a land inhabited by people foreign to them in every conceivable way and impose upon them white man's laws and penalties I cannot understand. These Arabs who were being transported thousands of miles over the seas would in but very few cases ever see their native land again. To all practical intents and purposes they might just as well have been exterminated and saved the suffering ordained by the code of their conquerors.

"Liberty, equality, fraternity" is the watchword of the French Republic. In no country in Europe is there less liberty. The French Revolution never brought freedom in its train; instead, it inaugurated an era of official oppression which exists to this very day. It is rather significant that of all the great civilized nations of the world France is the only one to maintain convict settlements overseas. It is a form of barbarity which the whole world, with the exception of this land of "Liberty, equality, fraternity," has agreed to abolish.

Life on board the *Loire* was not noticeably unpleasant. The society below decks—we lived in the big holds with the hatches off all day and night—if not exactly like a Mayfair drawing-room was at least tolerable. Of course, when you find yourself thrown into the companionship of murderers, burglars, robbers of all sorts and description, forgers and the scum of the world generally, it is no use complaining. You have made your bed and you must lie on it.

We had no work to do whatever; practically the only thing we did all day long was to sit around and play cards, gossip, tell each other the story of our lives, and, occasionally, squabble. One hour a day we were allowed up on deck in batches of about twenty for exercise. Four guards armed with rifles kept watch over us. They didn't bother maintaining a very strict vigilance and probably would not even have troubled to look if anybody had jumped overboard. In fact, I daresay that they would have shrugged their shoulders in true Gallic fashion and delivered themselves of the national equivalent concerning good riddance to bad rubbish. Once clear of the Straits of Gibraltar we rarely saw a ship. The *Loire* ploughed her lonely way across the Southern Atlantic, veritably a ship of despair carrying a human cargo doomed to a living death.

I have eaten worse food. We had tinned beef—didn't it bring back memories of Chicago!—soup and bread, all of which was served to us down below. Every morning each prisoner had a loaf of bread and a tin of coffee given to him. The heat was terrific, but, strange to say, not so noticeable as on deck. In each hatch there were about a hundred prisoners sleeping in hammocks slung close together with men on guard night and day. But, generally speaking, considering the nature of their charges, they had very little to do. Fighting brought swift reprisal in its train; there were special cells on the boat where the quarrelsome ones were locked up to stew away in savage silence until our destination was reached.

On going aboard we had been given two suits of clothes, one of linen and the other woolen, a pair of boots, a shirt and cap. You could have a sea-bath below decks; it used to give the old-timers who had already served a term at the Islands vast enjoyment to see the new hands lathering themselves all over with the rough soap provided and then trying to get it off with sea water.

So it went on for fifteen days, stewing, smoking, sleeping and swearing, this freight of human souls bound for the wind-swept islands where they were to toil away for many years before they could gain their liberty. I had not often indulged in the habit of introspection, but it was forcibly brought home to me as I looked around my fellow-prisoners on the *Loire* what a blind, unbelievable fool a man must be to get himself into the position of being nothing better than a common slave fated by his own foolishness to spend his life in servitude. It brought to my mind a piece of prison doggerel written by an American friend who had fallen foul of the law:

It's curious, isn't it, Eddie,
The changes a few years may bring.
Last year I was at Saratoga
As happy and rich as a king.
I was raking in pools at the races
'Midst women and wine and men
And sipping mintjulep by moonlight,
While to-day I am here in the Pen.

That's not so bad, is it; at any rate no worse than some similar effusions I have seen recently.

Devil's Island! It looked anything but that as I glimpsed through a porthole and caught my first sight of my tropical home-to-be. Judging from the exclamations of delight emanating from some of the prisoners the Île du Diable must have appeared to them as the Garden of Eden. Dense tropical vegetation ran down to the water's edge, mango trees laden with thickly clustered fruit were to be seen everywhere, while the sparkling sea, with the islands rising sharp out of the water, gave you a vision of languorous ease too deceptive to be real.

But we did not stop at the Île du Diable, which is slightly to the north of St. Joseph and Royale. Instead, the *Loire* steamed slowly onward until we reached Royale, when the order went round to prepare for debarkation. We were instructed to put on a straw hat, linen jumpers and trousers and to keep our hats on, whatever happened, unless we wanted sunstroke.

The dawn had come, heralded by a blood-red sun that presaged a scorching day. The six hundred men who had come from Europe were mustered on deck, counted, and then instructed to climb down to the tenders bobbing below. Convict prisoners who looked curiously at us rowed us ashore and a crowd of soldiers in the French Colonial uniform took charge and formed us up in long lines. In the blinding sunlight, before a smartly-dressed Commandant sitting at a table in front of an open tent, with half a dozen armed men around him, our names were read out while the Commandant asked a few questions and then sent us to the right or the left for despatch to the different islands.

"Eddie Guerin!" he called. I answered my name.

"St. Joseph," said the Commandant curtly, and I moved off to a batch with whom I subsequently found myself on the island of that name.

It took the greater part of the morning before we were finally disposed of and I was ravenously hungry when I arrived at my destination to serve the punishment to which my foolishness had led me. Truly a case of "where every prospect pleases and only man is vile." I looked around at my companions in adversity and all my savage instincts rose to the fore as I realized that they, and the officials, represented the only people I would see for I knew not how many years to come. The thought occurred to me to jump overboard and end my life in the sea, but as I glanced over the rail of the little steamer conveying us to St. Joseph and saw the sharks swimming alongside, I changed my mind and decided to await the time when I might make a proper bid for freedom.

A great many of the prisoners were taken on to the mainland, to Cayenne, the capital of French Guiana, others to Kourou further west and the remainder to the *Commune Pénitentiaire du Maroni.* There were mostly men sentenced to five, seven or ten years, and the bulk of them were boys from eighteen to twenty-five years of age! Imagine it, boys some of them barely old enough to know better, flung into the company of the most hardened criminals in the world, with nothing to hope for, condemned to a living death. The irreclaimables, the men who had previously served a term on the islands, were to be kept on the Île Royale, which they would probably never leave alive.

The Commandant's headquarters were at Maroni. At one time, I believe, Cayenne had been the principal convict settlement, but owing to innumerable complaints from the residents a special camp was formed at Maroni close by the river of that name which intersects French and Dutch Guiana.

St. Joseph, I found, was the biggest island of the three, although its circumference was only about three miles. All around the island ran a road made by the convicts, while in the center stood a large hill on which was situated the seclusion prison. It was a typical tropical vegetation with thousands of coconut tree and mangoes, but practically nothing else. No vegetables grew on the island; apparently it was nothing more than some volcanic eruption heaved up from the deep in time gone by.

There was no beach such as can be seen in the small islands of the Pacific. A roughly-made pier ran out into the water to allow of flat-bottomed boats landing their cargo—no steamer could have got near the place.

At the time I landed on St. Joseph, early in 1902, I found about two hundred and fifty men on the island, the majority of them engaged in building roads and blasting rock. There seemed to be no particular object in the work; it had been given to them merely to keep them occupied. Practically nothing was cultivated; rank vegetation grew wild, and when the officials were not looking some of the more agile of the prisoners would climb the coco-nut trees and drink the milk from the green nuts.

There were five or six block-houses scattered all over the island with armed men on duty. Down towards the jetty lived the guards and their families; the womenfolk of these men were the only females I saw after leaving France. Near-by was the house of the official executioner, an ex-convict who had won a sort of liberty by guillotining fellow-prisoners who had grown desperate and struck the men over them. But that, apparently, was a thing of the past. In days gone by prisoners accused of striking their guards, for which the penalty was death, were tried at Cayenne or Maroni, and then taken to the islands for execution.

I made the acquaintance of this overseas Monsieur de Paris. He seemed a decent sort of old fellow, a reprieved murderer condemned to drag out the remaining years of his life for a crime committed in a moment of passion. At the time I made his acquaintance he had lost his job of executioner, but was allowed to remain on St. Joseph, where he seemed to be getting a snug little sum of money cultivating a few bananas around his hut and selling fish to the prisoners. There was a big walled-in tank close to the jetty in which the prisoners were allowed to swim. When the tide was up it filled with water. When it went down there would be a lot of fish remaining, and this old guillotine-expert, who I daresay had cut off the heads of dozens of unfortunate men, had been given the right to dispose of the fish.

He was a chatty old gentleman. He informed me that he had retired from business and proceeded to show me how the guillotine worked. A prisoner sentenced to death would be executed in the full view of the other men so that his fate might for ever be before their eyes. There would be a ceremony similar to that in England when a man is drummed out of the army.

But Nemesis overtook this cold-blooded servant of officialdom who had become quite rich selling his fish and bananas. Whilst I was there he contracted leprosy. One day, officials from the mainland visited St. Joseph and took him away and I never heard of him again. His shack was burnt down and his banana trees were destroyed, so that all the money he made did him no good in the long run.

It was a strange life. Here we were, two hundred and fifty of us, steeped to the eyes in crime, living a lonely existence on a volcanic isle, hopelessly looking forward to the future. There was work for everybody. The stone quarries claimed some, the roadmaking others, while I, unused to a hard physical task and unable to do it, found myself appointed to the menial job of sweeping out the block-houses. For a companion I had a Russian whom I had known over in England, a notorious bank-robber who at one time used to patronize all the expensive cafés in the West End of London. He had already been sentenced to twenty years in the French convict settlement of New Caledonia, but after being there two or three years he succeeded in making his escape to Australia. Then he was foolish enough to go back to England and from there to France, where he was recaptured and sent to Guiana to work out the remainder of his term.

I at once began looking round for the means of escape. The staff of thirty guards as against two hundred and fifty desperate prisoners, did not appear particularly formidable. While there was nothing to prevent a mutiny, and probably the murder of the officials on the island, there was little or no possibility of getting away. Only one boat ran between the three islands and this was kept at the Île Royale. It brought the provisions, rowed by four prisoners with an armed guard in charge. I had a good look at it, but gave it up as a means of salvation. Even if I could succeed in disposing of the guard it would have been impossible to put to sea in it. All I could hope for was to sit tight and hope for something to happen.

We were not worked hard; so long as we were kept doing something the officials did not worry us. But it caused me a certain amount of petty annoyance to realize that our work did not matter; the island was not exploited to make us earn anything but merely to keep us employed. And it was undoubtedly a healthy existence, much better than the mainland. Prisoners from Maroni, Cayenne and Kourou stricken with malaria fever were sent to the Île Royale, which contained a big hospital, in order to recuperate. Royale was practically a barren rock in the middle of the sea, devoid of telephonic communication and compelled to use the semaphore whenever the officials wanted to send a message. On a clear day we could see across the water for twenty or thirty miles.

At night time we were confined in the big stone block-houses covered with roofs of corrugated iron. They were blazing hot in the day, but we never occupied them then except for the midday siesta when it became too warm for any work. Most of our time was spent in the open, idling at work that was nothing better than a farce. The guards leaned on their rifles dozing, nobody had sufficient energy to lift a hand beyond what was absolutely necessary. Those of the prisoners who had managed to smuggle in some money could always contrive to get coffee, tobacco and other little things. It was a serious offense to be found in possession of them, but nevertheless they were regularly brought over from the mainland and found their way to the men by ways and means which need not be mentioned.

At six o'clock in the morning we turned out and went off to our work. About eleven o'clock, with the sun blazing overhead, the tasks became almost impossible. Then we were marched back to the blockhouses and kept there until two o'clock. We had our midday meal, lay around and wondered, as I did, how long we would be fated to continue such an existence. Very few of the men wore anything on their feet; some even discarded their linen jumpers and went about half-naked, black as negroes. Some of the old-timers passed away the hours by tattooing their fellow-prisoners, anything, in fact, to divert their thoughts. There were Arabs on the island but they kept to themselves as much as possible. The Frenchmen hated them and never lost an opportunity of picking a quarrel with the poor devils.

Life for the guards could not have been much better. They lived in little houses near the quay, prisoners doing their washing and cooking. Water for the island was obtained during the rainy season and stored in huge cisterns. Every day there were tropical showers; immediately afterward the sun would shine brilliantly, enabling us to take off our wet clothing and get it dried in a few minutes. The strangest part of this strange existence was that many of the prisoners seemed to enjoy the conditions amongst which they lived, but after all, they were of the peasant class who had probably been working in France for a few francs a week with only an occasional taste of meat. Here, under sentence of life, they were not compelled to work hard and were given tinned beef and many other things they had never known before their imprisonment. Nine out of every ten of these men, I truly believe, would have declined to go back to France even if they had been given the opportunity. They certainly would not attempt to make their escape. It was only the men who had seen and tasted life, such as myself, who were continually railing against their lot. To me it was a living death, toiling away day after day underneath a broiling sun with nothing on earth to live for. Sooner or later I determined to make a bid for freedom even if it cost me my life.

Chapter Thirteen
THE LEGION OF THE LOST

Over twenty years have come and gone since I made my escape from the convict settlement of French Guiana, but I still wonder what fate has overtaken many of the men who, like me, had been doomed to drag out the remainder of their lives in penal servitude.

There was a Frenchman named Louis Verdiez, an anarchist, or, as he would be termed to-day, Communist, who had allowed his political opinions to carry him away to the length of throwing a bomb into the Chamber of Deputies. Verdiez escaped to London but was extradited and subsequently sentenced to transportation for life to the Islands.

He did not look upon himself as a criminal at all, and I daresay, among the heterogeneous collection of murderers, burglars, forgers, bank-robbers, and God only knows what else that composed the population of the Island, he was fully entitled to regard himself as a political prisoner who should not have been there at all. He was certainly a man very well liked by all his comrades in adversity, veritably a cohort of the damned.

The guards both respected and feared him, and, if they had dared, would have accorded him privileges, different from those of the other men. Verdiez and I came to know each other very well, and afterward, as I shall relate in the proper place, I asked him to come with me when I made my successful attempt at freedom.

Strong in my recollection also is an Englishman whose name I shall not give because he is now at liberty earning an honest living. When I first knew him he was a convict on Île St. Joseph in charge of a few wretched tubercular cows which supplied the officials and their families with milk. Many years afterward I met him in London. He came up to me in the street, held out his hand, and said to me: "Hullo, Eddie, do you remember the old Devil's Island days?"

Stranger still was a meeting with a man I had known in Chicago many years before, Billy O'Brien, gambler, card-sharper, bank-robber, anything, in fact, but an honest citizen. When the States grew a little too warm for his comfort he emigrated to Paris, the great Mecca of American crookdom. In Paris Billy must needs get mixed up in a shooting affray which cost him his liberty for evermore. He had been rash enough to steal an Apache's demoiselle. The aggrieved lover pulled out a knife, while Billy, a famous man at the draw, responded so quickly with half a dozen shots from his pistol that the rat of the underworld had no chance whatever. Billy might have got away with this little escapade in any other city but Paris. But the French people then, as now, heartily detested the Yankees, and Billy was convicted of willful murder and only saved from the guillotine because his victim had first threatened Him.

He wasn't a bad fellow by any means, but, of course, his life, like mine, proved right up to the hilt that you don't win out in the long run. Here was a man of the most pronounced intelligence living the life of a dog when he ought to have been making a name for himself in the world. He had been on the Islands some time before I arrived and was then under strict surveillance because he had attempted to get away.

"I'll tell you what happened to me," he said when we came to know each other well.

"After I had been here for about three years I got them to send me to the mainland" (the *Commune Pénitentiaire du Maroni* which I have previously mentioned). "Three of us planned to get away into Dutch Guiana, but failed. When they catch you at that game you will pay for it in a way you will remember for evermore.

"I was put into a block-house and remained there for three months shackled to the wall. I had nothing to do, nothing to read. Every day they brought me my food and occasionally allowed me to wash myself. No one was allowed to communicate with me, and I was only released when the doctor came along and said that I would surely die if I were not given some sort of freedom. So I've got no intention," said Billy, "of trying to get away again. I'll live here and I'll die here. I don't suppose they will ever send me back to the States."

An attack of scurvy, terribly common among all the prisoners, had resulted in Billy being sent to the Île St. Joseph for six months to recuperate. It was like a whiff of the old days to meet a man I had known in both Chicago and New York, and for hours on end we could talk over mutual friends, speculating, maybe, as to what had become of them. Billy had a bit of a job making mats out of palm leaves, a strange occupation, when you come to think of it, for a man who had been one of the greatest gamblers of his time. He used to get a bit of money smuggled in from the mainland at Cayenne, but every cent of it went in playing poker of a night when the guards were out of the way.

Billy and I were so friendly that I wanted him to help me in making my escape when my plans were more fully matured. I had good friends in Chicago and London who were secretly preparing the get-away I had in mind. The time wasn't ripe when I was on the Islands. I intended to wait until I could be sent to the mainland and then to make no mistake. One day, however, I saw Billy in close confabulation with Dutch Gus and that finished me with him. When a man betrays his friends he will do anything, and as far as Dutch Gus was concerned I was not foolish enough to harbor any delusions about his goodwill for me.

I would have nothing further to do with Billy O'Brien after that. I had helped him in innumerable ways, given him money which used to be brought over to me, and made his life ten times easier than it had been at Maroni. But I wouldn't stand my friends mixing with my enemies and especially in a penal settlement where men would snitch on the slightest provocation in the hope of currying favor. Fortunately for me, Billy was soon afterward sent back to Maroni, where I believe he died. I never heard of him again.

So the dreary life in these Islands of Disenchantment dragged on. One day succeeded another with nothing to distinguish it but the weather. Terrific thunderstorms, in which the heavens would grow inky black and then burst forth into frightening flame, followed by a downpour of rain which submerged everything within a few seconds, were the principal incidents in the enervating existence we led.

What a place to condemn a man to spend the remainder of his life! There were times when the hopelessness of the future so completely took possession of me that I felt impelled to throw myself in the sea and allow the ravenous sharks to end it all. Stuck on an island in the middle of the broad Atlantic, wearily dragging out the barren days, wondering when it would all end, waking up each morning to the knowledge that nothing could possibly happen to relieve the dreadful monotony, what wonder that a man should grow desperate and commit murder?

There was no necessity to lock up the prisoners when they had finished their work for the night. The sharks swimming around the islands constituted a far more dangerous barrier to freedom than all the rifles of the guards.

Both St. Joseph and Royale contained prisoners of every conceivable walk in life. There were young fellows serving short sentences of five years and old-timers who had been on the Islands ever since they were old enough to commit a crime of any sort. One poor old fellow I came to know well had fifty odd years to serve! He had originally received a life sentence and then, for attempting to escape, the authorities in Cayenne had maliciously given him another ten years! What for I could never understand. He was then about sixty years of age and had spent fully forty years of that time in jail. But then, the French take a grim delight in telling a man that he will be a prisoner until the end of his days. They will not actually subject you to physical violence, such as flogging, as is done in England. But they will certainly inflict upon you the infinitely greater punishment of depriving you of your liberty to the day of your death. And for all I know they may try to claim your freedom in the life hereafter.

On St. Joseph I came across all the ordinary types of men one sees in the streets of London, Paris, and New York. Clad in their convict dress of dirty white drill with their big Panama hats they all looked much of a muchness. It was only the Italians who managed to keep up their spirits. Of a night time, when there was nothing to do but lie in your hammock trying to get your tortured brain to sleep, the Italians would get together and sing songs from the grand operas half-way through the night. Volatile, never worrying, content if each day brought them the luxury of a cigarette, they were easily the happiest of all the prisoners. Most of them were murderers, but I don't think they allowed that fact to interfere with their contented frame of mind.

There were also Arabs on the islands, broken-spirited, down-trodden, as unlike the fierce Bedouin as it would be possible to imagine. The French convicts hated them like poison, and but for the restraint of the guards would have manhandled them all. I remember one day an Arab being set upon by half a dozen Frenchmen and nearly killed. Three or four of the guards had to come to the rescue with the butt-end of their rifles before the Arab could be saved. Every evening at sun-down, as regularly as clockwork, the Arabs turned to the East and prostrated themselves, praying, no doubt, to Allah that he would release them from their sufferings. They never complained; they just did what they were told, living, possibly, in the hope that death would put an end to an existence utterly devoid of hope.

They were about the only prisoners who made the slightest pretense at religion. The white infidels had long ago been abandoned by the French priests at Cayenne, and all the time I was on the Islands I never saw a chaplain or a priest. Whatever one may say of the French they certainly possess a strong sense of the eternal fitness of things. We were indeed a Legion of the Lost. Some time prior to my arrival there had been nuns on the Île Royale who looked after the hospital, as there had also been a resident priest. However, it seems to have dawned on the authorities they were wasting their time with any of the refining influences of life. Probably one could not blame them; their own existence must have been a shockingly dreary one, with nothing to look forward to but a return to France plus a meagre pension to eke out the remainder of their days.

The guards of St. Joseph, where I spent the first year of my imprisonment, were not a bad lot of fellows. Most of them were old soldiers and sailors, skilled in the use of arms, and always ready to earn a few francs from affluent prisoners. The precautions to prevent money getting into the Island were never-ending, but nevertheless men with friends outside could always get something. I had money from Chicago within three months of my arrival and I continued to receive it practically up to the day I got away. I wrote regularly to the people in the outside world, practically as often as I liked, and was allowed to receive unlimited letters in return. Of course everything was opened and read, but most of the prisoners were certainly permitted the indescribable boon of writing to their friends and relations. They were also allowed to have books and magazines. I had the *Illustrated London News* and the *Scientific American* sent to me as soon as my friends were apprised of my whereabouts. What the authorities didn't know was that I regularly received sums of money which I carefully hoarded for the time when my plans to escape would be reaching maturity.

It has always gone against my nature to knuckle down to anything. As many of my acquaintances among the different detective forces of the world can testify, I never plead guilty to any charge, any more than I am prepared to accept restraint placed upon me by people who think they are doing it for my good. Maybe it is the old Irish in me, but I am quite certain that if I hadn't been possessed of plenty of fight I would have been sent back to France to serve the remainder of my term on the Island when I was recaptured in England in 1906. And it is quite certain this story of mine would not have been written if I had weakly said to myself: "Oh, well, what's the use of fighting against Fate?"

I've never done that all my life. Possibly people will say it would have been a good thing for me to have utilized such strength of mind to turn over a new leaf and give crime the go-by. I suppose they are quite right; I won't attempt to argue with them.

For most of the time I spent on St. Joseph I kept out of serious trouble. Bitter experience of years before had drummed into me the foolishness of making myself a marked man, and so I continued to sweep out the block-houses, the paths around the Commandant's house, and generally to comport myself like a well-trained domestic. I don't say that I might not have done something desperate if the opportunity to get away had been thrust under my nose. When a man is under sentence of life imprisonment he can well be excused for contemplating even death as the only way out, and quite naturally he will be equally prepared to take life if he can thus win his way back to freedom.

But although I saw the Commandant often, and frequently had a chat with him, I never looked upon his life as the gate through which freedom lay. It is a sound principle, when you are intending to defy authority, to do it secretly and silently. Trumpet forth your intentions to the whole world and you ask for the trouble you will surely get. So although I saw the Commandant day by day I merely saluted in his person the system that had made me what I was. I wanted his friendship— not his enmity. And in a way his lot was just as hard as mine. To all intents and purposes he was a prisoner, with the difference that once every four years he was permitted to go to his native land for a holiday, and also to give himself a chance of relieving the savage moroseness of nature which naturally afflicts a man penned in the company of desperate criminals ready and willing to take his life if the opportunity offered.

The same old routine went on day after day. Every other morning there came over from the Île Royale a boat which brought bread, and once a week, the other provisions required for the men on St. Joseph. We could see this boat coming but no one was a allowed on the quay in case an organized mutiny took place. Every man had his ration of bread and water served out to him in the early morning. At eleven o'clock there would be a meal of soup, preserved beef and potatoes. Green vegetables we saw none. Scurvy was rampant, not only on the mainland, but also on the Islands, and all that would be done for a man was to send him to another place for a change. The wonder was that this dreadful disease did not wipe out the whole population of French Guiana.

Our next meal would be in the evening and consisted of coffee, bread and anything you had managed to save from the day. The old guillotiner down by the quayside sold us a bit of fruit if we had any money and religiously abstained from giving any credit. That, with a smuggled cigarette, had to do us for the night.

Once a week there came over to St. Joseph from the Île Royale a doctor who sat with a grim face at a sort of sick parade where the malingerers and weaklings whined out their tales. It isn't necessary for me to remark that they didn't receive much sympathy. When a man voluntarily occupies a position of medical officer in a prison he is usually, to start with, a third-rater who would never succeed in civil life. And secondly, it isn't his business to coddle convicts. I knew all this, so all the time I was on the Islands I carefully abstained from going sick.

Everybody dressed in white—Commandant, guards, doctor, prisoners, and the occasional visitors we had from the mainland. The guards were clothed in the French Colonial uniform of white drill, plus a big army pistol fully loaded, with a pouch filled with extra cartridges. On top of them were other guards with rifles ready to shoot if you tried to get away by sea.

I always had a proper respect for force, but I would not have been a man worthy of the name if I had not been filled with a determination to try and make my escape sooner or later. Whatever a man may be, he wants his liberty, and I meant to get mine, whoever died in the attempt. There were three of us on St. Joseph: Luigi Delonda, an Italian serving a lifer, Franz Hoffman, a German burglar, and myself, who planned a scheme which for quite a time seemed very promising.

When the boat arrived from Royale there were usually left behind a number of hammocks to replace those worn out. In the tropical heat clothing rotted within a few weeks. These canvas hammocks were continually being replaced, and the three of us got the idea that if we could steal about twenty of them we could use them to make some sort of boat with which we might reach the mainland.

It was a mad scheme, but the only thing that offered itself. The idea was to make a framework out of any odd pieces of wood we could find and sew the canvas around it and then, trusting to luck, to launch ourselves in the sea and paddle ourselves across the waters to the coast of Dutch Guiana. What might have happened to us if the plan had been put into execution I shudder to think.

We succeeded in getting the materials all right and hid them in the cavities of rocks on the edge of the water. For weeks we worked on the hammocks, sewing them together and fondly hoping that the time would come when our boat would be made. We knew, of course, the fate that lay before us if we were caught. If a man happened to be serving a definite term of imprisonment he got another five years added to it. If he was a lifer, which in the Islands really means life, he would probably go about night and day for six months or a year with a fourteen-pound chain riveted to his legs. There were many such men on the Island. Once they had failed to get away the officials took all sorts of precautions to prevent them making another attempt.

One fine afternoon—I could not for the life of me tell the exact date—Delonda had been down at a cave working on the boat while everybody else on the Island was at siesta. But as luck would have it he was seen creeping away by one of the French prisoners with whom he had already had a fight. This man carefully watched Delonda out of the way and then went on a tour of discovery which brought about disastrous results. Some of the partly-sewn hammocks were discovered, and the sergeant who was brought on the scene ordered that all the prisoners should be locked up for an extra hour while the rocks were searched from top to bottom.

It was only a matter of a few hours before the whole plot came to light. The following morning Delonda and Hoffman were paraded before the Commandant where they were taxed with attempting to escape. They denied all knowledge of the matter, but some needles and stout twine found in their possession which they had been using to sew the hammocks, exactly the same as that found in the cave, quickly sealed their fate. The Commandant ordered them to be sent to Royale, where they could be confined in a place from which escape would be a little more difficult. They were also to wear chains on their legs for six months as a reward for their ill-starred enterprise.

What happened immediately afterward I cannot say. I have no doubt, of course, that both Delonda and Hoffman were either induced or intimidated into a little snitching because the day after their departure I also received orders to collect my few worthless belongings in readiness for a trip to Royale.

"Well," I thought, "anything for a change." On my way across the sparkling blue sea I utilized the opportunity to take a good look at the coast line only a few miles distant. It possessed, at any rate to my unskilled eye, the advantage of being perfectly flat. There were no rocks to hinder an easy landing. Always at the back of my mind was the idea to get away from the Islands by boat under cover of darkness, in the hope that I would be able to land on the Dutch coast unseen. It was only after I had been on the Île Royale for some months in the company of convicts who had all been sentenced to life that I came to realize the utter impracticability of my plan. Men who had spent twenty years in this settlement laughed scornfully when I told them that it ought to be possible to make a boat and get away to Dutch Guiana.

"Ah, ha!" they exclaimed, tapping their heads significantly, "the sun has got him."

When I reached Royale I discovered that I was only suspected of attempting to escape. They didn't even bother punishing me, but I daresay I was watched. The Commandant-in-Chief, who only came over to the Islands about once a month, had me specially brought before him. I took heart to myself as soon as I caught sight of him. He seemed a good-humored sort of fellow, with a pair of sharp twinkling blue eyes, very smart in his white uniform, thoroughly efficient from tip to toe. No nonsense about that gentleman.

"Well, Guerin," he said to me, "I've heard a lot about you. It is said you have been trying to escape. Do you admit it?"

"No, sir," I lied stoutly. "I know nothing about the matter."

"Ah, well, it is of no importance. If you had got away in your boat the sharks would have had you within an hour. You are better off here."

I thought this was the prelude to six months in irons, but, lo and behold, the Commandant seemed in a far too amiable mood to punish a man for what after all was only a natural desire. Also, he seemed to like me, as most of the decent prison officials I have met will do if you won't betray a fellow culprit. They will certainly ask you to give away your pals—that is their duty— but they won't blame you if you refuse.

Anyhow, this Frenchman and I got on famously.

"I'm going to give you a good job over here, Guerin," he said. "You will be the officers' valet. It will be your duty to keep their clothes washed and mended, and all that sort of thing. Your food will be better and you will have a much easier time."

I couldn't very well protest, but if I had anything to do with it I had no intention of becoming a fixture on the Île Royale for the remainder of my life. Being a trusty is all very well. Personally I had no ambition in that direction.

"I'm afraid I can't wash clothes, sir," I replied, watching the Commandant closely out of the corner of my eye. "I've got an injured hand, as you can see," holding it up for him.

"Ah, I forgot that," the Commandant said. "Still, I will think about the matter," and with that dismissed me.

The next day the local Commandant called me over.

"Do you know how to cook?" he asked.

I was still dodging the domestic jobs.

"No, sir, I don't."

"Have you ever done any cooking at all?"

"Well, sir, I can make coffee."

"How do you make that?"

"I put the coffee in cold water and let it boil," I replied.

"*Ma foi!*" exclaimed the Commandant, holding up his hands in horror, "that won't do at all. I must find you something else to do."

If there was one thing more than another I wanted to avoid it was to become a fixture on the Island. From one point of view it was a good move to get a job apart from the ordinary prison

EDDIE GUERIN

labor, but it also meant, if you gave satisfaction in your work, that you stopped there for evermore. That I had no intention of doing. I couldn't see myself twenty years hence still a prisoner on the Islands. I would either be dead or free; of that I was firmly resolved.

With a servant's job you got certain privileges denied to the other men. In the Commandant's household there would be plenty of food and wine. There were even chickens and fresh beef to eat. Cattle were kept on the Island specially for the purpose of keeping the Commandant and the other officials in meat, wretched diseased beasts which had been brought over from the mainland and either had to be eaten quickly or else killed and thrown into the sea for the sharks. Periodically the doctor would condemn the whole lot *en bloc,* when they would be shot and subsequently provide a meal for the sharks.

A few days after the incident I have related the Commandant once more sent for me.

"I've got a job for you," he informed me. "You shall be my gardener."

He had a house situated on a promontory overlooking the island, surrounded by a garden in which tropical plants grew like wildfire. But the place was choked with weeds and I was given the job of pulling them up, keeping the paths clean and tidy, and digging the soil until my back ached. Regularly seven days a week did I curse my fate, wondering how long it would be before I would be able to make a dash for freedom.

However, the job had its slight compensations. For instance, when a convict died on the Island his body was sewn in a bag and then rowed out to sea by four of his fellow-prisoners with an armed guard, and then tumbled overboard, when no doubt the sharks speedily got an unexpected meal. They didn't bother burying anybody on the Islands. A couple of heavy stones carried the body to the bottom of the sea where no trace of its subsequent fate would ever be revealed.

Twice a week there came a boat from Cayenne with provisions. I also had a good look at that to ascertain whether I might secrete myself on it and thus leave the Island, but never a chance came my way.

Royale itself was a much more important settlement than St. Joseph. There must have been over two hundred men on the Island engaged in clearing scrub, making roads, carpentering, building, work, in fact, much more useful than the abortive labor of the other place. But the idea was, of course, that most of the men on Royale were serving life sentences and therefore had to do something to maintain themselves. There were something like thirty houses on the Island occupied by the guards and their families, all of whom were kept right away from the prisoners. The Island also possessed a bakehouse where the bread was cooked for the three places, Royale, St. Joseph and the Île du Diable. To all intents and purposes it was a self-supporting community, except that the food and clothing had to come from Cayenne. There was a big hospital on the island staffed by convicts, with the doctor in charge, who was assisted once a week by the inspecting Medical Officer from the mainland.

The very first man I met on the Île Royale was one of the Apaches who had been sentenced at the Seine Assizes at the same time as Dutch Gus and myself. Joyously did he greet me and grab my hand in a fierce grip, demanding to know how I had been getting on. I told him all my adventures since we had last seen each other and of how I hoped to escape.

"Well," he said, "I can tell you you won't do it from here. Your only chance is to be disinterred and sent to the mainland. Those great big sharks will never let you get far."

Chapter Fourteen
MY SENSATIONAL ESCAPE

I am now coming to what is probably the most momentous period in my life, namely, the time when I succeeded in making my escape and returning to civilization, to be followed by a world-wide blaze of notoriety from which I have suffered ever since.

Before I go on to narrate the true story of my actual escape I would like to take this opportunity of saying that *no prisoner has ever succeeded in getting away front the Île du Salut, or at any rate living to tell the tale.* There have certainly been attempts innumerable, and I shall tell of one which took place while I was on the Île Royale on the part of my courageous little Italian friend Delonda who, even after he had been punished for our little affair on St. Joseph, never abandoned hope of winning his freedom.

The outside world has the impression that the penal settlement of French Guiana consists of nothing but Devil's Island. It is easy to see how this delusion came into existence. When the unfortunate Captain Dreyfus was condemned by a court-martial of his brother officers to transportation for life, he was placed on the Île du Diable, or, in plain English, the Island of the Devil, an eminently suitable name for a desolate and dreary rock jutting up out of the sea.

I even doubt whether many people outside France ever knew there was a great penal settlement in French Guiana. But when the Dreyfus case flamed into one of the greatest *causes célèbres* of all times, and it was revealed that the victim of this terrible plot had been condemned to drag out the remainder of his life on Devil's Island, it was generally thought that that name applied to the entire colony.

I have already explained that the greatest number of men were kept on the mainland at a place called Maroni. The Islands were only used as a place of detention for the very worst characters, and until a man had shown to the officials that he could behave himself he was kept there more or less indefinitely. Nevertheless, after the *affaire Dreyfus* the picturesque appellation of Devil's Island, appropriate enough in the circumstances, was bestowed on the entire settlement.

Why I want to make this clear is because when I had succeeded in making my escape, and following in its train became the "hero" of two continents, it was generally believed that I had got away from Devil's Island. That impression still exists and probably will do so until the end of all time. *But it is utterly untrue.*

When I reached Chicago in 1905 a free man once more, the American Press came out with a tremendous story of how I had done what Captain Dreyfus with all his friends could not do. I shall tell the full story of my escape and the intensely dramatic events which followed it in its proper place. In the meantime I would like to say that Devil's Island is not inhabited except by an occasional prisoner who is taken over there to cut coco-nuts.

It was certainly on the Île du Diable that Captain Dreyfus was kept when he reached French Guiana. There he lived in a little shack surrounded by a wall, guarded night and day by soldiers who never let him out of their sight. The wall had been built when the agitation for his release was threatening the downfall of the French Government, because it was thought and believed that Dreyfus would be rescued by his friends at whatever cost. Three men followed him as he wandered about day after day, ready to shoot if the necessity arose. Food was brought over from the Île Royale. I think I am right in saying that Captain Dreyfus was the last prisoner ever condemned to serve his punishment on Devil's Island. Whatever men may have been there before his time there were certainly none sent there afterward. It is to be doubted whether the French Government would have dared to have used the place after the revelations that were made when Dreyfus was released.

There were no prisoners at all on Devil's Island when I was in that part of the world and as far as I know there are none now. Now that I have dealt with this important matter I will continue the story of my life in the settlement on the Île Royale. I ran across my accomplice in the American Express robbery, Dutch Gus, whom I had not seen for many months. While I was on St. Joseph, Gus had been sent to the mainland, right across to the middle of French Guiana. Malarial fever took hold of him with the result that he was sent to Royale to recover. I saw him wandering about the hospital ground looking like a ghost, but even then I could feel no sorrow for him. When a man will betray you to save his own skin he is beneath pity of any description. I have never done it in my life and I never shall.

As the months dragged on, with nothing to distinguish one from another, I began to lose count of time. Day by day under the blazing sun I went about my tasks, watching, waiting and hoping for the opportunity that never came my way. Occasionally there would be an interlude in the form of an arrival from St. Joseph of some one I knew, as, for instance, the Frenchman who had given us away when we tried to escape some months previously. He, also, had fallen foul of authority because every man on St. Joseph made a dead set at him. Then he began to go in fear of his life and the Commandant sent him to Royale to get him out of the way.

I lost no time in telling my fellow-prisoners there was a snitch amongst us. Once or twice he nearly got knifed and eventually the Commandant got rid of him for good by sending him off to the mainland where his reputation would not be known.

The mainland was also my ambition. I had not been on the Islands for two or three years without carefully sifting all the information obtainable from the old-timers as to how I might make my escape. They all told me the same thing—that it would be utterly impossible to make any sort of boat in which I could reach the shore. I would have to be disinterned and sent either to Maroni, Kourou or Cayenne to give myself the slightest chance of seeing civilization once again.

But the numerous ventures I made in that direction proved none too successful. Several times I approached the Commandant, who knew me very well because I was always about his house, asking whether I might not leave the Islands. I caught him one day as he came down the garden path, stood to attention as we were all required to do when we spoke to one of the officers, and said to him:

"M. Commandant, is there any chance of my getting disinterred?"

"Why do you want that, Guerin?" replied the Commandant with a smile. "You know it is unhealthy on the mainland, don't you?"

"Maroni is not bad," I said, that being the place I had been told to make for if I wanted to try and escape. But I daresay the Commandant knew all about my thoughts.

"It is not so healthy as here," he informed me with a certain amount of significance. "Still, I will see what I can do for you. What did you work at when you were in prison in France before?"

"I was a machinist in the tailor's shop," I answered. "I used to make tunics."

The Commandant promised to meet my wishes if he could. However, I heard nothing further of the matter for some time. He told me he had made application on my behalf to headquarters, but that it had been refused, so for the time being I had to contain myself waiting and wondering how long it would be before I did something desperate.

It must have been some six months later—for the life of me I couldn't give anything near the exact date—that Delonda and two other men conceived a daring plan to get away from the Île Royale. I had always been friendly with the little man. He trusted me, which was more than we would do with any Frenchman. There was a mutual bond of hatred in the whole settlement. I think the French prisoners were of the opinion that no foreigner ought to be there, an idea with which I thoroughly agreed. The Italians, the Germans and the English-speaking men for their part cordially hated the Frenchmen. If it hadn't been for the incessant watch kept upon us by the guard there would have been murder done every day.

Delonda had a scheme, a mad, desperate plan of trying to get away whatever the consequences. For his part anything was better than doing nothing. He had about thirty years to serve, and when he told me that he would either escape or die in the attempt I promised him my help.

"I don't think you've got a million-to-one chance," I warned him. "Still, if you've definitely made up your mind to risk it you might as well go forward."

I thought it utter madness for three men to try and launch themselves on the Atlantic Ocean, as they intended to do, in baths stolen from the officers' quarters. The intention was to obtain enough wood to float the baths and leave the rest to fate.

It was not a great deal I could do to help them. Being in and out of the Commandant's house all day long I certainly had the opportunity of obtaining plenty of food. That was all Delonda and his friends wanted from me. For the better part of a week I purloined every eatable article I could lay my hands on, hid it away in the scrub and just wondered how long it would be before they made their attempt.

When the momentous night arrived it was blowing half a gale. The baths were laboriously dragged down to the water and around them were lashed wooden scantlings torn off some of the buildings. For oars each man had a piece of wood, and it was thus perilously equipped that the three of them with dauntless courage pushed off into the ocean when it seemed inevitable that they must be swamped immediately.

What actually happened to them was more or less what might have been expected. After tossing about for two days and nights on the sea they were eventually thrown up on the shore of French Guiana, exhausted, drenched from head to foot, and starving. After hiding themselves in a wood for the better part of a day they succeeded in stealing a native boat and put out to sea, once more hoping this time to reach the Dutch coast. They had not gone very far before the Indians saw them and sent information to the authorities. There was then, and probably still is, a standing reward of one louis for the recapture of an escaped prisoner. Delonda and his two friends were caught long before they reached Dutch territory and ignominiously brought back to the Islands. I remember seeing them return and saying to myself as they were dragged ashore with the chains clanking on them: "My God, what chance have I?"

There were many such of these attempts, but I never heard of one that succeeded, even when the men had managed to reach Dutch Guiana and could reasonably hope to avoid being taken. But there were even greater perils to be encountered. When I was fighting my way back to freedom accompanied by a Belgian named Stoup, I came across the rotting skeletons of many men who had gone under in making a bid for liberty. Their origin could be easily traced by the fact that the French penal settlement mark was still on their decayed clothing.

Time did not go altogether unpleasantly on the Île Royale. The Commandant's wife treated me very kindly and I got on very well with most of my fellow-prisoners. It is strange, indeed, how an Englishman is looked up to all the world over, even among convicts. I was the confidant of half the men on the Island, and as I was also in the fortunate position of receiving money from friends, who had better be nameless, I could lead an existence which might easily have contented a man of a weaker turn of mind.

All the time I had been on the Islands I had taken the greatest possible care of my health. I knew that when the time came to make my dash that I would want all my strength, and for that reason it was more than a little fortunate that I had not yet been sent to the mainland where I would surely have contracted fever.

I had practically forgotten all about going to Maroni when one day to my great astonishment the Commandant stopped me to say that I was to get ready to leave for the mainland. He himself was leaving the Île Royale for France, and he evidently wanted to do me a good turn before he went away. I will even go the length of saying that the probably knew I intended to try my luck as so many other men had done and I have no doubt he sympathized with my desire. I recollect saying to myself: "This is fine; now I have got something to look forward to." From that moment onward I led a cool, calculating life with the thought ever present at the back of my mind that I would do or die.

There were about a dozen of us to be sent ashore, and when the time came to take our departure we were the recipients of congratulations as though we were embarking on a tour of the world midst the sighs of our envious friends.

The *Commune Pénitentiarie du Maroni,* to which we were bound, was then, and still is, easily the biggest convict station in French Guiana. The idea of sending men there was to allow them to lead something like a normal existence after they had served a probationary period on the Islands. It contained, I should think, fully three-quarters of the entire convict population.

The settlement at Maroni is a big place, twenty times as large as either St. Joseph or Royale. When a man had served two or three years on the Islands he was permitted the privilege of living on the mainland where, in course of time, he would gradually settle down.

It was penal servitude in the fullest sense of the words. The prison itself, a huge building accommodating over a thousand men, was surrounded by a great wall which would have enabled the authorities to keep all the prisoners in confinement if they wished to do so. But actually speaking it was a *dolce far niente* existence; provided you did a certain amount of work and gave no trouble you could lead a carefree, aimless sort of life, merely waiting for the time when you would be released on license, at liberty, if not to return to your native land, at least to remain in French Guiana and make the best of a bad job.

Men under sentence of transportation for life were not permitted to leave the colony. It struck me as strangely ironic that most of the men who had been released were wandering about outside the settlement practically starving. They were pathetically glad to receive the odds and ends of food we used to throw them as we marched out of the prison to our work. Many of them had married female convicts out of the convent. These women, poor spiritless creatures, walking about the settlement like lost sheep, were only too glad to link their lot with men of any nationality, and whether they were murderers or anything else did not greatly matter. The authorities granted them a plot of land, built them a hut to live in, and then left them to fend for themselves.

What the future of French Guiana will be no man can predict. In Cayenne itself, there were released convicts married to Negresses, French officers living with beautiful Creole women, Negroes, Indians, and hundreds of discharged prisoners wandering about unable to earn enough to keep body and soul together.

Still, I did not greatly worry myself about problems such as these. I had achieved the first part of my ambition towards getting away from this Never-never land when I found myself on the mainland, and from that time onwards my thoughts and energies were concentrated solely on the infinitely more difficult part of finding the ways and means of crossing over into Dutch Guiana. There was only one way it could be done. The River Maroni divides the two territories. If I was to make my escape I would have to get over the river and more or less trust to luck what happened afterward.

My old flame Chicago May recently told the world—through the medium of an American journal—that she found the money which enabled me to return to my native land! It is a nice romantic tale, but totally devoid of truth. May, according to her story, found 50,000 dollars to bribe a dozen officials.

I won't say much about this matter. The men who actually helped me I will not name, because there always remains the possibility that they may still get into trouble for what they did. The facts I am about to relate speak for themselves; there is not the slightest necessity for me to embellish a narrative which has already undergone more journalistic exaggeration than any affair since the days of our old friend Louis de Rougement.

Some months elapsed before I even contemplated making an attempt to get away. Prisoners fresh over from the Islands were closely watched by the guards until they had shown themselves thoroughly amenable to discipline. So I settled down to work in a sort of tailor's shop about a mile out of the prison, where a party of thirty men were marched every day in the charge of an armed guard. I gave no trouble whatever, I did exactly as I was told, and merely went on working from day to day, taking in everything, saying nothing, living only for the time when I might be free. I regularly received money from the States; how I got it cannot be revealed here.

I was a tailor and, I have no doubt, a pretty awkward one. On the verandah where I worked stitching away I made the acquaintance of an Italian who was shortly to be released, which meant that he would still be about the settlement but that he would not to any extent be under the supervision of the guards. He was the man to whom I looked for help, and if he is alive still I would like to express here the tremendous gratitude I feel for what he did. His name does not matter; for all I know he may still be dragging out his life in Guiana, and therefore I do not want to do him any harm if it can possibly be avoided. I paid him, as far as my limited means would permit, for the service he rendered me, but after all the few francs I was able to give him were as nothing compared to what he gave me.

This Italian arranged to provide me with clothing in place of my convict dress and he also did something infinitely harder. He found a Chinaman living on the banks of the Maroni who was willing to hire us a boat by which we might cross the river.

I need hardly remark that there was quite a considerable traffic in getting prisoners into Dutch Guiana. Money was needed, of course, but provided you had that you could make reasonably sure of escaping from the settlement. Many men had done it previous to my time and a good many others have done it since. Some of them have succeeded in escaping to South America, while others reached Dutch territory and then made their way up country, where they worked in the mines and lost their identity altogether. At the time when I made my attempt, I believe, there were no arrangements in existence with the Dutch Government by which escapees could be brought back, and it is easy enough to understand the reason. Dutch Guiana, like the greater part of French Guiana, consists of wide stretches of swamp land practically uninhabitable. The only white population of any consequence was to be found in the capital of Paramaribo, and naturally the Dutch people had no particular concern in capturing men who had escaped from the well-known horrors of the French penal settlement. A good many men settled down in Dutch Guiana, married native women, and were completely forgotten. There are still numbers of them there to-day, and I don't know of any reason why they should not be permitted to enjoy the liberty they were successful in winning.

It has been stated that in the course of my escape I went away with two other men, and that I was the only man of the three to reach safety alive, as it has also been said that I got away from Devil's Island in a boat and in it reached Dutch soil. It is grossly untrue.

The idea of going by myself did not appeal to me. I was no woodsman, whatever else I might have been, and I realized the peril of trying to make my way unaided across some hundreds of miles of unknown swamp and forest. To find a companion to help me was absolutely imperative, and I looked around for some one who might accompany me. Before I left the Islands I had had many discussions with the anarchist Verdiez as to whether or not I should wait until he was sent to the mainland. He was a man of the greatest intelligence and I trusted him fully, told him of the people who were helping me, and invited him to come with me.

But he steadfastly refused, pointing out that the hue and cry after him would be so great that our chances would be reduced to a minimum. Then I fixed upon the Belgian Stoup, only to be warned by Verdiez that he was a man who would probably betray me if the worst came to the worst.

Why I decided upon Stoup was simple enough. He was a country-bred man who would probably be able to find his way without much difficulty. Verdiez had advised me to use anybody who could possibly help me, and ultimately, with a good deal of misgiving, I let the Belgian into the secret and went forward with my plans.

I wanted to slip away from the place where I worked without attracting the attention of the guard. Almost every day my thimble used to drop off the verandah. The guard became so accustomed to seeing me go down for it that he grew tired of reviling me for an awkward fool and I don't suppose for one moment that he dreamed I would shortly disappear for good.

Everything was in readiness for the escape when there came a dramatic interlude. Only the day before I intended to make off Dutch Gus arrived from the Islands to be tried for escaping. While in Kourou he had managed to get away from the guard, when he was caught by some Indians paddling off in a canoe. I saw him at Maroni when he was brought in, looking the picture of misery. He looked eagerly towards me, hoping, no doubt, that I might lend him a helping hand. But I turned away, not only desiring to have nothing further to do with him, but too full of my own hopes to bother about the man who had attempted to save his own skin at the expense of another.

The great day dawned. The clothes provided for me by the Italian were already hidden in the prison. When I rose in the morning I wore them under the convict uniform. All day long I sat on the verandah sewing away unconcernedly, watching the guard like a cat, waiting for the time when the sun would be going down. Darkness comes quickly in a tropical clime. Unless I got across the river under cover of the night my chance would be well-nigh hopeless.

It must have been about half-past four, when the hour of return to the prison was shortly due, that the opportunity I wanted came. The guard had disappeared around the other side of the building. I flung my thimble over the verandah, went down the steps after it, and like a flash vanished into the scrub. Off came my white jacket and trousers while I wondered, my heart thumping with excitement, how long it would be before the chase began.

The guard came back. I heard him say: "Hullo, where is Guerin?" and then come running towards the bushes where I lay hidden. Some one shouted out that I had gone after my thimble, and I didn't wait to hear anything further. I was off to the river as fast as my legs could carry me.

The Italian had already received the money to pay the Chinaman and would be waiting for me on the river-bank. Stoup was also to be there, the arrangement being that the Italian should row the pair of us across the river and then bring the boat back in the hope that nothing would ever be discovered.

Three hours of breathless traveling, my heart going pit-a-pat with fear, eventually brought me to the rendezvous. When I reached the Chinaman's shack I found Stoup already there, lying in a hammock with a mass of old clothes over him. There were a couple of armed guards who constantly patrolled the river front. They frequently searched all the buildings along the water side, ready to shoot at sight any escaped convict. It was just touch-and-go whether or not they found us. The moment a man escaped they took up the hunt, and woe betide you if you were caught.

But there had been no time for anything like that to happen. Stoup, already dressed in a change of clothing, complete with hat, was waiting for me. Inside of five minutes of my arrival we were being rowed across the river towards the land that would give us freedom. In the black darkness the Italian pulled us out into mid-stream, and after a journey that seemed like a month, although it could not have been more than an hour or two, we were across the river and into Dutch territory.

Truly, a momentous event in my adventurous life! Pitch dark, completely ignorant of where I was, unable to do anything then and there except wait for the dawn, I could only console myself with the thought that the gates of freedom were open and that it rested with myself whether or not I would win through.

Our Italian friend left us. We shook him warmly by the hand, thanked him in the all too insufficient words we could muster, and faithfully promised him, if the opportunity came our way, that we would one day help him as he had helped us. He wished us good luck, gave us his word that whatever happened he would not betray us, and then got into the boat again to disappear into the black night.

So there we were, the Belgian and I, two men who barely understood each other, standing in a swampy country two hundred miles from the place we were making for, mutually wondering what fate would overtake us. We knew nothing of the perils that must inevitably lie ahead. All we could do was to fight our way forward, grimly determined that we would not go back to captivity alive.

Chapter Fifteen
I WIN MY FREEDOM

Ever since the time I made my escape I have suffered under the suspicion of having killed two men who accompanied me in my flight. How the story arose needs but little explanation.

When I ultimately got back to America my old friend Pat Sheedy, whom I had known for twenty years, was the first person to greet me. He sent me on to Chicago and there, a very untrue friend, he sold to the Press a wild, lying tale that I and two other men had got away from Devil's Island in a boat, that we had put out to sea to get outside the line of communication between French and British Guiana, and that finding myself in the perilous position of being without food, I had shot dead my two companions and arrived in Dutch Guiana alone.

For the present I will say no more about that, but I would like to remark that when the Press of all Europe and America were screaming out the story of my escape, there were various improvements made from time to time, about the best of them being a tale that I had not only killed my fellow-voyagers but also, to prevent myself starving, eaten them! Even de Rougement, himself, in his wildest flights of imagination, never got so far as that.

I never escaped from Devil's Island for the simple reason that I was never on it. I got away from the penitentiaries at Maroni in exactly the same way that other men have done both before and since—the only way that is possible. To talk about three men putting out into the Atlantic in a small rowing boat, and especially out into the open sea, is arrant nonsense. I know I have been guilty of the most incredible foolishness in the course of my misspent life, but this much is certain, I escaped in the manner that gave me chance of success. Any man attempting to leave the Islands in a boat would be found in a very short space of time, added to the fact that the French officials didn't exactly give you any facilities for acquiring boats.

As to shooting dead my two companions, I might just as well explain that the Frenchmen were rather unreasonable in a matter of allowing you possession of pistols. If you posted one to-day to any friend you might happen to have in a penal settlement I don't think he would get it. I certainly received money while I was there. That was the only help I had from abroad. I had never asked for any glorification because I succeeded where so many other men had failed, and I do not consider there was anything heroic in what I did. Anything was better than rotting away your life in the swampy fastnesses of a tropical country where the flies drove you mad by day and the mosquitoes sucked your blood by night. If there was anything heroic about it, it would be to remain in a country like that.

My return to civilization did undoubtedly create a world-wide sensation, but nothing might ever have been heard of me had it not been that my friend Sheedy sought to make profit out of my misfortune. For my part I would have been fully content to return to America or England unseen and unknown. When Sheedy basely betrayed me to the extent of telling the newspapers about my return, he drove me out of the States and thence to England to avoid the extradition proceedings that were launched by the French Government. The full story of what took place I will narrate in its proper sequence.

Of all that happened when Julian Stoup, the Belgian, and myself were struggling through the forest and swamp endeavoring to reach Paramaribo a book could be written by itself. We possessed the clothes we stood up in, a little food, while I also had hidden away, unknown to my companion, a few hundred francs.

It must have been for the better part of a fortnight that we slogged our way through the marshes and creeks that abounded in Dutch Guiana. Our clothing was torn to tatters as we struggled across the rough country, daily we got soaked from head to foot fording water-logged wastes. At nighttime, under the shelter of a bivouac made by Stoup, we would lie awake in a state of fear while the wild animals of the forest came sniffing around. Gigantic snakes struck at us as we fought our way through dense patches of undergrowth. Unkempt and unshaven, our feet a mass of blisters, starving but for the tropical fruit we could pick, it was nothing short of a miracle that We ever found our way at all. Times innumerable did the Belgian have to be dragged along by me, crying out that he wanted to be left alone to die. But I still struggled on, fiercely determined, as long as I had a breath in my body, that I would win through.

It must have been about ten days after getting away that we came to a big river and saw a large flat-bottomed boat being poled down-stream by a party of Creoles and Indians. Some of the Creoles spoke French and called out to know where we were going. I daresay they were fully aware we were escaped prisoners, because when I informed them that we were on our way to Paramaribo they demanded to know my nationality. I said I was an Englishman and told them that if they would take us down the river I would give them fifty francs.

The money worked wonders. We were taken aboard and after a journey of a day and a night came to a settlement which one of the Creoles informed me was about fifteen miles from Paramaribo. There everybody disembarked and we discovered that our saviors had been on an expedition to French Guiana to obtain a supply of the native spirit, taffia, on which they immediately proceeded to get blindly and riotously drunk.

Stoup and I thought it wiser to remain in the camp all night with them, but I don't want to undergo another such experience. I thought any moment that our throats would be cut for the money they had seen in my possession. I lay awake all night holding in my hand the only weapon I possessed, a razor I had brought from Maroni which bore upon it the French Government stamp.

However, the morning came safely enough. All that could be seen was a crowd of drunken men lying around the camp snoring off the effects of their overnight dissipation.

"The sooner we get out of this," I said to Stoup, "the better it will be. We'll get a boat of our own and chance what happens."

Once again did I bless the friend in America who had sent me money. With the help of a note for a hundred francs one of the Creoles got us a canoe and in it we started off down the river in the full knowledge that we were now entering upon the most dangerous part of our journey. I had no faith in the Dutch people. I thought it long odds that if we were seen news of our whereabouts would be immediately sent to Paramaribo and that on our arrival there we should be held to wait for instructions from Cayenne. So, paddling the canoe by night, tortuously creeping along expecting any moment to be sunk by one of the numerous trees floating down the river, hiding ourselves on the edge of the river by day, we slowly struggled on. The mosquitoes at night raised huge lumps all over us, while in the daytime, hidden in the scrub, ants and stinging flies of all descriptions did their best to complete anything the mosquitoes may have left undone.

We came across a Dutch settler who wanted to know where we were going.

"Down the river," we replied.

"Where have you come from?"

"From the gold mines."

"Ach, you do not look like miners. You are escaped prisoners, yes?"

"No, no," I replied boldly. "See"—pulling out an official-looking paper—"this is my passport." As a matter of fact it was my marriage certificate, but the Dutchman couldn't read any English and left us shaking his head, fully convinced we were liars.

Then a rare stroke of luck came our way. A lumber boat came slowly crawling down the river in charge of a white man. I hailed him and to my great joy he answered me in the purest Scotch.

"What will you be doing in the middle of a country like this?" he inquired, naturally enough. "I've never heard of you before."

"Take us aboard, there's a good fellow," I said, "and I'll tell you all about everything."

I wanted to get rid of that canoe. The idea of creeping down the river at night momentarily expecting to be sunk, to say nothing of the man-eating mosquitoes, had so got on my nerves that I would have willingly undergone any risk. When I heard that broad Scotch accent and saw a big brawny fellow with good honest Briton written all over him, I could have embraced him then and there. I daresay he knew what we were, but he had his barge poled into the river-bank and took us aboard without troubling to ask any awkward questions. He told us he was on his way to a lumber camp lower down the river, the owner of which employed three or four hundred coolies cutting up the mahogany logs from the back country. I told him straight out I had a story to relate.

"Ah, that will be all right," he replied, looking at me pityingly, "don't fash yersel' now. Ye'd like a tot of whisky, no doubt," going down below and producing a bottle of something I hadn't seen for a few years.

There have not been a great many people in my life for whom I could entertain feelings of gratitude, but I would like to pay my tribute to that kind-hearted, sterling Scot who took Stoup and me down the river, and all the time tactfully forbore to ask a single awkward question. He must have known, of course, that we had come from French Guiana because the river on which we were traveling was both roadway and waterway. Bedraggled, our clothing and boots torn to pieces, our faces telling the tale of the ordeal we had gone through, it would have taken a far less shrewd man than that Scot to conclude that we had come across country fugitives from justice. However, he said nothing.

The lumber camp was indeed a big place, with hundreds of Javanese coolies busily employed. I was at once taken to the owner of the place, when, seated on the verandah of his house, I looked him straight in the eye and gave him a full account of everything that had taken place. He asked me what I had been sent to prison for and I plainly told him, attempting nothing in the way of extenuation except that I thought I had been visited with an outrageous punishment in being transported for life.

The owner—also a Scotsman—heard me through in silence and never said a word, as is the way of his race. I began to fear I had made a mistake in revealing my plight. When it was all over and I had finished my story, he thought for a long time and then said:

"Ah, weel, I'll help ye, if it does get me into trouble. Man, ye've made a sad mess of your life. Will ye not turn over a new leaf before it's too late?"

I promised that I would—and no doubt at the time I meant it. But like many more of my good resolutions, it ultimately went astray.

Before I left the place Stoup and I fell out for good. It seems that he got to plotting with a Frenchman in the camp who had quickly come to the conclusion that we were escaped men with a price on our heads. Whether the Frenchman wanted money for his silence, or whether he had told Stoup that his only hope of getting away was by himself, I do not know. One of the black overseers warned me of what was going on, and told me it would be well to keep a tight hold of my money.

Lying in a cabin one afternoon pretending to be asleep—but with an open knife in my hand—the door opened softly. A man came creeping in. Like a flash I jumped at him and had just got the point of the knife in his shoulder-blades. It was the Frenchman. With an agonized yell he flew out while I followed hot on his tracks. I didn't catch him, but later that day I saw Stoup, when there was nearly another tragedy. He denied all knowledge of any attempted robbery. But I told him then and there that I was finished with him and that from then onward he must fend for himself. Thanks to the kindness of the Scottish owner a clean suit of white duck was specially brought up from Paramaribo while I waited for a boat to take me down. It was a passenger vessel which had come down the river some considerable distance, and I went aboard looking, I trust, a perfectly respectable human being who had never done a moment's wrong. Stoup had cleared out. Where he had gone nobody knew, but I readily concluded that if he were captured it would not be long before the same fate overtook me. I leant over the side of the vessel like any ordinary passenger, waved my hand to the men who had gone out of their way to befriend me, and thus sped on the way to Paramaribo and what I hoped would be salvation.

Nobody took the slightest notice of me. I went ashore in my white ducks unnoticed, found Paramaribo to be a rambling, comfortable-looking old town dozing in the hot sunshine, and inquired my way to the residence of the English consul. He was not at home, but a clerk advised me if I was in any hurry to go and see the American consul. I did not state my business, but here again I daresay I bore in my face evidence of the truth. I was lean, hungry-looking, pitted all over with mosquito bites, and no doubt appeared an out-and-out desperado. Anyhow, I went post-haste to see the representative of the Stars and Stripes, a decent good-natured young fellow named Bradley who afterward became an officer in the American army during the Great War.

I was shown into his office and he asked me what I wanted.

"Well, in the first place," I began, cautiously sizing him up, "I want to know if you will help a man in distress."

"That all depends," he replied. "I can't tell you until I know more about the matter."

He asked me where I had come from. I told him the truth—that I had spent the greater part of my life in America, that I had been in France and got into trouble there, ending up in the sentence which had resulted in my being sent to French Guiana for life.

"H'm!" said Bradley dubiously, drawing his hand down over his chin, "you are asking me to do something. I suppose you don't need me to tell you that if I am caught helping you to get away from here I will not only lose my job but that I will also render myself liable to be prosecuted by the Dutch authorities?"

To that I could say nothing. All I could do was to look at him, mutely hoping for the best. However, he would promise me nothing immediately.

"I'll tell you what I'll do, Guerin," he said at length. "I'll put you up at the house where I live. It doesn't belong to me, but the people who rent me the rooms won't ask questions and they'll take it for granted that you are all right. But I want to warn you right here not to walk about the streets by day or to tell a soul who you are."

"You don't need to tell me that," I answered. "Just give me the chance of getting away from this town and you'll never regret it to your dying day."

Bradley's fears about my presence in Paramaribo becoming known were soon realized. He came back to the boarding-house one evening to inform me that the Dutch police had called upon him to know if it were true that he was harboring a French prisoner from Guiana.

"I've told them nothing," he explained. "They are only guessing who you are and I've put them off with a story that you are a friend of mine from the interior. They may come along to see you and they may not. The best thing you can do is to keep out of the way."

I could sympathize with him in the worry he revealed. If there was trouble he would inevitably end up in disgrace, and sooner than have that happen to him I would have cleared out to chance what happened. He was expecting his partner back from New York in the course of a few days, and until that occurred he warned me on peril of my liberty to keep myself hidden.

I had to sneak out at night to get a breath of fresh air. It was absolutely intolerable shut up in the house all day having food brought up to me for all the world like a prisoner in a cell. What with the terrific heat and the maddening anxiety of my position I nearly went off my head.

I discovered on going out one evening that I was being followed.

"They know you're here all right," said Bradley, when I told him about the matter, "but you won't be touched while I have you under my protection. They've already got a couple of Frenchmen locked up in the town awaiting extradition proceedings. We'll get you away before they can make up their mind about you."

Bradley's partner returned from New York right on time and the three of us consulted as to what should be done. I had little or no money left—nothing much more than fifty francs—and all I could do was to throw myself on the mercy of the two Americans, who, to their eternal credit, never for one single second thought of throwing me down. They asked me where I wanted to go.

"To New York," I said, "but if I can get to Demerara (in British Guiana) first I can communicate with some friends to send me some money there to pay my passage back."

"Are you likely to get it?" asked Bradley's partner. "Now that you've got this far towards home you might just as well make a certainty of it. You daren't cable in your own name and you'll be hanging about for weeks if you have to write.

"The best thing you can do," continued this prince of good fellows, "is to take a boat on to Georgetown and from there catch the *City of Quebec* to New York. We'll stand you a third-class ticket, which is the best we can do. If you get back all right you can repay us the money, but in any case it doesn't matter much if you don't."

I am not given to displaying emotion or in any way making a parade of my feelings, but on this occasion the tears did well up into my eyes as there opened before me the vision of freedom. Foolish of me, no doubt, but quite spontaneous. There are not many men in this world, however hardened, who will not respond to kindness.

I said good-bye to Bradley and his partner, sorry in one way to leave them, but full of a kind of nervous joy at the prospect of once more reaching safety. I realized, of course, that I had still a long way to go. The *City of Quebec* touched, among other ports, the French island of Martinique, and there was always the bare possibility that the boat would be searched. I could not possibly know whether the French authorities were making any strenuous efforts to bring me back.

I reached Georgetown from Paramaribo in a small coasting steamer, intending to wait there until I could get some money from New York, foolishly thinking to go back in some sort of comfort. I tried to get work, only to find that no one would employ me. The menial labor of the town was done entirely by the natives and I had no trade to make my services worth while. I can still remember the truth hitting me in the eye of how useless I was, stranded in a busy little place like Georgetown, among my own people, literally living on the verge of starvation. Believe me, I knew then that you don't win at the crooked game.

After hanging about Georgetown vainly trying to obtain employment, with nothing but a franc or two in my pocket, I gave up the idea and went aboard the *City of Quebec.* My steerage ticket took me into the company of niggers and coolies, who easily decided I was poor white trash worthy of nothing but contempt. I shouldn't have had any false pride, but it cut me to the quick, herded down below with black men, while up above in the saloon were my own race going about in lordly ease wondering, possibly, when they saw me what I had done to bring myself to the society of plantation hands traveling back to Martinique, Barbados and Trinidad after serving their time in the sugar mills of British Guiana—another illuminating example of the ignominious position to which a man brings himself through his own criminal foolishness. You haven't won anything worth speaking of, have you, when you are forced to travel in the steerage with a gang of niggers good-naturedly aware of the fact that you are down and out? The only consolation I had was the knowledge of being on my way to New York with friends awaiting me.

The *City of Quebec* called at Martinique, unloaded a few passengers and took more aboard, worked a little cargo in and out, while I lay hidden below wondering whether I would be hauled forth to captivity. I don't think they would have taken me alive. Secreted away inside my jacket I had a big knife; it would have needed a courageous man to tackle me.

But, as is always the case when you feel the worst, my fears were groundless. The boat steamed away from the tiny little harbor without anybody coming for me, and I was free to continue ruminating on the future and what was in store for me when I stepped ashore at New York.

I must have been a pretty sight. The white suit which had been bought for me in Paramaribo was filthy dirty. I had purposely gone unshaven so that I might not be easily recognized, and I daresay I bore all the signs of a man who would stick at nothing. I had a fortnight's beard on me when I ultimately arrived at New York with precisely ten cents in the world. My razor, the one relic of my prison life, I foolishly sold to one of the stewards, when I left the boat, for twenty-five cents, so that I could have something to eat. I knew at the time I did it that I was chancing my liberty, but I took the risk.

I won't attempt to describe my feelings when New York loomed up on the horizon and I realized that all my dreams had come true. A more picturesque pen than mine would be required to set down in cold print the inner feelings of a man returning from a life-long sentence of captivity to the land of his boyhood. I know that I stood against the rail of the steamer in a fever of impatience, fiercely determined that nothing would now stand between safety and me.

There was no necessity then, as there is in these days, to have a certain sum of money in your possession landing in America—which perhaps was just as well for me. The *City of Quebec* tied up right alongside Brooklyn Bridge. I was down the gangway like a shot, paid five cents to cross the bridge—another five cents to reach Broadway—and there I was, in the city I had not seen for over twenty years, penniless, homeless, but full of a joy that made me jump about like a little child.

The very first thing I did was to go into a saloon and order myself a long glass of beautiful cool bock. I had another, a bite of food off the free-lunch counter, and went out absolutely stone-cold broke.

Then I bestirred myself to find some of my friends. I called at an hotel in Seventh Avenue where Pat Sheedy used to stay, only to find, as I expected, that he was out. I was sitting in the lounge writing him a letter when he came in and absolutely jumped ceilingwards in astonishment when he saw me.

"Eddie!" he shouted. "By the Holy Ghost, you've got back after all!"

He grabbed me by the hand and wrung it until he nearly pulled my arm out. I never saw a man so excited in my life.

"Come upstairs," he cried; "we'll have a bottle of champagne on this and you shall tell me all about it."

Talk we did—or at least I did—all through the morning. Lunch was brought to us upstairs and then Pat took me out downtown to buy me some clothes so that I might once more appear a decently clad citizen of the United States. What I looked like in my grubby ducks I can't imagine; a plucky man was wanted to be seen walking down the street with me.

What a wonderful feeling it is to be back in civilization with new clothes on your body, money in your pocket and a cigar in your mouth! My only anxiety was that the story of my escape might get into the American papers, when, of course, anything might happen to me. I remained in New York for some days at Pat's expense enjoying myself in a way that I have never experienced before or since. The novel sensation of it made the captivity almost worth while.

I left Sheedy on the understanding that I would go to Chicago to look up some of my old friends, and particularly Hinky Dink, who I knew would help me to a fresh start. Pat gave me a hundred dollars to see me on my way, shook hands with me, and never gave me the slightest inkling of how he had betrayed me. I nearly dropped dead with astonishment on reaching Chicago when I saw newspaper placards on the street with the picture of a man dressed as a convict paddling a canoe. The letterpress read:

GUERIN'S
SENSATIONAL ESCAPE
FROM
DEVIL'S ISLAND.

I read the story that was printed, a highly colored sensational account of how I had escaped from Devil's Island—which was quite untrue—with a long and fanciful tale of the blowing up of the American Express Company, the trial, and sentence of transportation for life, with a lot more dragged in about Captain Dreyfus and other men who had been in prison on the Île du Diable.

I didn't care a damn for the lies. It struck me like a blow over the heart to realize that my escape had now been blazoned forth to the entire world and that I would be a very lucky man indeed, if I succeeded in dodging the extradition that was bound to be demanded. Later, after I had met Bill Pinkerton in Chicago, I discovered how the story had leaked out. Immediately he had left me in New York, Pat Sheedy rushed round to a newspaper office and thought it worth while to sell for a paltry fifteen hundred dollars a man who had been a friend for twenty-odd years. Even Bill Pinkerton himself, who ran the Chicago branch of the famous detective agency, would have nothing to do with sending me back to the horrors of French Guiana. He was approached about the matter, some one saying to him:

"Do you know Eddie Guerin is back?"

"Yes, I do," replied Bill, "and I wouldn't lift a hand to hurt him. He has suffered more than enough for what he has done."

This, mind you, from one of the protectors of the American Express Company! Bill Pinkerton wasn't a man who often excited himself. But on this occasion he went out of his way to tell the individual who suggested that I should be sent back to captivity, that he wouldn't send a dog to a place like Devil's Island. Bill, like everybody else, had read all about the treatment to which Dreyfus had been subjected, and I daresay he agreed, as did the bench of English judges who afterward decided my fate, that whatever I had done it was not sufficiently bad to condemn me to a poisonous hole where men rotted away and were never heard of for evermore.

I don't know even now whether Pat Sheedy considered the full effects of what he had done, or if he even realized that it might mean going back to drag out the remainder of my life in chains. What I do know for certain is that I never spoke to him again.

Chapter Sixteen
A WOMAN SCORNED

I am not the man to whine. I had made my bed and fate, willy-nilly, compelled me to lie on it. But it was certainly brought home to me in full, when I returned to Chicago in the summer of 1905, what a heavy price I might yet have to pay for the crimes of the past.

The few friends I had left were aghast when they realized the probable effect of the sensational stories that were printed every day concerning my escape. I also knew that it would be utterly impossible for me to settle down again in Chicago. I went and saw the pal of my boyhood days, Hinky Dink, now one of the most prosperous men in Chicago. Loyalty to my old friend forbids me to relate the extent to which I am indebted to him for my freedom. But I do know this—he is the last man in the world to expect any printed acknowledgment of gratitude for the good he has done in the world.

I saw him at his big saloon, up to his eyes in work, but tremendously glad to welcome me once more. I had strained his friendship in a way that he would have tolerated from few men, but nevertheless he shook me warmly by the hand, pulled me into his office where we could talk privately, and requested that I should relate to him the full details of everything that had taken place, and how it had come about that the story of my return was now being shouted out by the Press for all the world to hear.

I can see Hinky now, looking at me reflectively with his shrewd but kindly eyes, as he pulled hard on a cigar.

"Well," he remarked at last, when I had reached the end of my tale, "it's made things a bit awkward. You are getting on in life now and it's just about time you settled down to something that won't land you in prison again.

"You can take it from me, Eddie, that hard work is the best in the end, and you'll certainly get more money at it than at the jobs you've been doing. What you have just been through ought to be a lesson to you for the remainder of your life. You've brought off a million-to-one chance."

I knew, of course, that Hinky was quite right. But to me it seemed hopeless to turn over a new leaf at forty-five years of age. To be quite truthful, I couldn't tackle hard work, just the same as I realized that I had no trade by which I might earn a decent living.

I daresay Hinky Dink knew everything that was passing through my mind and in all probability he knew I would never go straight. As we were parting he gave me two hundred and fifty dollars and told me to have a look round Chicago to see if I couldn't find something to keep me out of mischief.

I remained in the city for about a month untroubled by the police. Most of the old-timers with whom I had been acquainted had retired and I suppose the new men thought it would be only fair to give me a chance to behave.

But one day Hinky Dink sent for me, locked the office door when I got there, his face telling me that there was more trouble ahead.

"Eddie," he said, "I've got bad news for you. The French Ambassador in Washington has made application to the State Department to have you sent back to France. I've had the tip from the police captain that you will have to be arrested.

"Now," he went on, "you'll have to get out of the country quick. It's no good your stopping here, and I can't possibly help you the moment the State Department grants the warrant. You'd better get across into Canada. I'll give you some more money and see what I can do for you when you are over the border."

I am no coward, but it will be foolish of me to deny the fear I felt at the idea of going back to French Guiana to drag out the remainder of my life in captivity, shackled, starved, maltreated in every possible way. The privations I had already undergone had made me as thin as a lath. I still felt the effects of my prison life, just the same as I was beginning to appreciate what a misspent life really means when you are approaching middle age. I had plenty of aunts, uncles and cousins in Chicago, but none of them wanted to have anything to do with me. For help of any sort I could only depend on a friend like Hinky Dink. Most of the men I knew had long ago drifted away from their home town. Some were in England, many of them were in prison. And in any case they were no good to me. Above all things, it was absolutely imperative that I got out of Chicago posthaste.

The newspapers were still supplying their readers with lurid details of my escape when I cleared out and safely made my way into Canada. The Chicago police had already received instructions to arrest me, but I don't think they made any serious attempt to find me. I am not cadging for sympathy, but I will say this: there was a strong feeling throughout the United States of America that the privations I had suffered in making my escape were such as to arouse a certain amount of admiration. Often of a night in Chicago had I heard people discussing my case and saying that I deserved to go free.

I planted myself in Toronto for something like six months, using a false name and being careful to do nothing that would bring me in conflict with the police. I tried my hardest to get work, but no one would employ me, for the all-important reason that I had no trade.

Not for all the money in the world would I go through such another period of tension. A man under sentence of death could experience no greater misery than the suspense of living from day to day never knowing when he might fall into the hands of the police and eventually find himself doomed to lifelong imprisonment.

Friends in Chicago kept me supplied with money and regularly wrote to me urging that I should find employment of some kind or another. The only work I could possibly obtain was manual labor of a type I could not do. And so it went on until the strain nearly drove me insane. I determined to get back to England and chance what happened.

By way of Montreal and Nova Scotia I travelled to Liverpool and thence on to London. A cautious look round the West End for some of my old friends revealed that most of them had disappeared. But Chicago May was about, the French authorities having released her from prison after she had served about two and a half of her five years. The tale went, according to May, that a prison doctor had succumbed to her fascinations and had ordered her release on the grounds that she was in bad health. That was what May said; I never came across a woman in all my life who possessed such an exaggerated idea of her own attractions.

At all events, I decided that London was none too healthy for me just then. Besides, I had firmly resolved to steer clear of crime and the possibility of falling into the hands of Scotland Yard, knowing full well that once the French Government were apprised of my whereabouts application would be made for my extradition. The experience of 1888 had taught me one lesson; I didn't want another fight like the one I had then.

What did I do? I went up North, to Leeds, where I found a job at the only trade I had ever learnt. I became, for the time being, a tailor. It wasn't what I would call congenial work for a man who had done things that had set the world aflame with excitement. The men I worked with pretty soon sized me up, but I stuck at it for three months, stitching away and wondering day after day how long it would be before my good resolutions cracked. There was nothing in the English papers to worry me, but I found it utterly impossible to stand the strain of slaving away in a tailor's workshop for two or three pounds a week, with nothing to do of a night except drinking around the public-houses in the company of men I despised. So, towards the end of February, 1906, I threw down my needle and thread and made off to London, not caring very much what happened.

I did not go near my old haunts in the West End for some little time. For a week or two I lived in North London and also in Shepherd's Bush, wandering about scrambling for a living as best I could. Occasionally I ran across old friends who nearly dropped dead with astonishment when they saw the man whom they believed to be imprisoned for life on Devil's Island walking about the streets of London. Nevertheless, they were all glad to see me, but I have no doubt that the news of my return got around and incidentally paved the way for other and still more dramatic events.

I also discovered that during my imprisonment three or four men had been arrested in London putting down the checks stolen from the American Express Company and that they were now doing time thereby. The extraordinary part of the affair was that all of them were strangers to me, so I could only conclude that they must have been working with Chicago May, Dutch Gus, or Kid McManus. One of them was an old flame of May's, picked up after I had been captured on the train to England. There was just the possibility, of course, that there might still be a bit of money knocking about and I made a few discreet inquiries.

Unfortunately, as it turned out, these inquiries inevitably led me to Chicago May. I had been in London for a week or two when I went one day into a public-house in Great Portland Street, the Horse and Groom. There, sitting down in the saloon bar, whom should I find but May? She rushed over the moment she saw me.

"My God! Eddie," she cried, "I am glad to see you."

She had not heard of my return to England, and for quite a time she couldn't contain herself. I particularly want to emphasize the fact that she didn't know of my whereabouts because she has recently been informing the world that it was she who arranged my escape. She had nothing whatever to do with the matter, although that is neither here nor there.

For my part, I wasn't particularly anxious to see the lady. However, we had a drink together, when she took the opportunity of pitching me a pitiful story of all the woes and troubles that had overtaken her since we had been in Paris in 1901.

"Well," I said, giving her a critical look over, "you don't look so bad on it?"

To be quite truthful, May's story was sadly belied by her appearance. She wore an expensive dress. Her hair was peroxided as brilliantly as of old, in fact, she looked to me very much like a well-groomed bird. The last time I had seen her, of course, was in the dock in France. Here she was, drinking in a London public-house, apparently as young as ever.

I couldn't calm her excitement. She demanded to know all the details of my escape, what had happened to Dutch Gus, had I heard from Kid McManus, what was I going to do in the future, and a million other things. One after another she lowered whisky and sodas, interspersed with an occasional brandy to calm her fluttering heart, while I, also becoming a little softened by the liquor, began to delude myself that poor old May wasn't quite so bad as I thought.

May herself had a bit of a story to relate. She had made up to the prison doctor, successfully kidded him that she had water on the knee, and extracted from him a promise that if he ordered her release she would marry him. I had to laugh when I heard this, which rather annoyed May, but she soon recovered and went on to relate that the authorities had nipped this little idea in the bud by promptly deporting her as soon as she was set free. That, however, didn't worry May. She meant to go back to France and find the enamored old gentleman, confident that if he wouldn't marry her, at any rate she would get some money out of him.

She wanted to know if I could help her.

"I'm not a doctor," I said.

"Ah, but you are clever, Eddie. You know how to manage women." This with a languorous look telling me as plainly as a woman could tell that she loved me as well as ever.

Well, I've been a damn fool all my life, and once more under the influence of booze I did something I afterward bitterly regretted. I again took May to live with me and resumed the old life of six years before. There were several little schemes I had on foot. One was a Continental tour—not embracing France, I may say—in company with my old friend Ed Rice. May persuaded me to take her with me, the idea being that she should have her water on the knee cured by a course of treatment at the baths in Aix-la-Chapelle.

I must have been suffering from water on the brain to have consented. But anyhow, I took her with me, all the time hating myself for associating with her. Once or twice, in reflective moments, I used to cast my eyes over her and ask myself what on earth any man could see in her. I suppose I am the last man in the world who ought to be fastidious, but when I looked at May, even then beginning to get a bit coarse and blowsy, it began to dawn on me that she might grow to be a bit of a nuisance. In her early days, I believe, she had been a dishwasher, and she certainly possessed a pair of hands like a prizefighter. There was no doubt that she could fight like a man; some of the policemen who had had cause to arrest her had occasionally received a good deal more than they had ever bargained for.

I used to meet her at the baths at Aix-la-Chapelle when she was coming out. One day, going as usual to pick up the lady, I discovered to my intense astonishment that she was not alone in the baths. The attendant informed me that the fair May was in the company of a wealthy old gentleman with whom she seemed to be getting on famously.

"All right," I replied, "you may tell Madame that I shall not wait for her."

May was very indignant when she made her appearance.

"What's the matter with you?" she inquired. "Can't I pick up an old guy without you kicking up a row? I've got to live somehow."

"The best thing you can do," I said, "is to pack your bag and get back to London as soon as you can. I've had enough of you. You're no sooner in one man's company than you begin to look round for another. I've been a damn fool ever to trust you again. You tried it with 'Dutch Gus' and now you're at it once more."

May, like most ladies of her profession, was never satisfied with one man. Her idea of a good time was to have half a dozen of them fighting for her favors, and I might just as well admit that I didn't think enough of them to get into any trouble. So we had words, most of which won't bear repeating. The upshot of the matter was that May returned to London while Ed Rice and I went on to Berlin. I didn't dream that she would ever go to the length of doing what she did.

I had returned to London myself about the end of April, 1906, when I met a friend of May's named Emily Skinner. She showed me a letter from May, in which the lady said that she was sticking to me because she knew I was sure to get hold of some money on the Continent.

It was quite an informative little epistle. It went on to say that after I had got hold of money she, May, was going to play me up in London, and suggested that she and Emily should get me drunk, rob me of all my money, and then inform Scotland Yard that the man who had escaped from French Guiana was back in London. Quite a pretty little scheme!

Emily Skinner didn't in the least approve—nor did I.

"You'll have to help me in this," I told her. "I'll give her (May) something she'll remember to her dying day."

That very night, in the Hotel Provence, I met May and Emily, made no mention of what had happened in the past, and apparently became as drunk as a lord. There were half a dozen of us drinking together, but I remained as sober as a judge. Most of the booze that came my way I emptied on the floor while May, growing more and more flushed, and more repellent than I had ever imagined possible, kept casting at me glances that told me more plainly than words that Emily Skinner's tale was true.

About midnight we made a move, the intention being to go to Emily's flat in Kenton Street, Bloomsbury. I don't know for certain, but I think quite likely that I might have been murdered that night had the opportunity come May's way. I do know that she had a pistol in her possession and that if the worst came to the worst she would have shot me dead, locked up the flat, and left it to chance what happened. In all probability the police would not have troubled about the matter, because they would have known it to have been a vendetta of some sort not worth worrying about.

However, I had all my wits about me and I think I successfully deluded May with the idea that I was ready to let bygones be bygones. We were quite a loving couple when we took our departure from the Provence, and remained affectionate until we reached Emily's flat. As soon as we got into the dining-room I showed her her mistake. Quick as lightning I locked the door, put the key in my pocket.

"Now," I began to the astonished May, "you thought you were going to do me in, did you? Get all my money and then give me away to the police. I've seen your letter to Emily and I know all about the matter."

May collapsed in a fright. Cowering, she lay in an arm-chair with the fear jumping out of her eyes. She must have expected me to murder her, and I was undoubtedly in that maddened mood when I would have committed any crime. The wonder was that the noise of my shouting did not bring some one hammering on the door.

"Take off that sealskin coat," I yelled at her. "Take off that dress you are wearing and tell your thieving friends or anyone else you like that the fellow who gave you these things is taking them away again because you are a dirty damned traitoress of the worst type."

I didn't wait for her to take them off. I tore them from her body, gave her a thrashing which I wager she still remembers, and then flung her outside the door.

"Now," I shouted after I had finished with her, "you can go and tell the police all about me and tell them to go to hell with you. I'm leaving the country now and I don't care a curse what happens."

In all likelihood the flat I was in—one of many in a neighborhood notorious among the women of the West End— had seen and heard many such scenes as the one May and I had that fateful April night. No one took the slightest notice of May's screams and I cleared out of the place in a mad, fighting mood when I would have readily killed anybody who attempted to bar my way. But, as is so often the case, not a single thing occurred. I went back to the lodgings I occupied while May got some clothes from somewhere and hurriedly made her way to the Tottenham Court Road Police Station where she saw the celebrated Detective Inspector Kane and told him a story which I have no doubt set the police telephones buzzing all over London. And I daresay the wires between London and Paris were equally busy.

I never seriously thought that May would fulfil her threat of sending me back to prison, which only goes to show how little I knew her true, vindictive nature. In the course of our fight at Kenton Street she had screamed out that she would send me back to Devil's Island to die like a dog while I, no doubt, had told her a few other choice things about herself which must have bitten deep even into the treacherous nature of a double-dyed harlot.

A couple of days after the affair I was walking down Oxford Street, London, early in the morning, when I met a friend who literally jumped with astonishment.

"Good heavens, Eddie," he exclaimed, "how is it you're about?"

I thought he was referring to my escape from prison and proceeded to tell him how I had got away. But he pulled me up short.

"Don't you know," he said, "that in yesterday's French papers there was a report that you were in London and that you were going to be extradited to France?"

It was my turn to be astonished—and also intensely dismayed. Having heard nothing more about my case ever since I had landed in England I had thought that the French Government were bothering no more about me. I didn't wait to say any more just then but immediately rushed down into Soho to a foreign newsagent's where I often bought French papers. If I had stopped for a moment and thought I might have come to the conclusion that it was one of the most dangerous places in London for me to visit.

Why? It didn't even hit my addled brain, so thunderstruck was I, that Chicago May had carried out the threat she had screamed at me of betraying me to the police, and if that was the case the paper shop in Soho was dangerous, because she knew I was in the habit of going there.

But I didn't dream of my peril. I hurried off to the shop in Charlotte Street—it was only two or three minutes' walk away—went inside and bought the *Petit Parisien* and *Le Matin,* exchanged a word or two in French with the woman behind the counter, came outside, when—crash! three burly policemen jumped upon me, whipped a pair of handcuffs on me before I knew where I was, and informed me—quite unnecessarily—that I was in custody.

"What the hell is this for?" I panted. "Can't a man buy a paper without a bunch of coppers jumping on him?"

A crowd gathered like wildfire. The policemen started to drag me up the street and in reply to my expostulations would only say that I was wanted.

"What for?" I demanded, struggling like a lunatic. I knew pretty well what I was wanted for. It didn't require any special intelligence for me to realize that unless I got out of their clutches soon I was due for another trip to the Islands. Fighting, kicking, biting, I was hustled into a cab and taken to the police station in Tottenham Court Road, where I found Kane awaiting me.

I knew him, of course, just as well as he knew me.

"Well, Eddie," he said to me grimly, "we've caught you again. You know what it is for."

"I don't know anything about it," I replied, still panting. "You've had me dragged in here for nothing and I want to know the reason."

"I'll tell you," explained Kane, "though there is really no necessity. The French Government has applied to Central to have you arrested for escaping from prison. Don't blame me; I'm only doing my duty. You'll be extradited, and that, as far as I am concerned, is all there is to it."

"I don't think I shall," I retorted.

"But you were sent back before," said Kane.

"Quite right, but if I knew then what I know now I would never have gone."

Kane only smiled, at which I told him that I had to congratulate him on being the instrument of the law to send a fellow-being back to a human hell-hole, and I daresay I added, without any unnecessary equivocation, a few pungent words to the effect that he might enjoy a similar fate. I also told him—and he did not deny it—that it was Chicago May who had given him the information which had resulted in my arrest.

However, my passionate protests had no effect. I was thrust into a cell, left by myself for the day, and then, the following morning, taken to Bow Street Police Station where the Chief Magistrate of England opened the hearing of what was destined to be an epoch-making case.

Chapter Seventeen
MY CELEBRATED EXTRADITION CASE

I have mentioned in an earlier part of this book the pitiful pride which a prisoner feels in making his cell one of the show spots of the jail. In much the same way I can still take a certain amount of pleasure in the thought that the tremendous fight I put up against the French Government from April 29, 1906, to June 14, 1907, is now an historic event in the annals of the British law.

It is utterly unfair, of course, to take any particular credit myself. The man I have to thank was a stern-natured, clever Scottish lawyer named Richard Muir, who for eight months, tooth and nail, fought the extradition proceedings like a terrier. He won in the end because he would not be beaten. He is dead now, after a long and eminently honorable career, and I can only take this opportunity of tendering to him the grateful thanks of the man whom he saved from rotting away his life amid the fever-stricken swamps of French Guiana.

The fight for my liberty opened at Bow Street and went on for the greater part of a week without any definite decision being come to. One of my friends who was allowed to see me told me that a solicitor named G. W. Ricketts, who did a great deal of police work at Clerkenwell, would be a good man to have charge of my case. I certainly wanted a lawyer of that sort, knowing, as I did, how much I had at stake. So I sent for him and asked him who was the best barrister I could get. I suggested Charles Gill, who had previously appeared for me at the time of the Lyons robbery in 1888.

Gill, however, probably because he had not been successful before, refused to take the case. There then came into the matter an Irishman who seemed to have a good deal of sympathy for me. He was what they call in Ireland a "broth of a boy," breezy, confident and about him the genial manner that only an

Irishman can assume. As a matter of fact, he came from the same part of Ireland as my father and knew him well.

"Well, Guerin," he said, "ye're just loike your father. Oi'll get ye out of this in next to no time."

I didn't altogether believe him, nevertheless I felt grateful and only hoped he would be as good as his word. Bitter experience had taught me that once you were in the hands of the English police it was a none too easy matter to get out. My Irish friend informed me that he would come to court and give evidence to the effect that my father remained a British subject throughout the whole of his life, even when he was in the States. It appears that he had gone to America at the same time as my father, but had returned to his native land shortly afterward.

He advised me to get hold of a well-known Irish lawyer, Long John O'Connor, to plead my case, and I did so, dead against the advice of my solicitor. The proceedings had been going on for something like six months, during which time I had been kept locked up in Brixton Prison bitterly cursing myself for the folly that had ever made me have anything to do with Chicago May again. I knew by that time who had played the traitor. Emily Skinner continually visited me in prison and kept me fully posted as to what was transpiring outside.

The time came when the Bow Street magistrate had to say yes or no to the application for my extradition. Long John got up in court and started to talk. He told the magistrate that my name was Irish and that I was Irish. Then, with one of those dramatic gestures which he probably thought would have been made by Daniel O'Connell, he put me into the witness-box.

"Ye're British, are ye not, Guerin?"

"Oi am," I replied in my best Irish accent.

Evidently the magistrate did not regard me as an impartial witness on that score. He rudely interrupted the peroration Long John was beginning to deliver by demanding to know whether I had any witnesses. I said I had, but Long John waved his hand in a lordly fashion and said: "Oi am not callin' them, your worship."

That didn't suit me at all. I had a pretty good idea that on my own testimony I hadn't a dog's chance. I took the liberty of interrupting Long John by telling the magistrate that an Irish M.P.—with plenty of emphasis on the M.P.—was anxious to come to court and give evidence to the effect that I was a British subject.

"And now," I added, "Mr. O'Connor won't let him come forward."

The magistrate refused to listen to me.

"You've had plenty of opportunity to call any witnesses you wanted," he replied. "This case has dragged on for many months and I don't intend it shall go on any longer. I will make an order granting the application for your extradition."

It was indeed a stunning blow. Locked up in the cell at Bow Street awaiting the time when I would be taken back to Brixton Gaol I was miserably ruminating on all my folly of the past when the door opened and I saw Emily Skinner there. She, poor creature, faithful to her friends as are so many women of the underworld, had come to tell me that she had seen Long John, who had curtly informed her that it would be no use appealing from the decision of the magistrate.

"You can tell O'Connor to go to the devil," I retorted. "I know what the law in this matter is, if he doesn't. I am a British subject and before I am finished I shall prove it."

Next morning at Brixton Ricketts came to see me, and on this occasion, with things in a much more serious state, we discussed the pros and cons of the case with a view to appeal to the High Court. I had no intention of going back to France until I had exhausted every possible stratagem of the law.

"I think you have just one hope," said Ricketts. "I have been to Gill and he will have nothing to do with your case. But there is another very well-known man named Muir. He is generally for the prosecution and he is about the toughest man at the Bar to get over. If I can get him to appear for you I think you have got a first-class fighting chance."

Ricketts also told me one or two things which greatly comforted me. One of them was that there was no fear of Sir Edward Clarke appearing for the Crown. Clarke was the man who had got me sent back in 1888, as I still firmly believe, dead against the law. I will prove my words in narrating the events that took place when Richard Muir, together with Ricketts, pulled off his coat to fight what they both believed to be a grossly illegal demand for extradition. And what wasn't extradition law in 1888 wasn't law in 1906.

I had no huge sums of money to offer Muir. The only way Ricketts could approach him was from the point of view of humanity and it was on that score that Muir agreed to appeal on my behalf to the High Court. He told Ricketts that the first thing I should do was to obtain all the information possible as to the birthplace of both my father and my mother, and also ascertain definitely whether or not my father, on going to Chicago, had ever renounced his British nationality. The great difficulty was that all the records of Chicago had been destroyed in the great fire of 1871. In the meantime Muir went to the King's Bench of Judges and applied for a Writ of Habeas Corpus to have me brought up in court pending the result of his investigations in the United States.

I will not unnecessarily weary the readers of this story with a repetition of the tediously drawn-out proceedings that lasted for nearly eight months while all the time I lay in Brixton Prison eating out my heart. Day by day, week by week, month by month, I saw fresh faces come and go, while all the time the fight for my body went on. Brixton, of course, was, and still is, only a remand prison, and until you are finally disposed of you are allowed the privilege of a special cell, that is, if you have the money, and also to get your food from outside. In an ordinary way I would have done the fourteen months I was locked up without worrying, but it gnawed at my vitals night and day to think that the end of it all might be Devil's Island for the remainder of my life.

I spent hours and hours of my time writing out for Muir all that I could remember of my father and mother, and of everything that transpired in my early days in Chicago. I had always been led to believe that I was born in Hoxton. This much is quite certain. In the days of my extreme boyhood I was known in America as "Cockney Guerin," conclusive proof of the fact that everybody regarded me as a Londoner. Naturally, all the information with which I supplied Muir and Ricketts had to be corroborated, and something like eight months elapsed before the case finally came up for decision before what is known as the King's Bench Divisional Court. It is a court usually presided over by the Lord Chief Justice of England sitting with two other judges, and on June 14, 1907, before a court crowded to suffocation, there came up the matter of The King *v.* The Governor of Brixton Prison—*ex parte* Guerin.

Seated on the Bench, clad in their gorgeous scarlet robes trimmed with ermine, were the three judges, the severe, handsome Lord Alverstone, Lord Chief Justice of England, the more human-looking Mr. Justice Darling, whose reputation as a criminal lawyer was second to none in England, and the typical legal manner as personified by Mr. Justice A. T. Lawrence, kind-hearted, anxious only to do the right thing.

I had already done a number of things which might have got me into serious trouble. On my own responsibility I had written to both the Home Secretary and the Earl of Dysart, who held the office of Director of Public Prosecutions, saying that I had been the victim of a prostitute's jealousy and that the police had gone out of their way to have me arrested. However, I presume the authorities took no notice of my indiscretions in that direction.

Many other things had happened during the time I was lying at Brixton. One Sunday morning while attending church service a man with an American accent made himself known to me. He was only a young fellow, who told me his real name was Cubine Jackson, adding that he had given the police the name of Charles Smith. Scotland Yard detectives had arrested him in the neighborhood of Park Lane for suspicious behavior, and on taking him to the police station found a pair of nippers on him. I daresay he had heard all about me—one of the penalties of being famous, or infamous, whichever you like. He wanted to know, this human skunk, whether I could help him out of his trouble. It seemed that the Marlborough Street magistrate, aware of the fact that he had already served four years' penal servitude in Africa for house-breaking, had sent him to the London Sessions to be tried by a jury.

Foolishly, never for one moment suspecting any evil, I gave him the advice to tell Sir Robert Wallace, the judge at the

Sessions, that he had got into bad company and if he could only get another chance he would immediately go back to America and give the police of England no more trouble. Sir Robert Wallace, of course, is the kindest-hearted judge in England. He has saved more men from becoming confirmed criminals than all the other judges put together. I am quite sure that if I had known him in my younger days I would never have gone wrong for good. He has a way of talking to the man in the dock that makes the prisoner thoroughly ashamed of himself. And it pleases me to add my humble tribute to such a man, and also to hope that he will long be spared to administer justice as he sees it.

I even went to the length of writing out for this Cubine Jackson what he should say to Sir Robert Wallace. Evidently it was pretty effective because, to the great mystification, and not a little annoyance, of the police, Jackson was bound over to be of good behavior for twelve months. How he utilized the liberty I obtained for him and how he paid his debt to me I will narrate in due course.

He had heard all about my case, as had everybody in the prison. To all intents and purposes I had become one of the fixtures. Every remand going in and out knew all about the Devil's Island man. Cubine Jackson and I became very friendly. I told him more frankly than I had ever told anyone except my lawyers exactly what had happened with Chicago May, and I daresay I added, without any unnecessary disguise of words, that if I ever got out of prison alive I would surely kill her.

Jackson, for his part, told me a few things. Being an American, he also had the honor of May's acquaintance, and he informed me that May had spoken to him about me, adding, if I did succeed in getting out of prison that she would shoot me, with a few other lurid details which need not be mentioned. What Jackson and I said to each other in prison subsequently became very important. I shall not detail the matter here; instead I shall relate the dramatic end of the proceedings in the High Court when I stood in an improvised dock with the Governor of Brixton Prison at my side and my heart thumping up and down waiting to hear my fate.

Never, I beg of any boy thinking of committing a crime, expose yourself to that awful ordeal of waiting in a court not knowing whether you are going to lifelong imprisonment or whether you will ever be free again. Want of courage I never had, but I will confess to dying a thousand deaths that beautiful June day in the year 1907 when I sat in the Law Courts in the Strand wondering whether the day would see me free or back in a cell awaiting the time to be sent over to France, and thence to Devil's Island for evermore.

Well, if there is one thing about the law of England worthy of admiration it is the impressive manner in which important cases are conducted. High over the heads of the three grave-faced judges were the Royal Arms of England, while down below the Bench there was an equally awe-inspiring array of bewigged and begowned barristers who had crowded into the court to hear the decision of the judges.

Tense drama if you like! As I sat down in the little dock, the cynosure of all eyes, I felt an odd thrill of pride that I, Eddie Guerin, should have been the cause of all this imposing gathering of the law. Nobody seemed to feel the slightest animosity towards me; if anything, every person with whom I came in contact seemed to be sympathetically inclined. Dozens of people, including even the warders at Brixton, had wished me good luck.

Muir himself had no doubt about the result, and as I looked at his strong, clever face and listened to his cold, confident voice all my doubts disappeared. He intended to present my case in a manner that would shift the onus of proving my nationality, not on the defense, but on the prosecution.

The Attorney-General of England opened the proceedings and in a profound silence told the court that I had been arrested at the instance of the French Embassy for breaking prison, that offense being within the Extradition Act of 1870. I, the prisoner, alleged that I was a British subject because I was born in Hoxton, and after my counsel had obtained the order to produce me in court permission had been received to collect fresh evidence in Chicago, with the result that witnesses had been examined and cross-examined before the British Consul of that city. Apparently, said the Attorney-General, the order was procured with the object of showing that my alleged British nationality did not rest on my birth in Hoxton, but on the fact of my father being a British subject.

Here Muir interrupted and said that he had applied for permission to take evidence in America on the ground that my father was a British subject who had never lost his nationality. The Attorney-General admitted that under certain sections of the Extradition Act of 1870 nationals were not extraditable.

With that opening presented to him, Muir proceeded to detail the result of his long and arduous investigations in Chicago. He stated that my father was named Edmund Guerin, and that he was born in Knockany Parish, County Limerick, on June 11th, 1824. Somewhere between 1854 and 1857 he left his home in Ireland and arrived in Chicago, where he married a widow named Fox.

In 1859 or 1860 the self-same Edmund Guerin and his wife came to Europe, leaving behind them in Chicago a boy named Patrick Guerin, who was my eldest brother. From 1860, the date of the outbreak of the Civil War in America, until 1867, my parents were not in Chicago and there was every reason to believe, apart from whatever value might have been placed on the testimony of the witnesses who previously stated that I had first seen the light of day in Hoxton, that I could not possibly have been born in Chicago. My parents returned, accompanied by me, in 1867, and evidently my speech was so peculiar that I was at once nicknamed "Cockney Guerin."

"It rested with the Crown," said Muir emphatically, "to prove that there was any change of nationality on the part of Edmund Guerin. He had always refused to vote at the elections in the United States.

"My case," he concluded, "is that the prisoner's father having been a natural born British subject, the onus is on the Crown to show that he had changed his nationality, there being in fact evidence that he never did change it."

The Attorney-General made no attempt whatever to influence the Bench. He agreed with Muir that there was strong evidence that my father would not vote and would only say that it was the Court to decide whether it could be accepted. He could not suggest any reason why it should not, as he had no evidence to meet it.

Then, deliberately, in a densely-packed court where you could almost have heard a pin drop, the three judges conferred. After a few minutes they resumed their seats and the Lord Chief Justice gave judgment. He did it so quietly, and so unassumingly, that I had to strain my ears to catch his fateful words.

"There is a large body of evidence," he said, "that the prisoner's father always said he was a British subject and for that reason persistently declined to vote in America under considerable pressure, and the onus rested on the Crown to prove naturalization. That had not been proved, and, therefore, the prisoner was a British subject, and this rule must be made absolute."

I did not understand the actual meaning of the Lord Chief Justice's concluding words. "Rule absolute" was to me so much double-Dutch. I sat blankly staring at the Bench wondering what it all meant while the lawyers were hurrying out of court. The bewilderment I felt must have expressed itself in my face, because Mr. Justice Darling looked over to me, called one of the ushers, and said to him: "Tell the prisoner he is discharged."

God! I couldn't believe my ears when the usher told me I was free to go. I had to ask him again and again if it were true.

"Yes," he replied, "they can't take you back to prison now. Get your things and clear out as quick as you can."

I had no words at my command to express fully the tremendous joy I felt as I hurried out of the Law Courts that day. Think of it, lying for fourteen months expecting all the time to go back to purgatory, sleeping and waking only with the thought of the fate before you, suddenly to find yourself flung free into the world! I don't know what my face showed. Muir, I believe, subsequently said that it lit up with the most unspeakable relief he had ever seen in any man's face and I daresay he spoke nothing but the bare truth.

A crowd of newspaper reporters held me up as I got out into the Strand. Unceremoniously I pushed them on one side, jumped into a cab, and drove off to Emily Skinner's flat in Kenton Street, where my few belongings had been left. It didn't greatly trouble me whether they were still there or not. I had my freedom, which was the only thing in the world that mattered. I wasn't even thinking of Chicago May.

Chapter Eighteen
CHICAGO MAY'S VENGEANCE

Now comes what might be aptly described as the grand climax of my adventurous life. When I got back to the flat I found Emily Skinner waiting for me, overjoyed at my release and full of news of a rather ominous nature. It appeared that after Cubine Jackson, or, as he was generally known, Charlie Smith, had been released from prison he had gone to Chicago May and repeated to her all our conversation in Brixton. May, cunning as they make them, had soon extracted the full story.

According to what she had told Emily Skinner, it was my life or hers. I had told Charlie Smith—according to May—I would either shoot her or burn out her eyes with vitriol. I can quite believe she expected something to happen to her. My name would not have been Eddie Guerin if I had calmly stood the diabolical trick she had served me. That I wasn't back at Devil's Island was no fault of hers.

However, I didn't bother about May just then. Instead, I went off to the old Provence to enjoy myself, where I met dozens of the fellows I had known in days gone by. Incidentally, I learnt that Chicago May was going about with Charlie Smith, and that the pair of them had sworn to do me in. That didn't very much worry me. When you have been threatened with death a hundred times you cease to concern yourself about such little trifles. "Eat, drink and be merry" has ever been my motto in life.

The newspapers were full of my case and I could not have received more congratulations if I had just won the Derby which Boss Croker had pulled off that year with his horse Orby. For twenty-four hours the wine and wassail went round—and then came tragedy.

On the following evening Emily Skinner and I were at the Provence drinking, no doubt more than was good for us. About half-past ten we decided to go back to the flat in Kenton Street. We walked along Long Acre, crossed over into Holborn, and I waited outside the Russell Square tube station while Emily went in to buy herself a paper. I stood at the corner waiting for her. Suddenly a cab drove by and I heard a female voice I knew very well call out: "There he is."

The cab drove on a few yards further and stopped. Out of it jumped a woman and a man, Chicago May and Charlie Smith. In less time than it takes me to relate I was the target of a popping fusillade of shots aimed at me by the drunken Charlie. I could hear May screaming in an adjacent doorway while I jumped about dodging the gunman. Not for me to be killed stone dead in that fashion. If Smith hadn't been drunk he must, of course, have killed me. All he succeeded in doing was putting a bullet into my foot, which certainly made me yell a bit.

May in a doorway near the tube station kept screaming out: "Oh! oh! oh! oh! Kill him, Charlie. He's got a pistol." Poor Emily was also doing her best to make a noise, so that one way and another we were creating a bit of excitement in the neighborhood.

I don't altogether know what happened because when you've got a bullet in you, even if it is only in the foot, you become rather uncertain of things. Smith ran off into the darkness and I called out to May, still cowering in the doorway: "When you couldn't succeed in sending me to Devil's Island you would stoop to murder, you unmentionable something—"

"I'm only sorry he didn't succeed," cried May.

The strange part of this affair was that she didn't attempt to run. A policeman on duty near-by was already hot on the trail of Charlie Smith. A regular hue and cry took place, another constable, reinforced by a couple of civilians, also taking up the hunt. Bloomsbury became alive with people running here and there wanting to know what all the trouble was about.

Smith, nearly caught, stuck his pistol in the face of one of the civilians and threatened to blow out his brains if he did not abandon the chase. He pulled the trigger at a police constable who came up, found there was nothing in the pistol, and promptly flung it in the officer's face. That finished him. Like a flash the policeman jumped at him, downed him, and eventually hauled him off to the Hunter Street station to be charged with attempted murder.

All the time this was going on other events were transpiring between May and myself. Police had also arrived at our part of the world and I made no bones about then and there giving May into custody for attempted murder. She, too, was hauled off to the station and on the way tried to get rid of a wicked-looking knife she had in her hand-bag.

One way and another, quite a pretty little mix-up. Another policeman took me off to the Royal Free Hospital to have my wound attended to while detective officers set about staging the second act of this absorbing little drama. There came to my bedside in the hospital Detective-Inspector Stockley, the officer in charge of the Division. We were quite old friends. He also knew May well.

"Eddie," he said, "who shot you?"

"I don't know," I replied.

"Oh, yes, you do. Come on, who did it?"

But I still protested I knew nothing about the matter and Stockley proceeded to set about what is known in the vernacular as "skull-dragging," that is, making a man give evidence when he doesn't want to. There even came my old friend Charlie Mitchell, the ex-champion heavyweight of England, who wanted to know, with a wealth of lurid adjectives, if I really meant to let Chicago May get away with it.

"Not me," I said, "she'll have to pay for this all right." As a matter of fact, what was worrying me more than anything else just then was the fact that I had given the hospital barber some money to put on a horse that had won. I had £30 coming to me, but instead of paying me the barber took the knock and disappeared.

Although I didn't particularly want to, the police compelled me, as soon as I was well enough, to go to Bow Street and give evidence against May and Charlie. The most amazing part of the whole affair was that they seemed to regard it as a huge joke.

They were laughing all the time I was in the box, Heaven only knows what for. Attempted murder isn't a nice charge to face in England. Still, there they were, defended by a well-known police court solicitor named Arthur Newton, sublimely confident that everything would come all right. Newton seemed to have the idea that I was a witness who would not stand much cross-examination.

"Now, remember," he warned me in the witness-box, "you are on oath."

"I don't want you to tell me that," I replied.

"I want you to tell me the truth. Have you ever worked in your life?"

"Yes."

"Oh, and where did you work?"

"On Devil's Island," I retorted pertly.

"Don't try to be funny," said Arthur in his lordliest manner.

"It's you who are trying to be funny, asking silly questions," I answered. "I'm not here to be made a fool of by you." Nor was I.

The actual trial itself, which took two days at the Old Bailey, created a tremendous public sensation. It seemed that May had completely burnt her boats behind her when she wrote a letter to one of her old lovers in which she said that Charlie Smith was the man I had got to throw vitriol on her, and that she had lost no time in turning the tables.

So the third act opened on July 25th, 1907, before Mr. Justice Darling, with Charles Smith, twenty-five years of age, tinsmith by trade, and May Vivienne Churchill, thirty-five years of age, humorously described as an artist, charged with shooting at your humble servant with intent to murder him and wounding him with the same intent. Both of the prisoners pleaded not guilty.

The late Mr. Huntly Jenkins and Mr. Fordham, now a London magistrate, appeared for Smith, while May had an advocate whom I had known well in 1888, the late Mr. A. A. Purcell.

I have said before, and I still say it, that I didn't want to give evidence against either of the prisoners. Smith had shot me, true, and Chicago May had put him up to it. But as far as I was concerned personally I would have preferred to settle with them at my own time and in my own place. If it wasn't that Stockley kept me under close observation all the time I would have cleared out of London and allowed the charges to lapse. But I didn't get the chance. I had to go into the witness-box at the Old Bailey and subject myself to the cross-examination of Huntly Jenkins and Purcell, both of whom, I will readily admit, had plenty of material at their command. The defense wanted to prove that I had both vitriol and weapons in my possession on the night of the crime. Huntly Jenkins also suggested that I had been wandering about the public-houses of the West End looking for Smith to shoot him. Purcell even asked me if I did not still think that Chicago May was deeply in love with me.

"I'll take her word for it," I replied, "even if some of the more recent events have made me rather doubtful of her affection," which aroused great laughter in court.

I had to go through it all: how May had come over to Paris to save me and herself had been arrested, how I had escaped from Devil's Island, to say nothing of an accusation from Purcell that I had shot the two men who had got away with me. Then the policeman I had shot in America came up for discussion, as also did all my previous convictions. But I took the occasion to inform Purcell that I felt no ill-will towards either of the prisoners, and that I was not the prosecutor. And so it went on for the better part of a day, and by the time the three lawyers for the defense had finished with me I didn't want to see another criminal court for the remainder of my life.

When the proceedings terminated for the day I said to Detective-Inspector Stockley: "You won't want me here again, will you?"

Stockley realized what I meant. There was a distinct possibility that I might still get a bullet from one of May's friends. Besides, I have been inside courts too often for my liking. You couldn't catch me going into one voluntarily for all the money in the world. I told Stockley, therefore, that with his kind permission I intended to absent myself from the final scene.

There wasn't much evidence for the defense worth speaking about. The shooting was admitted, while "Chicago May's" letters to her old inamorata conclusively proved that she had been the instigator of the whole affair. The Crown prosecutor, Arthur Gill, who now sits as a Metropolitan police magistrate, summed up the case for the prosecution and said he did not dispute the fact that May was in a state of deep fear at the time of my release and quite evidently she determined to be first in the field.

The gentlemen on the other side urged, having nothing better to put forward, that I was a terrible desperado who would kill anybody at sight and that my dear old friend May was only protecting her own precious life in deciding to kill me first.

I am not trying to throw any bouquets at myself, so I will merely repeat what took place. The jury, without leaving the box, brought in a verdict of guilty of shooting with intent to murder. Detective-Inspector Stockley then went into the witness-box to inform the court that Smith was an American by birth who had served several terms of imprisonment in South Africa, and that he had come to England after being deported from that country. Chicago May was one of the most notorious women in London. She made it a practice of getting men into compromising circumstances and then blackmailing them. She had even driven men to suicide.

They told me afterward that May's jaunty attitude had gradually deserted her as the trial went on. It began to dawn even upon her cocksure nature that she wasn't going to see the lights of London for many a long day. Any uncertainty about the matter finally disappeared when the judge, passing sentence, said that the verdict the jury had returned was the only possible and logical one. I, Guerin, was a bad man in many respects, but I was entitled to the same protection in regard to my life as the best of them. It was not for the prisoners to judge me or seek to take my life. He thought there was a difference in the case of Smith and that of Churchill, although they were both undoubtedly guilty—the one of having shot at me with intent to murder, and the other of having counselled and procured the shooting with that intent; and therefore they were equally guilty of the criminal act charged.

Smith had no excuse whatever; it was no quarrel of his, but he took it on his shoulders. Churchill evidently believed that I intended to harm her, and for that reason he would make a distinction between the two prisoners.

Then the judge dramatically paused amid a deep silence while he passed sentence.

"You, Smith, will go to penal servitude for life. You, Churchill, will be kept in penal servitude for fifteen years."

They told me that May's face went absolutely green when she heard the terrible words. She had never believed right up to the end that she would get anything more than ten or twelve months. The fight went out of her instantaneously. She had to be practically carried out of the dock in a swooning condition and taken to a cell to be revived.

Even greater was the shock to Smith, and even I could not help feeling sorry for a man receiving a life sentence when I knew all the time he had merely been the tool of an insanely jealous and vindictive woman. Before they could remove him from the dock he began cursing the judge in the worst language ever heard at the Old Bailey. But for all the good it did him he might just as well have saved his breath. The warders hustled him below and from there to the obscurity of a convict prison where he spent something like fifteen or sixteen years before the authorities decided to release him and send him back to his native land.

I was not in Court when the judge passed sentence. For one reason—as I have already explained—I thought it distinctly possible that May might have another admirer anxious to finish me off altogether. I also firmly believed in steering clear of courts as much as I could. As a matter of fact, I was in a café in the West End of London with Charlie Mitchell when the news came through that Smith had got life and Chicago May fifteen years.

It would be hypocritical for me to pretend that I felt any pronounced regret for the fate of the two people who had attempted to kill me, but I thought then, as I still think, that their punishment was terribly severe. But, of course, English judges have always gone out of their way to put down private vendettas which are settled with pistols. Unless there are extremely extenuating circumstances, cases of attempted murder are almost invariably punished with penal servitude for life, which is no doubt the principal reason why there is so little shooting in the United Kingdom.

Now let me here deal with the case of Chicago May as an illuminating example of the truth that you can't win at the crooked game. May was an Irish emigrant girl who went to America in the late 'eighties endowed with all the advantages that Nature could give her. In her girlhood days she must have been strikingly beautiful, but evidently she took to the easiest way a woman knows of earning money and speedily got herself into trouble.

When she was only in the early twenties she came into conflict with the police at Denver for robbing men, and by the time she had returned to England, which would be about 1898, she had acquired something like an international reputation as an exponent of what they call the badger trick. This little game, like most money-making grafts, is remarkable chiefly for its simplicity. The first essential is a good-looking woman. She picks up a client, takes him home to her flat, and there, with the aid of a confederate—usually a woman—hidden under a table covered with a cloth that reaches to the ground, robs the man of his pocket book and any other valuables that may be in evidence.

When the row came, as it usually did, May could truthfully say that she couldn't have stolen the money because she hadn't been near the victim's clothes. With all the hardihood in the world she would invite the visitor to search the flat. He, of course, wasn't to know that a lady concealed beneath the table had already crawled out and taken his wallet, and then as cunningly and carefully crawled out by the door, nor did May bother to tell him. At any rate, there would be a violent scene, ending with the victim declaring his intention of going for the police.

"Oh, do what you like," May would say. "The police can come here and search as much as they like. They won't find anything." Nor did they.

May played this game for some years in London, her *tapin,* as the French describe the promenade of the *demi-mondaine,* being principally Northumberland Avenue, on account of the fact that the two big hotels in that thoroughfare were extensively patronized by American visitors. The good-looking, supremely confident May certainly possessed a wonderful eye for sizing up American people, and especially middle-aged gentlemen with fat wallets who would not care to make too much trouble if they happened to get into her clutches.

There were three or four women who worked together, using one another's flats in turn and managing to keep out of jail despite the innumerable occasions on which they fell afoul of the police. Stockley, then the detective-inspector at Bow Street, who knew May's little ways as well as any man in England, ran across her one night in a West End public-house, seated by herself. It was probably a bit early for business. Just about this time he had been receiving numerous complaints about the lady, so he took the opportunity of sitting down beside her and relating to her what might be termed "The Fable of the Pheasant."

"I suppose you know, May," he began, "that every year in England, just when the autumn is drawing on, all the well-to-do people in London shut up their town houses and go to their country estates to shoot.

"Now, on those estates, May, they preserve some beautiful game birds called pheasants. Keepers are specially employed to rear them so that when they have reached maturity their rich master may come down and shoot them.

"The pheasant is a difficult bird to kill. It flies high and at a tremendous speed. It frequently happens that despite all the efforts of twenty or thirty crack shots it succeeds in escaping its doom that particular autumn.

"But I want to tell you this, May," Stockley continued. "Although the pheasant may dodge its fate that year the time will come when it is no longer so fast on the wing as it used to be. There will be another shooting party and on this occasion the pheasant, older and not so agile as of yore, will come rocketing down to earth with a terrible thud and never rise again."

May looked at Stockley with her calculating blue eyes, and remarked:

"Say, ain't you the wise guy?" and ended up by requesting him to have a whisky and soda and to mind his own damned business.

There is a sequel to this little story, as there should be to most good tales. Cold print will not bear repetition of the actual words involved, but the main incidents of the affair may be related. After May had been sentenced by Justice Darling to fifteen years' penal servitude she was in a cell below the court, awaiting removal to Holloway Prison—and subsequently to the female convict jail at Aylesbury—with her nose lugubriously stuck through the bars of the spy-hole of the door when Stockley happened to come along. Just previously he had been relating to the judge some of the spot-light episodes of May's lively life.

Feeling rather sorry for the lady, he paused, commiserated with her, and then rather unwisely said: "You remember, don't you, May, what I told you that night in the West End about the pheasants?"

May did recollect the matter, but obviously she was not in the least grateful for the good advice then given her. She told Stockley, in words which are still vividly imprinted upon his mind, exactly what she thought of him, of Scotland Yard in general, of the judge, of me, and everybody connected with the affair. And as I say, the exact phraseology cannot be repeated on any decent printed page.

May did her time with the usual remission of three months every year without getting into any serious trouble. But even while she was in Aylesbury Convict Prison she couldn't forbear to stop playing her old tricks, though to be sure she did not get much opportunity for practice. The late Lord Rothschild, whose country house at Tring was close to Aylesbury, frequently visited the prison. May, being one of its most distinguished inmates, had the honor of being introduced to his lordship, who apparently was quite struck by her personality. Anyhow, I'll say this: It wouldn't be May's fault if he wasn't.

His lordship even went to the length one day of presenting May with a bunch of violets from his buttonhole. For weeks afterward May's attitude towards her fellow-prisoners was absolutely unbearable. When the violets withered May carefully hung them up in her cell, until one day a jealous rival stole in and destroyed the precious keepsake. Poor May went raving mad; there was a stand-up fight which she won hands down, and although it did cost her fourteen days' bread and water she roundly declared it was well worth while.

For quite a long time afterward May continued to make eyes at the famous head of the wealthy Rothschild family. When the news went round the prison that his lordship was about to pay a visit. May used to bestir herself. The peroxide had long faded out of her hair, and I daresay the rough prison food and the hard open-air life had coarsened her creamlike complexion. However, she used to succeed in toning down the somewhat ruddy color of her skin by a judicious application of whitewash from the wall of her cell, which no doubt satisfied her vanity even if it made Lord Rothschild laugh consumedly when he had bidden the lady good-bye. May was a born masher if ever there was one in this world.

Chapter Nineteen
THE BALANCE SHEET

Now that I have fully related the entire sequence of dramatic events that followed the robbery of the American Express Company in Paris, which to all intents and purposes ended at the Old Bailey in London with the sentencing of Charlie Smith and Chicago May, it would no doubt be fitting for me to be able to record that I turned over a new leaf and never sinned again.

Just allow me a moment to reckon up the pros and cons of the Great Game, setting out all the people who had been concerned in the American Express job and exactly what they received for their trouble. After all, it constitutes the essence of this book.

Let me first of all deal with the man who did get away—Kid McManus. His share of the loot was about $75,000, for which he would be lucky to receive half. But the Kid won for the time being because he never went to jail for that and he also had the use of the money.

Dutch Gus had his share, also amounting to about $75,000, for less than forty-eight hours, and for all the good it did him he might just as well have been without it. In May, 1901, Gus was in prison, and, unless he has died in French Guiana, is still there. I have never heard a word about him since I made my escape. He will spend his entire life—if he still has it—in paying for something he never received.

The French police said that I also had $75,000 which I gave to Chicago May. I never admitted having the money, though I daresay they didn't believe me. The Goddess of Chance being on my side, I paid a comparatively small price for my part in the grand *coup*. A month or two under five years' imprisonment, counting everything in, including the time in France when I was awaiting trial and the fourteen months I lay in Brixton Prison represents about the sum total of the law's exactions in my case, plus, of course, a bullet in the foot, which is hardly worth mentioning.

Chicago May came out of the deal much worse than I did. True, her cut turned out to be much bigger than mine, but she had to pay for it. Three years in France plus twelve years in England, are nasty slices out of the life of a woman whose principal assets are her charms. When May had completed her English sentence and had been deported to the States she was to all intents and purposes finished. She, it is quite certain, would unhesitatingly subscribe to the view that as you sow, so will you surely reap.

And what of Cubine Jackson, alias Charlie Smith, cheap cracksman and poor foolish tool of a designing woman? What had the American Express robbery brought him? It must have been a bitter reflection to him as the long and dreary years dragged on that he should be frittering away the best time of his life behind prison walls for the sake of what? "A rag and a bone and a hank of hair"—as Kipling puts it. He, I am absolutely sure, would corroborate the opinion that crime is an unprofitable profession for any human being.

There were also the unfortunate individuals who did time for passing the checks stolen from the American Express safe. They, also, could have had but little opportunity of enjoying the proceeds of their share. So, with the exception of Kid McManus, nobody won in this particular little episode of real life. And even the Kid only escaped for a time. When funds began to run short he must needs try his luck at a Canadian safe, which only brought him seven years' penal servitude. It is the old, old story of taking the pitcher to the well once too often. The trouble with all crooks is that they don't know when to leave off.

It might be thought, then, with all this undeniable proof right before my eyes, that I would immediately abandon the ways that are dark for an honest, if impecunious, existence.

I was getting on in years a bit. When a man reaches the age of forty-seven years he ought to have some sense—if he is ever going to have any—and he should also have some money, that is, again, if he is ever going to have any. I am quite certain I was absolutely lacking in the latter qualification; of the other I will leave the readers of this book to judge. There comes a time in the life of all men and women who have been pursuing a foolish course some realization of the goal to which they are heading. But in ninety-nine cases out of a hundred, even if there comes to them the awakening of mind which will fully bring home the idiocy of their behavior, they are devoid of the necessary strength of mind to turn aside and make a fresh start.

Now, here I was in London in 1907, notorious throughout the length and breadth of the world as a man who had effected a daring escape from a foreign penal settlement, the recipient of a good deal of unnecessary admiration for what I had done. For the time being I became a veritable lion of the underworld. Newspapers literally fought for the favor of an interview, while Press photographers chased me wherever I went, desperately anxious to obtain for the edification of the public the picture of the man of whom everybody was talking. Undoubtedly fame sufficient to turn the head of anybody.

There happened shortly after the Old Bailey trial of Chicago May and Charlie Smith a somewhat amusing episode over which I could afford to chuckle for many a day. The enterprising clerk of a lawyer connected with the case one day found himself in Emily Skinner's flat in Kenton Street. Standing on the mantelpiece he saw the photograph of a very good-looking woman whom he rather rashly concluded to be my wife. Promptly did he purloin it and dispose of it to an equally enterprising newspaper, which printed it with the inscription underneath of "Mrs. Eddie Guerin." I would have been highly flattered to have been able to say that such a beautiful woman was my wife. Unfortunately, it happened to be the photograph of a very well-known London actress who, naturally, did not appreciate the connection with such a notorious person as myself. The matter cost the offenders something like £500 to settle, so I daresay that they would also reckon themselves among the people who did not win.

The people who wish to exploit me as the leading figure in this great drama also had to pay for the privilege, but in their instance they probably did so with profit. However, I got a little out of it, so I didn't complain. One of the slight compensations of notoriety—especially nowadays—is that you are frequently given the opportunity of turning the more unfortunate side of your life into money. I don't for one moment allege that it is altogether worth while, because if I were offered the alternative of doing, say, ten years' penal servitude, and then receiving £10,000 for a detailed account of what I had undergone, or remaining out of prison altogether, I would choose the latter every time. *There is no money on this earth that can compensate any man—or woman—for wasting what should be the best years of his or her life in a prison cell.*

However, on the proceeds of what the Press paid me for various matters connected with Devil's Island I managed to lead quite a comfortable existence for over twelve months without lapsing into crime of any sort. I followed the races with varying fortune and at one time found myself in such affluence that I could take a trip back to the States. I discovered then that most of the old crowd were slipping out of the game. Sophie Lyons, for instance, had married Billy Burke and announced her intention of turning respectable. It was while I was over in Chicago on this occasion that Billy wanted me to kiss his blushing bride and be friends, instead of which I slugged him.

Sophie, of course, like one or two other friends of mine, made a success of crime, and got out of the business in time to die a rich woman.

She settled down in Detroit, and with the dollars obtained from her various misdeeds of the past began to operate in real estate. She was so successful at it that when she died a few years ago she left behind a fortune of no less than $1,000,000. Whether or not she ever managed to keep Billy straight I doubt. This much is quite certain, that when Sophie passed away she left the bulk of her money in trust for the education of the children of convicts. I have already stated that she didn't remember me in her will.

The most amazing part about Sophie's life was the manner in which she threw off all her criminal associates and became known all over America as a straightforward business woman. When you come to think of it, it is almost incredible that such a thing could have happened. Her grandfather was in his day a noted cracksman, her mother was a convicted thief, and her father a notorious blackmailer. Sophie herself, as befitted such breeding, was a blackmailing thief. She married one of America's most celebrated burglars, Ned Lyons, deserted him, and for a time took up with another well-known crook known as Jim Brady[51]. When Jim failed to come up to expectations she fastened on to Billy Burke[52], reformed him as well as herself, and then lived on until 1921[53] to show the world that she, at any rate, was an exception to the rule that crime doesn't pay. I was told that what really made Sophie turn over a new leaf was the fact that her two daughters, who had been decently brought up and educated in a Californian convent, refused to recognize her in any way. There was already a son who had gone wrong. He, true to his ancestry, used to put what they call the "black hand" on his long-suffering mother, but as he ended up by getting twenty years' penal servitude for shooting at a policeman I daresay he can be put down as one of the failures of the profession.

Sophie's death was as mysterious as her sudden reformation. Three men had called at her Detroit home and while they were there she was heard to cry out: "Quint, Quint, for God's sake, don't do it!" Nobody took much notice at the time, but shortly afterward neighbors went in and discovered Sophie in a state of collapse. She was hurriedly removed to a hospital and found to be suffering from a terrible blow on the head which brought on cerebral hemorrhage. The police never got to the bottom of the matter, although it was known that her visitors had been three gunmen with a long and bad record of crime. Whether they had called to rob her, or whether she had threatened to expose them for something, could never be ascertained. She was about seventy years of age then, and there is no doubt that at the time of her death she was honestly trying to make amends for the misdeeds of the past.

Another very remarkable personality in the world of crime was Adam Worth, who is still remembered in England as the man who stole Gainsborough's beautiful picture of the Duchess of Devonshire[54]. Harry Raymond, as everybody in London knew him, was still going strong when I returned to England in 1909, although, of course, he was then an old man. For many years he was recognized by the police of both Europe and America as one of the cleverest framers-up in the whole world. Harry originally fled to England after being mixed up with the man who is still recognized as one of the greatest crooks of all time, the notorious Mark Shinburn[55]. He got away with something like £30,000 as his share of a big bank robbery and settled down in London as a real master crook.

The worst deal Harry ever made in his life was the Duchess of Devonshire. The people from whom it had been stolen offered a reward of £1,000 for its return, and when it became known in America that Harry Raymond had it hidden somewhere the Pinkertons went to Pat Sheedy to invoke his assistance in getting it back. Pat sent over to me to see what I could do, and eventually Harry agreed to part with it after first assuring himself that he was in no danger of arrest. Then Messrs. Agnew, the art dealers to whom it belonged, wanted to be quite certain that they were getting the proper picture and not a fake, so it was quite a long time before the affair was settled. You couldn't teach Harry Raymond much. He was a German-American Jew who lived on the labors of other men, and he must have been clever because he remained in England for thirty years and never once fell into the hands of the police. But like most of us, he had a canker continually eating at his heart. In Canada he had an old sweetheart of whom he remained passionately fond to the end of his days, but he was afraid to cross the Atlantic because there were old crimes to be accounted for, another instance of how your past sins continually come home to roost.

I could go on almost indefinitely relating stories of famous criminals with whom I have been associated, most of whom either died in poverty or went out in prison. Men like Walter Sheridan, who specialized in bank-robbery, forgery, counterfeiting and the hypothecation of bonds, Joe Howard, Billy Porter, Michael Kurtz, Billy Burke, and dozens of others were all known to the London police when I first came here. Then there were the Bidwell brothers, who achieved great notoriety by forging Bank of England notes, Charlie Williamson, Johnny Curtin (who with Billy Porter pulled off over a dozen big robberies which had been laid out for them by Harry Raymond), Moocher Wigram, one of the greatest organizers of crime that ever lived, those famous forgers the Kennaway brothers, Big Ed Rice, notorious throughout Europe and America as a con man, and dozens more I could mention. To-day there are no serious robberies in England worth mentioning, not because Scotland Yard is more clever, but simply because there are not the men to do them. I know that the Yard men with whom I used to be acquainted in the 'eighties and 'nineties laugh sarcastically when the crooks of nowadays are spoken of; they say there are no "good" men worth talking about and they are quite right. I suppose I must be one of the last of the old brigade, and as I have gone out of the business for keeps, I can also be counted among the has-beens.

It is much the same in America. The yeggmen, as they are known in the States, used at one time to be a real terror to country banks. They not only robbed banks; they murdered people with absolute impunity, and it was not until the Pinkertons started after them in real earnest that the game began to grow unprofitable. In a well-policed country like England the yeggman wouldn't be possible, but in America, and more especially in the Middle West, he flourished exceedingly in

States like Minnesota, Nebraska, Indiana, South Dakota, Wisconsin, and Illinois.

They get their name from the gypsies. The yegg is the Romany word for the chief of a traveling band; it doesn't require much imagination to visualize the tramp thief, which is really what the yeggman comes to, adopting gypsy slang to fit his own particular needs. Very often they will travel the country a dozen strong, including among their number men skilled in mechanics and explosives.

They regularly send out scouting a novice at the game known in the vernacular as a "gay cat." This individual is entrusted with the job of finding what police are on duty in that particular town, what risks are likely to be met, and also to ascertain the likeliest means of a get-away. It is an extraordinary business in its way, something like the old bush-ranging game in Australia forty or fifty years ago, with this great difference, that whereas the "bail-up" experts in Australia used to content themselves with plundering a bank at the point of a pistol, the yeggmen travel the country looking for banks likely to be worth robbing and make it a part of their plan carefully to study everything before they make the attempt. For instance, they will not attack a bank on a moonlight night, nor are they at all keen on entering a place where there is a night watchman.

Pinkertons have practically put an end to the yeggmen by not only mercilessly hunting them down, but also by displaying a notice outside the cashier's desk which tells the gang that they will be looking for trouble if they try any of their tricks there. "This bank is under the protection of the Pinkertons," is sufficient warning for any gay cat. He returns to the chief yegg to inform him that there is nothing doing.

The yeggman took the place of the bank-sneak thieves with whom I served my apprenticeship. Of course, there is a vast gulf between the two. A successful bank-sneak requires to be well dressed and to possess a gentlemanly appearance. His profession necessitates quite a lot of nerve and the risks of capture are very great. Many years ago it was one of the most flourishing criminal games in America; I could name a hundred men who got a good living at it and then came over to Europe to try their luck. France used to be a particularly happy hunting ground, although that is now a thing of the past. As soon as the courts over there began serving out ten-year sentences it was generally agreed that the time had come to try something else.

There is no doubt that the Pinkertons did more than all the detective forces in the world combined together to smash up the big bank robbers. When Bill Pinkerton, who died only a few years ago, went after a man he didn't let up until he had got him, and if it cost him a million dollars he didn't mind. As he left a fortune of something like $15,000,000 it is quite obvious that he made more money out of crime than any of the people whom he hunted down. But, of course, a firm like the Pinkertons would have no chance in England. The power of arrest which they possessed in America would never be given them in this country. Besides, England is too small to allow bank thieves, however clever, to operate for long. There is no jumping freight trains and making a long hop from one State to another as there is in America. Also, the telephone plays sad havoc with your chance of escape. It only wants a crime to be committed in London for a full description of the suspects to be sent over England, Scotland and Ireland within twenty-four hours. And you can't hide yourself in this country like the yeggmen do in the illimitable stretches of territory across the herring-pond. So, as I say, all the big men have gone out of the business. Just now and again one of the old-fashioned type of burglar has a run for a few months and then gets put away for ten or fifteen years. The Prevention of Crimes Act, under which habituals can, in addition to the sentence that may be imposed for the offense with which they are actually charged, receive another ten years' penal servitude, has effectually stamped out what I call the real tradesmen. Most of the prisoners you see at the Old Bailey are novices at the game, or, at least, so they tell me. I never go near the place myself.

All sorts of deterrents have combined to terminate the day of what I should call the big crook. The strict passport system now in vogue makes it very difficult for the internationals to ply their trade between one country and another as easily as of old. When I came to London in 1887 the West End was full of Americans, bank-robbers, safe-smashers, forgers, con men and receivers. In the ordinary course of events you reported yourself to one of the fences and if you wanted money you could have it. However, there are very few of them in England to-day. Just now and again a mail train is robbed or a cat burglar gets a nice little pocketful of jewelry. No doubt education is playing its part. "Honesty is the best policy" is one of the fundamental principles of the compulsory learning with which the younger generation of to-day are brought up.

I never came across a more striking example of the fact that you can't win than the life of Mark Shinburn. Here was a man who in the hey-day of his career achieved more spectacular successes than any other bank-robber in the world. He returned to Europe after relieving a bank in America of a million dollars, although that was but one instance of the many *coups* he pulled off. But in Belgium, where he lived in great style for a number of years, he became short of money, and undertook another bank robbery for which he got seventeen years' imprisonment. I met him in America in the early 'eighties. He had just come out of jail after serving a long sentence, utterly impoverished, an old man, and with nothing in front of him but a bed in a doss-house and, as likely as not, death by starvation. Walter Sheridan[56], another very highly accomplished man in many ways, died in obscure poverty, as did dozens of others I could mention. With most of them it was the case of "easy come, easy go." They spent what they made, never knowing from one day to another when they might go to prison and thus be denied the opportunity to enjoy the money they got.

Chapter Twenty
YOU CAN'T WIN!

This is what I call an Epilogue. I said, in the very beginning, that I would prove, as all the prison statistics in the world could not prove, that you haven't got a dog's chance at the crooked game. I am now going to show, altogether apart from anything connected with money, how you will everlastingly suffer for your wins of days gone by.

In the year 1911, having got hold of a little money by various ways and means which I need not enumerate, I opened a tobacco and sweet shop in the West End of London. I was getting on in years; when a man reaches the age of fifty he wants to ask himself what is going to happen in his old age.

This little business of mine possessed the merit of being an accommodation address for the innumerable friends who were what I might call birds of passage. I didn't bother serving behind the counter myself, nor did I put my name on the premises. No doubt if it had become generally known that the Demon of Devil's Island—as one newspaper euphoniously described me—had turned shopkeeper it would have resulted, at any rate temporarily, in plenty of curious customers anxious to have a good look at the man who had achieved such astounding notoriety. However, modesty has always been my most consuming characteristic, to say nothing of the fact that I didn't want any Scotland Yard men nosing about the shop. So I engaged a girl to take the money while I busied myself with other and more profitable things. What I want to describe is how my previous lapses from grace were responsible for cutting short my career as a tradesman. I happened to be in Glasgow on one occasion drinking with some men in the Caledonian Hotel. What my business was does not really matter. On leaving the place I strolled up as far as Buchanan Street when a girl touched me on the shoulder and whispered: "There are two detectives following you."

For once in a while my conscience was perfectly clear.

"Are you sure?" I asked the girl, one of the right sort.

"Yes," she replied, "they're following you all right."

I thought I might just as well make certain. Telling the girl to come with me, I climbed on the top of a tram and asked my companion to see what happened. One of the detectives got inside, rode with us for a mile and then, apparently, disappeared when we got off and went into a public-house for a drink. I had sent the girl off with money for her trouble and started down the street again when suddenly a couple of the City detectives jumped out on me.

They were only local men, so, when they dragged me down to head-quarters and wanted to know my name, I didn't go to the bother of telling them that I was Eddie Guerin. Any old name does in an emergency. Then they brought out a camera and said: "We'll tak' your photograph."

"No, you won't," I replied promptly, giving the camera a kick which sent it flying. That was the signal for four men grabbing me and banging me into a cell. They left me there for a few minutes and then returned for the purpose of taking my fingerprints. Once more did I strenuously object, which told them, of course, there was something wrong. It took four of them twenty minutes' hard fight before they got what they wanted. In the morning the jailers told me to come out and wash myself prior to going into court, where I was to be charged with being a suspected person.

"After I leave the court," I said, "I will wash myself and not before. I don't think you'll keep me long."

A detective got up in front of the Bailey and said I had been acting suspiciously in the Caledonian Hotel.

"You did not arrest me in the Caledonian Hotel," I protested.

"No, but you were followed from there."

"Did you see me do anything wrong in the hotel?"

"No, but you answer the description of a man who was there three weeks ago and who stole some money from a guest."

I asked the detective if I was charged with that, to which he replied that I was not. But I could see I had no hope of being released forthwith; they had discovered I was Eddie Guerin and meant to hold me for a week on the off-chance of something turning up.

A week later two Scotland Yard men came up to Glasgow, went into the witness-box, and swore that I habitually associated with the most notorious crooks in London. I asked them for names and particulars.

"Well, So-and-so for one," mentioning a well-known thief.

"Where have you ever seen me with him?"

"In London repeatedly during the last two years."

"I have never spoken to this man in my life," I said to the Bailey.

One of the detectives—he is now retired from the Yard—added that he had known me for many years, at which I lost my temper completely.

"Known me!" I shouted, "yes, of course you have known me and you know all about me. Did you come all the way from Scotland Yard to tell us that?"

The C.I.D.[57] man also began to get a bit short.

"I was brought up here to testify that you are an associate of crooks," he replied. "I don't know anything at all of what you have been doing here."

Things went on in this manner for some time. The Bailey wanted to know what I had been in the Caledonian Hotel for.

"Merely to get a drink," I informed him.

The upshot of the matter was that the Bailey advised me to get a lawyer, and ultimately, after eliciting from the Glasgow police that the only evidence they had against me came from a porter who "thought" he recognized me as the man who had committed a jewel robbery at the hotel some weeks before, I was discharged. To prove that I did possess some reputable means of livelihood I had to disclose the fact that I had a tobacconist's shop in London. On top of the Glasgow affair there came another blow. The girl whom I employed had a sweetheart who got into trouble down Devon way. He must needs write to my shop, with the result that Scotland Yard men continually came nosing around on the supposition that I was running the business as a blind. Naturally, it didn't suit me to be everlastingly spied upon by the police, so I sold the shop for what it was worth and went back to the old life.

I could fill another volume with the ups-and-downs I have experienced since then. Being Eddie Guerin, of much undesirable notoriety, I am a marked man wherever I go. Every detective in London claims the honor of my acquaintance, but I think I am right in saying that it is only the old-timers such as Leach, Stockley, Froest, Arrow and a few others who have now retired from the police who can truthfully lay claim to knowing me by sight. I could pass by a hundred C.I.D. men without being recognized, simply because I am before their time. I doubt very much whether Wensley would know me, and I am quite certain that the younger men could only say I was Eddie Guerin on the strength of somebody else's information.

I fully realize that I am the possessor of a very bad reputation. It only wants the whisper of my name to bring the police around on a skull-dragging expedition. When a friend of mine, an ex-jockey, got into trouble over a jewelry job in the North, a snitch informed the police that I had been mixed up in the affair. I didn't even know the jockey at the time, but nevertheless it took me a week to prove my innocence. That is what you call the sins of the past coming home to roost with a vengeance.

What have I done in England? I certainly fell in 1888 for something that failed to materialize. Then I did ten years' penal servitude in France, and following that came the American Express affair, for which, it seems, I am doomed to be punished for evermore, because the memory of it remains and I am known as a man who will stick at nothing. The first really serious offense I committed in England took place at Brighton in 1917, and even then, as with most of my lapses from grace, I got absolutely nothing.

Money was very tight with me. I went down to Brighton to call on a friend staying at the Hotel Metropole, had a good many drinks with him, and probably lost my head. Coming downstairs I saw a lady leaving her room, when it suddenly flashed across my mind that here was the opportunity of getting something to go on with. Petty thieving was never much in my line; I always liked to go after something worth having. This, however, was a case of needs must when the devil drives, and so, like a shot, I whipped out of my pocket a little jemmy I had, stuck it into the door and snapped the lock open within a second or two.

I was into the room, trying to open a dressing-bag I saw there, hoping that it would contain jewels, when the woman suddenly came back. She screamed blue murder when she saw me, and without waiting to say anything I made a blind dash for the corridor followed by cries of "Stop thief!" A valet, hearing the disturbance, saw me come running along and made a half-hearted attempt to stop me. I easily pushed him on one side and went on. Then, as he didn't seem inclined to give up the chase, I threw the jemmy at him to get rid of him. It didn't hit him, but it gave me a little breathing time.

Down the stairs I ran and into the lounge with much clatter behind me. Somebody yelled out to the hall porter to shut the front door, and by the time I had reached the ground floor the Metropole was in a pretty state of confusion. I did not lose my head. Instead of attempting to force my way out I coolly took off my hat and coat, seated myself at a table in the lounge, and ordered tea! The ruse might have succeeded had not the valet come down and immediately spotted me.

"That's him!" he cried, pointing at me. I concluded that the time had arrived not only to go, but to go quickly. Up I jumped and ran through the lounge, determined to break my way through the front door by force. About sixteen men fell on me; breathless, coatless, marked all over, I was pushed into a room and locked up there until the police arrived.

This, of course, was a horribly unprofitable exploit—one of the very worst in which I had ever taken part. The local Bench committed me to the Sussex Assizes which are held at the ancient town of Lewes, where in due time I found to my dismay that I was to be tried by the formidable Judge Avory. Being under no delusions as to the fate that might overtake me with the man who possessed the reputation of being the severest judge on the English Bench, I came to the conclusion that it would be wiser to plead guilty to attempted larceny. But to this the judge would not agree. When I was put into the dock the prosecution wanted to make it an accomplished fact. Crown counsel said that when the woman came back into her room I had already cut open her dressing-case, and that when she disturbed me her jewelry went flying all over the place. The lawyer defending me contended that I had only attempted to steal and, what was only true, that I had not actually got away with anything. I went into the witness-box to tell the same story, but it did not avail. The jury brought in a verdict of guilty on this count, and also on a charge of assaulting the valet by throwing the jemmy at him. In all, I received sentence of two years' hard labor, which wouldn't have mattered so much if I had actually stolen anything. But what I got was precisely the same as I did in the American Express robbery—nothing.

After being taken from the Assize Court on my way to the station I ran across the Brighton detective who had charge of the case in company with the prosecutor and the hotel valet. I didn't mind the woman giving evidence against me, but I certainly went out of my way to tell the valet what I thought of him, asking him whether he didn't think that the twenty months I received for the attempted larceny was not sufficient punishment without another four months for throwing something that didn't hit him. However, that little outburst did me no good and I duly went on to Portsmouth Prison to serve my time.

When a man is getting on to sixty years of age and finds himself in jail it is bitterly brought home to him that he has made a sorry mess of his life. Here I was, fifty-seven years of age, penniless, with nothing to look forward to when I went out, sewing and marking mail-bags for the use of the Post Office. A child could have done the work. I daresay the Governor and the warders were rather sorry for me. There was not the slightest attempt at ill-treatment and so long as you did what you were told you got into no trouble. The English prison system of to-day is quite humane; men are not unduly humiliated, the food is plain but plentiful, and it is not worth while attempting to escape. But the two years I served there seemed fearfully long, because I rarely saw anyone to speak to.

The old Catholic priest entrusted with the task of safeguarding my spiritual welfare begged of me to come to confession, thinking, possibly, that he might induce me to tread the path of righteousness. I had to go to church the same as everybody else, but although I used to help to dress the altar, I made up my mind that I would have nothing to do with confession. When the priest expostulated with me I replied that I did not want to be a hypocrite and that it was utterly useless expecting me to pretend that I felt in a frame of mind to open my heart to anyone.

"How long is it since you went to confession?" he inquired one day when he came to my cell.

"A good many years, Father," I replied.

"If I ask you a question, will you answer it truthfully?" he requested.

"If it is a fair question."

"Well how long is it since you have been to confession?"

"Fifty years."

He threw up his hands in despair and left me, fully convinced, I am sure, that I was indeed hopeless.

I used to go round the prison with a taskmaster to give the men their work, and while doing this I occasionally went out of my way to talk to a boy who was going to be sent to one of the Borstal institutions[58] where they now take the young offenders. One of the Protestant chaplains saw me doing this one day and took it upon himself to tell the boy something of my past history. I complained about the matter to the old Father, saying I thought it unfair. I had only been giving the boy some good advice, but probably the chaplain thought I was filling his head with mischief.

Well, and so the time went on. I sewed and stamped thousands upon thousands of mail-bags, saw the prison steadily empty of its inmates so that they could be sent to the War, and myself requested that I might go. However, they wouldn't take me, and when I had finished my sentence the War was over. I received my discharge with nothing better to do than to look round and get a living as best I could. It would have been strange had I not gone back to the only life I knew—that of getting a living by my wits. Of all the impossible propositions any man can be faced with, there is nothing worse than that of living down a bad reputation. I happened to be in the Strand Palace Hotel one day when I saw Gough, then the detective-inspector at Bow Street. He was standing in the hall and I saw him trying to catch my eye. I knew he was Mr. Gough, although I wasn't quite sure whether he knew I was Mr. Guerin—a case of two "G's." He possessed the reputation of being a man who made no bones about arresting any suspicious character, and I began to wonder how I would get out of the place without being taken along to Bow Street and probably charged. When your conscience is not altogether clear you don't like looking the world in the face, more especially that part of it consisting of detectives. Suddenly I had an inspiration. I went to one of the lady clerks at the desk and as boldly as I could said:

"Would you mind sending upstairs for my silk scarf? I have forgotten it. The chambermaid will know where to find it."

Out of the corner of my eye I could see Gough all attention. The girl asked me for the number of my room and I gave the first one that came into my head. Both Gough and I were standing near the telephone boxes. I saw him sidle into one of them, evidently for the purpose of telephoning to Bow Street.

That was quite enough for me. The girl at the desk sensed nothing wrong; she didn't see the little by-play that had been taking place. Like a shot I ran out of the side door, bolted into an office opposite, and stood watching there when Gough came out, puzzled to know where I had disappeared. He took up a position on the corner of the street so that he could watch both exits from the Strand Palace Hotel, but he waited a long time without getting any satisfaction. A boy who came into the office got me a taxicab. I passed right by Gough, leaning far back, without being seen, and took advantage of the occasion to shake hands with myself on successfully dodging what would undoubtedly have been another six months. I saw Gough some time afterward, when he said to me, discussing things in general:

"We nearly got you in the Strand Palace, but you just managed to beat us that time."

But it only proves what I have been saying all along, that is, the unutterable foolishness of getting yourself a reputation that will enable the police to hound you from pillar to post. After all, there is nothing clever in subjecting yourself to the ignominy of being turned out of any public place for no reason whatever. Yet that is the fate which continually overtakes the old crook. Every man's hand is against him, and I think, all things considered, that it is far and away the worst punishment you can suffer. No man likes it everlastingly rubbed into him that he is not fit to associate with his fellow-beings. If there is one lesson I would like to bring home to any boy who is setting out on the path of crime it is that of the awful humiliation he will undergo long after he has paid the penalty demanded by the law.

Some little time after the Strand Palace Hotel episode I went into the American Bar at the Savoy opposite, for no other reason than that of the good drinks they serve. There were a good many American people in the place and I struck up a conversation with some of them, with the promise of seeing them on the following day. Next morning, on going in, I saw Gough. He had then left the police, but I knew it was morally certain that it would not do for me to go into the Savoy again. He was talking to the manager at the time. Beyond giving me a look, he did nothing, but I made it my business to leave the place immediately and never went back. I knew what would happen. One of the waiters would come up and more or less politely tell me that my patronage was not required.

It is this sort of incident that brings home to a man, as nothing else can, the foolishness of a criminal past. It follows you to the end of your days; the only hope you have is to clear out to a new country, to land there unknown, equipped with the determination to steer clear of anything in the least dangerous.

You may be eating a meal or having a drink in the most harmless company imaginable when some one calls you on one side and says: "I should not come in here any more if I were you."

"Why not?"

"Well, you know what it is. People don't like it. Take my advice, there's a good fellow, and don't make any trouble. You won't do yourself any good."

Having a glass of lager beer one day with some theatrical people in a West End hotel, I heard a whisper of my name. I said nothing at the time and went out. When I next entered the place the barmaid gave me a significant look.

"I'm sorry," she said, "I can't serve you."

"Why?" I inquired angrily. I knew the reason well enough; had I not experienced it many times before?

The girl informed me that she had been instructed by the manager not to serve me with anything. I demanded to see the gentleman and refused to go out until I did. He came bustling along, full of importance.

"Do you know me?" I asked.

"No," he said, "I don't recollect you."

"Oh, if that is the case, why can't I have a drink here?"

The barmaid whispered that I was the notorious Eddie Guerin, after which we had a few words. Ultimately a policeman was sent for, arriving while I was still telling the manager what I thought of him in some of the choicest language I could muster. I told the copper he ought to go upstairs and have a look at the young girls drinking themselves into prostitution with some of the worst women in London. And after that, if he thought the public-house was such an exclusive establishment as the manager pretended, he could take me into custody and charge me with what he liked. The policeman, being quite a wise youngster, declined to do anything of the sort and eventually sent me on my way. The moral is obvious: don't expose yourself to the possibility of such insults.

Chapter Twenty-One
THE HARVEST

In an idle moment one day I stood watching a Salvation Army meeting in London and got into conversation with one of General Booth's disciples. Possibly I looked like a brand that might be plucked from the burning; I don't know, I leave other people to form their opinion of me.

There I was, listening to some one they had got hold of saying: "Yes, brothers, I have been a wicked sinner and have been many times in jail," etc., etc., when the Salvation Army man, no doubt noticing that I looked slightly amused, remarked: "I wonder if this chap has been all he says he has."

"If you ask me," I said, "I think he is a damned liar. No man who has been in prison wants to shout it out for all the world to hear."

I must have looked as though I knew something about the matter, because after a little desultory conversation the Salvation Army man inquired:

"Why don't you join us? You say you have been to different parts of the world, and I am sure you must have a story to tell."

If he had only known it, I certainly had; but of course he hadn't the faintest idea he was talking to Eddie Guerin.

"I think I could tell you a few things," I replied, "but I shan't. You seem to be doing good work, and if you can impress upon all these young boys and girls the advantages of an honest life, you'll have done something worth while."

But there was no stalling off that ardent Salvationist.

"Can *you* give us any experience of a crooked life?" he asked.

"Not me," I replied hastily. "I've always gone straight."

The worst thing about me is that I don't look the part. Friends have told me that my appearance resembles that of a kindly old gentleman utterly incapable of wrongdoing. On one occasion I went up to Leeds, intending to stay there for York races. The town was absolutely full; I could not obtain accommodation anywhere and after hunting around for some time I asked one of the railway officials if he knew where I might obtain a room. He said he thought he knew of a place and took me round to a house where I found a vacant room. Just as he was leaving he said:

"You'll be all right here, old chap. This is where all the police on duty at the races are staying!" adding something about my money being quite safe in such a place.

That was putting my head into the lion's mouth with a vengeance. However, I thought to myself that I would get up early in the morning, have an early breakfast, and clear out. But when I got downstairs about eight o'clock there were about twenty policemen in the dining-room, one of them at the end of a long table serving out the fish. I must say they were very kind to me. All of them greeted me with a cordial good-morning and even went to the length of insisting that the "old gentleman" should be served first. I enjoyed that breakfast; they were a decent lot of fellows, and I daresay they wouldn't have known a good crook if they saw one. I didn't tell them who I was; instead, I gave them a tip or two and asked them if they thought I would be quite safe on a racecourse. I told a couple of my pals what had happened, but they wouldn't believe me.

This highly respectable appearance of mine frequently leads to all sorts of mistakes. Outside the Casino at Nice one day, one of the Australian con men picked me out for a mug and started off with the usual chatty opening.

"How do you do? It's quite a long time since we met."

"So it is," I said. "About how long would you think?"

"Oh, I can't remember just now. I've met you somewhere, but I can't quite place you. What part of the world do you come from?"

"Quite the opposite from you," I replied, smiling broadly.

My interrogator took what is vulgarly known as a tumble. He went off looking none too pleased with himself, while I strolled into the Casino, where I saw Charlie King, one of the big men at the game.

"Charlie," I said, "one of your men outside has been trying to pick me up."

"Good God!" he replied. "I'm sorry, Eddie; I'll see it doesn't happen again."

I underwent another experience of picking up which did not turn out so fortunately. I had come down from the North and had been in London about two days when I saw four men standing at the corner of a West End street who were pointed out to me as detectives. I made it my business to go and have a look at them, passing right by them without being recognized. I particularly want to emphasize this because of what happened shortly afterward. That very same night I was in a saloon close by, drinking with a dozen other people, when a woman suddenly said in a low voice: "Look out, the 'splits' are here."

"I don't care," I replied. "I've done nothing to get me into trouble." I didn't know then, though I was informed of it later, that a dirty little rat of a Yiddisher cocaine-seller named Solly

Solomons had seen one of the detectives and informed him—anxious to curry a bit of favor and probably expecting to be knocked off himself—that Eddie Guerin was inside.

Eddie Guerin! Quite a nice little capture for a detective then busily engaged in cleaning up London. Just as I was leaving the saloon three men jumped on me.

"Come on, you," they said.

I did not submit too tamely, be quite sure of that. In fact, there was a devil of a scuffle, in course of which I demanded to know why I had been arrested. They would not tell me, instead calling a taxicab and hustling me into it. Without any further opportunity of protest I was taken off to Vine Street Police Station, where, with the detectives standing on either side of me, the inspector in the Charge Room took down the precious information that I was accused of picking pockets outside the London Hippodrome.

I was absolutely dumbfounded and then, losing my temper completely, said a few things which provoked something like a free fight. Three or four of the detectives got hold of me, gave me a first-class beating up and threw me downstairs into a cell. They even took my boots away in case I might kick somebody. In the cell I remained all night, not greatly worrying, and not in the least disappointed when I had to wait until the morning before anything further transpired. Then the police took me off to Bow Street Police Station, where one of the detectives gave evidence that he had seen me outside the Hippodrome waiting for the 'buses, and also seen me slip my hand under a man's coat and feel for his leather. Evidently I did not meet with any success there, for I made another attempt, with the same result. Then, disgusted, I went to the saloon and had a drink. After a time I came back to the same place and made a third attempt to pick somebody's pocket. Then I was followed to the public-house and arrested in the circumstances I have already described. After the Scotland Yard man had made these statements the magistrate—I think it was Mr. Graham Campbell—asked me whether I had any questions to ask.

"Yes," I said, turning to the detective. "How long have you known me?"

"For several years."

"You know my past, don't you?"

"Yes, I do."

"You have got the cheek to come here and tell that rubbishy story that you saw me go three times to the same spot and did not take me in charge there and then but waited until some time later when I was leaving a public-house?"

Three more detectives got into the witness-box, all of whom, naturally, corroborated the first man's story. I found I was also charged with assaulting the police, and when it came to this I asked the magistrate who carried signs of assault and battery if it wasn't me.

I also put it to the Stipendiary that he must know, as all the witnesses knew, that pickpockets do not work single-handed, also if it was plausible that any man in his sane senses would go to one of the most brilliantly lighted corners in London and commit such an offense. The case went on for quite a long time and eventually I was sentenced to four months' hard labor. I decided to appeal: accordingly was allowed out on £300 bail, much against the opposition of the police. I succeeded in getting six witnesses, one of them included the licensee of the saloon, all of whom swore that I could not possibly be guilty because I was indoors drinking at the time the offense was alleged to have taken place. I will admit, excepting the publican, that my witnesses were not exactly angels. Still, they were no worse than the witnesses for the prosecution.

When the time came for my case to be heard at the London Sessions I had to undergo another ordeal. Two or three Press photographers, possibly anxious to obtain a good picture of the notorious Eddie Guerin, followed me about for some hours.

"If you don't clear off," I warned them, "I'll break my stick over your heads."

Up came a detective to inform me that if I touched the photographers he would put a charge of assault against me! This was the first time I ever knew that you had to have your photograph taken by the Press whether you liked it or not. Then when I went into court I spied a fellow in the gallery trying to sketch me. I put my hand over my face and was asked by the judge why I was doing it.

"I have been followed by men trying to take my photograph," I said, "and now I come to court to find some one in the gallery sketching me. I protest against it, my lord."

The judge fully agreed with me and ordered the man to be turned out. However, such little incidents did not affect the result of the case. My appeal was dismissed because the police witnesses were believed in preference to mine. *I was absolutely innocent.*

The Black Maria took me from the London Sessions Court House to His Majesty's prison in Pentonville, where the Governor of that time was Major Blake. He was a thorough gentleman in every possible way, much too good a man to be in the prison service. What I liked about him was the friendly way he greeted you, no animosity, no official frills, just a plain man-to-man talk. When I was brought up before him in the morning, he said:

"Well, Guerin, you've got four months."

"Yes, sir."

"It is not necessary for me to tell you that it is in your own interests to behave yourself while you are here. You know that from past experience.

"It is very remarkable," continued Major Blake, "but you seem to leave one prison to go to another. I am surprised at a man of your intelligence not realizing before now the uselessness of a life of crime. You are not a fool, Guerin. Why don't you give it up?"

When I am spoken to in this manner I have the proper feeling—shame. I told the Governor that on this occasion I was just as surprised as he was, because I had not committed the offense for which I had been sent to prison. I don't suppose he believed me, for he shook his head resignedly and merely requested me to think over what he had said.

Well, four months is nothing for a man who has done twenty-five years in prison, and I accepted the position philosophically, if privately I told myself that I was merely suffering once more for the sins of the past. There were many men in the prison I knew, all of whom were utterly astounded to see me there. All the time I had been in England, since 1888, I had never been arrested in London. There were many inquiries concerning the why and the wherefore of the matter. Also, to be quite candid, it rather galled me to find myself in the company of the average Pentonville criminal, the lowest of the low. Here was I, the once-famous Eddie Guerin, doing four months in the society of sneak-thieves and all the riff-raff collected from the police courts.

The news soon got round. Even inside a prison you have your fame, and as the new-comers arrived they were told to be sure and have a good look at me, the man who had been sentenced to transportation for life and escaped. Devil's Island made a tasty morsel for these gutter-snipes to roll over their tongue. One morning I caught a couple of them at it and threatened to smash their heads for them. They went squealing to the nearest warder, who immediately had me locked up and taken before the Governor.

"What's the matter, Guerin?" asked Major Blake with a smile.

"Nothing very much, sir," I replied. "I was doing my work and paying no attention to anyone when I heard this man"—nodding towards one of the precious couple who had made the complaint—"telling every one all about me and what I had done in the past."

"What did you do?"

"I only said I would knock his head off if he did it again."

"Quite right," murmured the Governor. He wrote something on a paper in front of him and sent me outside. I waited there for some time expecting to hear that I had been punished, when one old warder came up to me and wanted to know what I was waiting for.

"The Governor told me to stand here," I replied.

"Go up to your cell," said the old fellow. "It's all right. You're not going to be punished, but the other man will."

Major Blake ran his prison admirably. The only fault that could be found with him—if it could be termed a fault—was that he treated his charges too kindly. But I, for one, have never forgotten him. In a way I am glad he has left the prison service because I would have hated to have gone back and met that silent reproach which does more to shame a man into righteousness than all the lectures in the world.

I have never pretended to be a paragon of virtue. At the time of my arrest I admitted having been convicted many times previously. I told the court, however, that picking pockets was out of my line altogether, which was perfectly true. Most people imagine that it is one of the lowest forms of crime in the world. They ought to try it; they will then discover that it takes years of practice and not a little amount of nerve. Had the detectives who arrested me for what is known in the vernacular as "dipping" searched me properly, they might have found something worth very much more than a trumpery charge of attempted pocket-picking. They might, for instance, have come across a cloak-room ticket which on further investigation might have led them to quite a nice little parcel of jewelry. That ticket remained among my belongings all the time I was in Pentonville Prison and it was handed to me when I took my discharge. The very first thing I did was to go to the cloak-room, obtain the coat which I had deposited there, and wearing it walk to the river, into which I emptied the contents of the pockets. So much for the Criminal Investigation Department. On this particular occasion, I didn't bother trying to dispose of something that would have brought me in quite a substantial sum of money.

One more lapse—and one only—have I to record. As the years rolled on, so did it become harder to do a sentence. Nothing but stark, staring necessity ever made me take the risk of tasting the sorrows of prison life again. In sober truth it was for nothing much. In Edinburgh, at my wits' end for money, I went into an hotel in much the same manner as I had done at Brighton, hoping to find a jewel case that I might purloin. A chambermaid saw me in the room, and promptly gave the alarm, with the result that I appeared before the Bailey the following morning charged with attempted larceny.

The Scottish police were scrupulously fair in the way they treated me. They allowed no sensational newspaper headlines about the celebrated Eddie Guerin being in custody, carefully abstained from the slightest exaggeration in presenting the facts against me, and called only two witnesses. I remember feeling thoroughly ashamed of myself when the Bailey, a decent-looking old fellow, glanced up at me from his desk and said: "I am surprised at ye, Guerin. I thocht ye'd feenished wi' this game long ago."

He gave me just what I expected, six months' hard labor, all within the space of a few minutes. I daresay that old Bailey had read all about me, and although he didn't say so he just gave me a look as much as to say: "Well, fancy a man like Eddie Guerin coming down to this!"

The Scottish prison was quiet, well ordered, utterly free from quarreling, bad language, or rancorous officials. You couldn't fight, because there was nothing to fight for. There was no tobacco, no smuggling of prohibited articles. The Governor was a fair-minded man, probably very badly paid, and faced, like most of us, with the problem of an expenditure rising above his income. There was no bribery, nothing but an all-pervading calm wherein you might, provided you had the inclination, regain that balance of mind which should enable you to go out into the world again unfettered by hate or prejudice. Taking it all in all, the British prison system carefully abstains from anything calculated to make men worse. Solitary confinement, which I consider easily the most terrible punishment in the world, is now practically non-existent. The chaplains will come and talk to you, as they did to me in Scotland, frankly and freely, discussing anything but religion. They know, of course, that the average prisoner is utterly devoid of religious sentiment, and the moment a man pretends to possess it he is at once—and rightly—marked down as an errant hypocrite.

You get pretty good justice in Great Britain. In the ordinary course of events I would not be disposed to bestow any encomiums on policemen, but I will cheerfully grant the London City police—for what it is worth—my certificate of fair treatment. I was once arrested at the Three Nuns Hotel in Aldgate by a City detective who told the Alderman at the Mansion House that he had followed me in there from one of the banks and taken me into custody because I had been acting suspiciously. This detective knew, naturally, that I was Eddie

Guerin, the man who had done many banks in his time, so probably he thought he would do me.

He got up in the witness-box and told his little tale, after which I questioned him. I asked him if he had followed me into any of the numerous banks I was alleged to have entered.

"No," he replied, "but I saw you go in."

"You don't know whether I was transacting any business or not?"

"I can't say whether you did."

"You won't say I did not."

"No."

The Alderman, a comfortable-looking old City merchant, asked me why I had gone into the banks. I told him that a London journalist had wanted me, as an expert in such matters, to write a book pointing out why so few English people who went into banks were robbed by comparison with the French. It was part of my contract that I should go into the banks and, as it were, survey the battlefield. I informed His Worship, who appeared very interested, that in England intelligent precautions were taken against people being robbed. The case was adjourned to obtain the attendance of my literary sponsor. When he came to court he confirmed my story and the Alderman told me I could go, genially warning me at the same time that banks were good places for me to keep away from. Outside the Mansion House were the usual Press photographers. I'll wager nobody else in the world has had his photograph so religiously sought as myself. However, they were no more successful in this instance than they were before.

I am now spending the remainder of my life paying the price of things that have happened in the past. I can still remember the tears my poor old mother shed over me when I fled from Chicago after shooting the policeman, and there still vividly haunts my mind the words she spoke, that I would live to regret the day I had broken her heart. I am close upon the three-score years and ten allotted to man, and I possess practically nothing but what I stand up in. All I have to show for a lifetime of bitter experience is an unenviable reputation which I shall no doubt carry to my dying day. I have no proper home and simply lead a hand-to-mouth existence, trusting to luck to see me through. Stocks and shares I have none, any more than I possess a respected place in the community.

The difficulty I have, after a life that has been full of thrills, is to reconcile myself to the idea of settling down to some humdrum occupation that will keep me for the remainder of my days. But before I can do this I must cut myself adrift from all my old friends. They may not be very desirable people, but they are all I have.

I can allow myself the privilege, in common with other and more distinguished men, of writing my Memoirs. Probably there will be readers who will turn up their noses in disgust over a criminal setting down in cold print the unsavory experiences of his past. I am fully aware that I represent a phase of life which is not in the least worthy of emulation. Nevertheless, there is always the younger generation growing up, and if this story of mine will help the boys of to-day to appreciate the undeniable fact that a criminal career can only end disastrously, then all that I have gone through will not have been in vain.

There is no particular message I wish to convey to the public. What has happened to me tells, more forcibly than actual words, the fate that will surely overtake you if you persist in going astray. I have wasted fifty years doing things that have brought nothing but trouble in their train. If I had spent that time, aided by the courage and determination I am reputed to possess, in hard, old-fashioned work, I would have become a millionaire. And that is the lesson of book.

Notes

[1] Sidney T. Felstead (1888-1965), author of *The Underworld of London* (1923).

[2] Thomas Edward Guerin was born in London on August 20, 1860.

[3] October 8–10, 1871. Guerin would have been 11 years old.

[4] Mary Anne Duignan (1871-1929), a.k.a. "Chicago" May Churchill.

[5] Eddie Guerin was 15 when his father died On October 13, 1875.

[6] A safe-cracker.

[7] Persons easily deceived.

[8] Confidence man.

[9] Pitchmen.

[10] A pick-pocket.

[11] A card-sharp.

[12] A con-man whose role is to distract a victim and keep him engaged.

[13] Short for detective.

[14] A constable or police officer.

[15] Red-light district from 24th to 42nd streets between 6th and 7th Avenues.

[16] Thomas "Shang" Draper (1839–1883).

[17] John "Little Freddie" Irving (1844–1883).

[18] John "Johnny the Mick" Walsh (1852–1883).

[19] Michael "Sheeny Mike" Kurtz (1845–1904).

[20] Joseph Elliot (1853–1893).

[21] Born Jane Freeman (1856–1892).

[22] It was actually in May 1886.

[23] Thomas F. Byrnes (1842–1910).

[24] Richard W. Croker (1843–1922).

[25] Frederick Gebhard (1860–1910).

[26] To charge with vagrancy.

[27] Patrick Sheedy (1856–1909).

[28] *Within the Maze* (1872), a novel by Ellen Wood.

[29] A couplet from "To Althea, from Prison" (1642), a poem by Richard Lovelace.

[30] The café at 41 Blue Island Ave. was owned by Clemment Marcille and his wife.

[31] Although ambiguous, "Le Frebre" could be the name of the café.

[32] Originally published February 13, 1898.

[33] June 20, 1887.

[34] The equivalent of $32,000 today.

[35] "The Napoleon of Crime" Adam Worth (1844–1902).

[36] *Portrait of Georgiana, Duchess of Devonshire*, Thomas Gainsborough (1787).

[37] Lt. Colonel E. S. Milman (1870–1940).

[38] Sophie Lyons (1847–1924).

[39] Edward "Ned" Lyons (1839-1907).

[40] June 26, 1869.

[41] Fredericka "Marm" Mandelbaum (1825–1894).

[42] A messenger bag.

[43] The equivalent of $1.4 million today.

[44] Sir Charles Frederick Gill (1851-1923).

[45] Sir Harry Bodkin Poland (1829–1928).

[46] The equivalent of $40,000 today.

[47] Michael "Hinky Dink" Kenna (1858–1946).

[48] The equivalent of $8,000 today.

[49] The equivalent of $8 million today.

[50] A small, four-wheeled hackney coach.

[51] James "Yakey Yake" Brady (1875–1904).

[52] William "Billy the Kid" Burke (1858–1919).

[53] It was actually May 8, 1924. She was 76.

[54] Stolen May 26, 1876, from the London gallery of Thomas Agnew & Sons.

[55] Maximilian Schoenbein (1842–1916), a.k.a. "Max Shinburn."

[56] Walter A. Sheridan (1834–1890).

[57] Criminal Investigation Department.

[58] Reform schools for juvenile offenders.